David Bonavia
DENG

Longman

© Judith Bonavia
First published 1989

Published by
Longman Group (Far East) Ltd
18/F, Cornwall House
Tong Chong Street
Quarry Bay
Hong Kong
and associated companies throughout the world.

ISBN 0 582 99952 9

Printed in Hong Kong

To my father and mother,
Gran, Ian and Lillie,
Donald, Michael and Mary,
this book is dedicated with fondest love.

PREFACE

My husband worked on this biography of Deng Xiaoping during the last two years of his life, completing it in May 1988, only months before his death.

The bloody suppression of the student movement in Tiananmen Square in Peking on 4 June 1989 and the subsequent intimidation, arrests, and executions have left both Chinese and Westerners shocked and appalled.

Deng appears to have emerged, through the use of brute military force and ruthless political manoeuvring, with his power intact. But at what cost? To many observers he seems wantonly to have put at risk all that he had achieved since 1978. Now physically frail, he has too little time allotted him to restore his image and that of the Chinese Communist Party both at home and abroad. His reputation is forever poisoned.

David would not have been surprised at the tragic turn of events. His experience of both the Soviet Union and the People's Republic of China had been infinitely depressing. He felt inspired by the citizens of these two great nations, by their patriotism and courage and their capacity for long suffering. But he had no illusions about the way the leaderships of Communist countries respond to crisis.

My husband believed that Deng Xiaoping showed that some Communist leaders can learn from their own experiences of personal suffering in purges and thus moderate the degree to which they rule by state terror. That may mitigate the current repression. I suspect that David might well have argued that when the dust has settled it will emerge, despite current appearances, that Deng Xiaoping has not thrown away all the liberalisation efforts, particularly on the economic side, of the last decade, even though the nation is numbed and disillusioned.

Whatever the final verdict, however, it is clear that Deng has put himself in the dock.

My husband intended this work primarily as a biography for the general reader and did not wish to clog the text with a comprehensive mass of academic sourcing. He drew on a wide range of material, including memoirs of veteran Communist and Nationalist activists, military and official records, Red Guard sources, and the French press. Official diplomatic records were important in tracing the evolution of Deng's strategic and diplomatic thinking. Finally, the Chinese and Western press since 1973 provided valuable insights into his political, economic, and cultural policies.

My contribution has been an attempt to pinpoint sources in the text where possible, and I am very grateful to Penelope Hill who assisted in this task and in the final editing. But the text remains as my husband wrote it.

Judy Bonavia
Hong Kong
July 1989

FOREWORD

David and Judy Bonavia and I were last together on 16 November 1986, in Hong Kong, when a few friends joined us for dinner at Jimmy's Kitchen. Afterwards, David and I stayed in touch through letters, in which we discussed, among other subjects, Deng Xiaoping, who I found mystifying. Then silence fell until the news of David's death reached me and I called Judy in Scotland.

I first got to know David in 1966 when he was working on the *Far Eastern Economic Review* and I was on my sabbatical leave in Hong Kong, and apart from his time in Moscow as correspondent for *The Times* and my second exile in Toronto, we saw each other regularly. Despite the age difference, David being almost 20 years younger, it was a genuine personal tie which extended beyond our common concern with China. Now the divide between us is impassable. I have no way of telling whether it inflicts on him a sense of loss; it certainly does so on me.

His *Deng Xiaoping* violates in several ways the Chinese biographical tradition which still remains dominant after so many decades of republicanism and people's republicanism. The Chinese biography is not psychological but highly didactic. When the biographer has made a sketch of the subject's role in shaping history and an explanation of the lessons to be learned from him or her, the job is done. All the listed biographies in the official dynastic histories are therefore no more than caricatures, a few thousand words long, regardless of their being of the most brilliant statesmen or the least significant emperors, great reformers or skilled physicians. If a Chinese reader seeks understanding and entertainment in the emotional and intellectual growth of a distinguished individual, he has to go to less formal writings. Furthermore, the tradition also frowns upon the publication of a biography of an important statesman still in office.

In recent decades, there have been exceptions to this rule of course, thanks to the advent of the modern printing press, the emergence of publishing as an industry, and a measure of openness and democracy ushered into Chinese political life by republicanism. However, let us not forget the influence of non-Chinese authors on Chinese biographical writing. To refer to eminent Chinese Communists alone, without the initial and crucial efforts made by them the Chinese people would know even less of Zhou Enlai, Zhu De, and even Mao Zedong. Now I believe that David will exert his influence on the Chinese through his *Deng Xiaoping*.

But that generation of Titans has almost completely faded into history. Deng Xiaoping is one of the very few remaining key links between it and the present generation of leaders. His contribution to China's development since the end of the 1970s has been peerless. Yet there is to date not a single biography on him of a comparable scale and depth to David's in Chinese and published in Deng's own country. The other, younger leaders are treated with even more thorough neglect. Seen in this regard, one wonders whether the limited measure of openness introduced since 1912 has in fact become narrower. It also suggests that Chinese people seem to prefer to enshroud their leaders in mystery, which is often made more inscrutable by rumours and unverified anecdotes. To hope for a multi-volume biography on a Chinese leader comparable in stature to H. von Poschinger's *Bismarck* or Martin Gilbert's *Churchill* is tantamount to demanding greater openness and less reverence, neither of which appears to be possible under the present circumstances.

David Bonavia's *Deng Xiaoping* is to date the best to appear in print in any language. After all, he was more, far more, than a journalist who had reported on Chinese affairs for some of the most respected newspapers in the English-speaking world; he was a scholar who had acquired profound knowledge of the Chinese and their civilisation. He could raise questions as not many others in the same field can and proceed to answer them. The clarity and economy of his prose and the sureness of his grasp of details, including those of the evolution of Deng's ideas, strategies, and policies from the time when he emerged as one of the most brilliant strategists in the resumed civil war between the Communists and the Nationalists in the second half of the 1940s, make the chapters on the strategist, the moderate, the reformer, the statesman, and the commander-in-chief both dependable and satisfying. There David has offered cogent answers to two extremely complicated questions in Deng's distinguished career: how did he develop his statecraft to such a degree of consummation, and how did he become estranged from Mao? What David could explain, to my mind, only a little less satisfactorily are two other tough questions: what had Deng learned during his apprentice years in France, Russia, and China before 1945, and when all is said and done, in what sense is Deng a Marxist? The complexities of each of these two questions are of a different nature. The first is caused by the institutional and cultural restrictions imposed on any attempt to understand this and other Communist leaders; the second entails the dilemma of using Marxism to break the spell of a Malthusian agricultural revolution.

Jerome Ch'en
Toronto
March 1989

CONTENTS

Preface iv
Foreword vi
Introduction xi

1. Childhood and Early Youth 1
2. The Young Commissar 11
3. The Zunyi Conference 27
4. The Strategist 39
5. From Sichuan to Peking 61
6. Change of Emphasis 73
7. The Moderate 95
8. Russia Again 109
9. Cultural Revolution and Exile 113
10. The Return 129
11. The Reformer 165
12. The Statesman 199
13. The Commander-in-Chief 213
14. The Thoughts of Deng 225

Epilogue 245
Bibliography 249
Glossary 253
Index 261

INTRODUCTION

The reasons for attempting a biography of Deng Xiaoping — inadequate though many of the source materials may be — hardly need explanation. Deng is one of the outstanding statesmen of the twentieth century. By sheer determination he pulled China back from the often disastrous policies of the late Chairman Mao Zedong, expelled Mao's closest supporters from their posts, and instituted a relatively modern state, in which the cult of personality was eschewed and a form of limited *glasnost* put in its place to aid economic and political reform. Many of Mao's erstwhile devotees would accuse Deng of having betrayed that monstrous ego's policies, and of ignoring Mao's amazing ability to rally the nation behind him for useful as well as useless tasks.

One can only speculate what would have happened if China had pursued Mao's ideas to the end. The fact is that those ideas went against human nature, and Deng was the first high-ranking Party member after the Cultural Revolution to say so publicly, however many decried them in private.

The Chinese Communist Party was founded in Shanghai and Hangzhou in 1921, but its influence quickly became widespread among Chinese students in Europe. Deng is a walking history of the Party, from its beginnings among a leftist group of Chinese intellectuals in France during the early 1920s, through guerilla commands in China, political controversies, purges, military victories, and the initially successful post-war reconstruction. He eventually gained sympathy with the bourgeoisie and intellectuals who sustained the brunt of Mao's policies, subdued his own political rivals and installed what appears to be a stable, pragmatic regime loyal to his ideas rather than to Mao's.

Deng has also presided over the ebbing of the dangerous quarrel with the Soviet Union, the improvement of relations with the United States and most developed countries, and the solution to the problem of retrieving Hong Kong from the British. However the reunification of Taiwan with the mainland has eluded him, but he has been wise enough to let new links develop peacefully and gradually without resorting to arms.

The journalist's cliché describing Deng as a 'diminutive, peppery Sichuanese' though accurate enough, is as wearisome to the reader as it must be to him. He is short of stature, even for a Chinese, has a will of iron, a mordant wit, and is proud of eating Sichuan's pungent-flavoured foods. He seems to lack however, the vindictiveness and aggression often attributed to small men in public affairs. Common sense is his guideline.

The story of Deng's political development unfolds from a childhood uncharacteristically secure for a revolutionary. His easy adherence to Communism and his fortitude and organisational talent seem to have been surprisingly natural. On each occasion when the Party was riven by inner conflicts, Deng emerged, it seemed almost by chance, upholding Mao's line and reaping the benefits when Mao recouped his position of leadership. This changed from the early 1960s and the waning Great Leap Forward which had shown the first signs of Mao's growing loss of touch with reality.

Deng was apparently late in grasping the full implications of Mao's leftward swing from 1957 onwards, and this may have been his biggest single mistake. Since his political exile in 1967 and his rehabilitation in 1973, he has adhered to his own ideas of reason and the need for a peaceful environment to realise China's true potential for economic development in domestic policies as well as her role in world affairs. 'Modernisation' is his key word. Though he has disappointed radical leftists in the West and some champions of Third World causes who still look to Mao's works as a source of strength and vision, Deng has achieved renown in the outside world.

By his own decision, Deng is fading gradually from the political scene. China's future depends on his successors' ability to solidify and further develop his policies.

I am extremely grateful to Sallie Coolidge for her editing, and to Lynn Pan and Catherine Antoine for additional information in the writing of this book — and most of all to my wife.

The *pinyin* system of romanisation of Chinese has been adhered to throughout, except in the case of a few names like Chiang Kai-shek and Sun Yat-sen which are more familiar in alternative romanisations. If *pinyin* is a little misleading in its representation of phonetic values for speakers of Western languages, it is at least standardised. The main points to remember are that *q* is pronounced like English *ch*, *c* like English *ts*, and *x* like a light English *s*. The letter *a* as in *pinyin yan* is pronounced like an open English *e*, as in *hen*.

David Bonavia
Hong Kong
June 1988

Chapter 1

CHILDHOOD AND EARLY YOUTH

T he year 1904 was not a particularly happy one for China. In Manchuria, her territory was being fought over by the armies of Tsarist Russia and Imperial Japan; British Indian troops had occupied Lhasa despite China's historic claim to sovereignty over Tibet; armed rebellion was raging in the southwestern province of Guangxi; and the Yellow River burst its dykes, causing severe flooding in central China. In Tokyo, meanwhile, the British-educated Dr Sun Yat-sen was meeting with other would-be Chinese revolutionaries to plot the further course of their plans to bring down the Manchu Qing dynasty.

In the vicinity of Chongqing, a large city on the Yangzi River in the western province of Sichuan, an event took place in 1904 which would profoundly influence the course of Chinese history from the 1930s right up until the closing years of the twentieth century. On 22 August, a male child was born in a village called Xiexing in Guang'an county. The baby was named by his parents Deng Xixian.

His father, Deng Wenming, was a landlord whose fields yielded some thirteen tons of grain a year, the basis for a comfortable though not luxurious life-style. He was a secret member of the anti-Manchu society called *gelao hui*, or brotherhood association, but being on good terms with the local military commander he was given official appointments related to public security and had command over a squad of soldiers. Bandits were rife in Sichuan and most other parts of China at the time.

Deng Wenming was a Hakka from the north of Guangdong province in south China. The Hakkas, or 'guest people', originally came from central China but had fled the Manchu conquest in the mid-seventeenth century and settled in the south. They have the reputation of being tough, combative, and clannish. One of Deng's Hakka ancestors served as a high official under the eighteenth-century emperor Qian Long.

It is not known why Deng Wenming moved to Sichuan, except that after disastrous wars and earthquakes there, the Manchus promoted immigration from other parts of China to repopulate this large and secluded province known as 'China's grain basket'. To all intents and purposes Deng Xiaoping, a name he may have adopted in Moscow, is a Sichuanese born and bred, and he speaks Chinese with a strong Sichuan accent.

Deng Wenming had four wives who bore him five sons and three daughters. Of the five sons, Xixian — or Xiaoping (Little Peace), as he would later call himself — was the eldest. Altogether Deng Wenming had ten children. His first wife, Zhang, had none. His second wife, Tan, had Deng Xianlie, a daughter, and three sons, Deng Xiaoping, Deng Gen, and Deng Shuping. His third wife, Xiao, had one son and his fourth wife, Xia Bogan, had a daughter by an earlier marriage, a son who died young, a second son, and two daughters. Altogether Deng Xiaoping had three brothers, a sister, three half brothers, and three half sisters. Deng treated his family well in later years. His father died in 1938.

Deng's younger brother, Deng Gen, was born in 1910 and worked as a schoolteacher. In 1941, he went to the Communist base area of Yan'an to work as a journalist, became deputy mayor of Chongqing in 1949, and was eventually transferred to the same post in the Yangzi triple city of Wuhan. Deng Shuping, the youngest brother born in 1912, stayed at home to manage the family's property and became a local functionary of the Guomindang, the large Nationalist revolutionary party founded and led by Dr Sun Yat-sen until his death in 1925 which became highly anti-Communist under its subsequent leader, Chiang Kai-shek. Deng Xiaoping saw to it that Deng Shuping was indoctrinated with Communist ideas after the Communist victory in 1949; he was later appointed to a judiciary post in Chongqing. He committed suicide in 1967 after being 'struggled against' by the Red Guards.

The Deng household appears to have been a reasonably harmonious one, respected by its neighbours. After a conventional education in the Chinese classics, Deng was enrolled at a school teaching modern Western learning, rather than the traditional literary skills which used to be the chief means of advancement in a civilian career. Some of his most impressionable years coincided with World War I in Europe which weakened the faith of many progressive Chinese intellectuals in the benefits of European civilisation. Others, however, continued to advocate the use of European and American ideas to make China strong.

In 1911, the Manchu government was building railways with loans from British, Belgian, French, German, and American banks, but specified that the new system of transport would be under Peking's control. This enraged local magnates in Sichuan who wanted control of their railways for themselves, and succeeded in gathering a storm of mass protest in the province whose people are historically well-known for their resistance to interference in their affairs by the Chinese central authorities. There was violence on the streets. Students rioted and business ground to a halt, several demonstrators were shot by central government troops, and local magnates were arrested. The province united in its hostility to the Manchu dynasty. There was not long to wait before that hostility would be reflected in many other parts of China.

On 10 October 1911 — when Deng was seven — a military

uprising at the important garrison city of Wuchang further down the Yangzi River developed into a national upheaval, the so-called Xinhai Revolution. (Xinhai is the name for the year 1911 in the Chinese 60-year cyclic calendar.) Sun Yat-sen was invited to return to China from London, where he was living at the time, to take the office of provisional president pending the formation of a parliament and the drafting of a republican constitution.

The 1911 Revolution was essentially a nationalistic affair, inspired by the growing desire of the ethnic Chinese to throw off the yoke of the Manchus. In power since the eighteenth century, the Manchus had become increasingly inept and oppressive as they permitted the country to be carved up by the imperialist powers and exploited by foreign capitalists. The Russian revolution was six years away and the words 'communism' and 'socialism' were barely known in China at that time. The imperial powers were basking in the Edwardian afternoon. Britain, Russia, France, Italy, Austria, and Germany were eyeing each other with a view to war, and China was 'the sick man of Asia', of little account in the power game, the Western powers' only interest being her big markets and valuable products for which they vied. The rise of Japan was viewed by them with suspicion, especially since Japan clearly had further ambitions with regard to China after the annexation of the large island of Taiwan (Formosa) in 1895 and the stationing of Japanese troops in Manchuria.

The role Deng's family played in these events is not known, but it may be assumed that his father was sympathetic to the 'railway protection movement' and, tacitly at least, hostile to the Manchus. The revolution must have been discussed frequently in the family, so the eldest son would have absorbed some political knowledge and awareness. By the time he was fifteen, the May Fourth Movement (1919) had broken out in Peking. Under such slogans as 'Oppose feudalism and imperialism', students, merchants, and ordinary people were united in their opposition to the imperialist powers' attempts to reimpose territorial concessions on the parts of China which had sided with the Allies against Germany and allowed Chinese labour battalions to be sent to France. The May Fourth Movement was also aimed against the incompetent militarist clique which had set itself up as the government in Peking. Although Peking and Sichuan were a thousand miles apart, the influence of the movement was quickly transmitted and absorbed in the big western province.

Despite the growing hostility to the Western powers and Japan, some Chinese intellectuals and philanthropists continued to advocate the use of Western ideas to make China a strong and modern country. One of these intellectuals was the francophile educator, Li Youyong (alias Li Shizeng), whose New Century Movement helped to organise work-and-study programmes for Chinese students in France.

Li Youyong, who had been educated in the French town of Montargis about 60 miles south of Paris, notified the municipal authorities in 1912 that he had decided to found an association with the aim of sending more Chinese students to study in France rather than in Japan, the United States, Britain, or Germany. Only those with 'sufficient means to meet the costs of a fairly long stay in France' were to be enrolled for an appropriate fee and would be assigned to dormitories in institutions of education where they could learn adequate French in order to study their appropriate courses. Female students, whose educational opportunities in China were extremely limited, would be accommodated at the Montargis Girls' College, while the young men would go to schools in the districts of Chesnoys and Durzy. The Mayor of Montargis, the sub-prefect, and the local representative in the National Assembly gave their approval. It was agreed that the scheme to educate young Chinese was acceptable on condition that it should in no way interfere with the instruction being given to French girls and boys at those schools. The Chinese students would be from 'good' families and would pay fees and other expenses, such as laundry and hair-cutting, out of their own or their parents' pockets. The municipal officials noted that:

'On their return to China, they would help us to propagate French influence in the Middle Kingdom. They would become faithful clients of ours, deaf to the solicitations of American, English or German industrialists who are at present competing for the Chinese market. We must thank Mr Li Youyong for having thought of bringing this benefit to our city, where he has friends certain to enjoy the material advantages which cannot but accrue to our businessmen and to the city itself, since the Chinese students, without giving rise to the slightest extra cost, will pay the same fees as the present pupils, and the arrival of about fifty young men and girls of well-to-do families will add to the charm of our city an unexpected and picturesque tone. This would be in contrast to the high costs of maintaining schools in foreign countries such as China and Morocco as the expense of the spread of French culture in the Orient is particularly onerous for our Budget.'

When the programme for the education of Chinese students was initiated, there were only about thirty Chinese students in France, mostly based in Paris. Greater numbers went to universities in the United States, Britain, and Germany. The Mayor of Montargis and other dignitaries were not moved by entirely altruistic motives — they wanted to generate more commercial links with China and saw this as a good opportunity to create a generation of francophile businessmen. They had no suspicion that the students coming to France were increasingly motivated by nationalistic and revolutionary sentiments. As pointed out in the local newspaper *Le Gatinais*, it was cheaper to educate Asiatics in France than to set up expensive missions overseas.

Students who applied to go to France had to learn something of the language first. French was already quite widely taught in Sichuan due to the presence of numerous French missionaries who regarded the province and other parts of southwest China as France's pastoral domain, a natural extension of its colonies in Indochina. A Sino-French Educational Society had been formed and had set up free schools in Chongqing and other large cities. It attracted thousands of students, including Deng, who enrolled there for a one-year course, probably in 1919. Thus at the early age of fifteen he was already living away from home (he could hardly commute the 60 miles between Chongqing and Guang'an), in a large commercial city with a growing industrial base. Chongqing was politically sophisticated and possessed strong links with the outside world via the Yangzi River and the port of Shanghai. This may have helped him to become worldly-wise and self-confident at a time when most boys of his age, if their families could afford the instruction, were still studying the Confucian classics.

On 11 September 1920, Deng and nearly 200 other Chinese students sailed on a Messageries Maritimes liner for Marseilles. They travelled steerage since most of them had little money and life in France would be expensive by Chinese standards. On arrival, a contemporary source says, Deng was notable for the way in which he took charge of the ninety other Sichuanese students, arranging their luggage in an orderly fashion while students from other provinces of China hunted high and low for their belongings, scattered all over the docks. This talent for organisation was to become one of Deng's strongest points in his later career.

Whereas Deng's family may have tolerated his attendance at the French school in Chongqing, they almost certainly opposed his decision to travel to France and join the now popular work-study programme. As the eldest son, he would traditionally have been expected to stay at home and run the household after his father's death. His departure for France was an early sign of the implacable determination which he brought to everything he undertook.

Information on Deng's six-odd years in France is patchy at best. Li Youyong (or Shizeng) had close ties with the leading citizens of Montargis, which had a big factory making rubber footwear. Deng is believed to have worked there for a while, where he became progressively involved with Zhou Enlai and other members of the Chinese students' left-wing movement in France, the *Jeunes Socialistes* (the Socialist Youth League). One of the places of Deng's sojourn was Montargis — from 13 February to 3 September 1922 and again from 2 February to 11 June 1923. In 1923, he worked at Hutchinson's rubber factory.

There is no record of friction with the Chinese students, the first of whom arrived in Montargis late in 1912 and immediately wrote to the Mayor, M. Falour: 'We shall be only too happy if we can bring [back to China] some sparks of the French genius, the torch of the world and the glory of humanity.' Indeed, the local newspaper regretted that the celebration party for the anniversary of the Chinese revolution of 1911 was confined to the students and school staff. The students socialised very little and, though some of them might have been well-to-do by Chinese standards, many of them wrote home complaining of the northern French climate and their relative poverty. The local people for their part viewed the exotic strangers with reserve, and occasionally alarm.

On 20 May 1922, *Le Gatinais* showed itself tolerant and sympathetic when a young Chinese student, Li Heying, who had spent a short time at the Collège de Montargis fired on the Chinese minister in Paris when he was entering his car after a dinner party. Li Heying succeeded in slightly wounding the minister's companion, a Chinese railway engineer. The student was believed to have been motivated by resentment against the diplomat for his lack of interest in the affairs of Chinese students in France, who by that time numbered in their thousands. There had also been scandals concerning the use of funds intended for distribution by the Chinese Embassy to the students. So it was perhaps not entirely out of charity that the minister petitioned the French judiciary to handle his would-be assassin's case with maximum leniency. Li drew a one-year prison sentence, but there seemed to be sympathy for him on the part of the people of Montargis.

Deng must have read of these events and they could only have stirred his awakening consciousness as a Chinese revolutionary. The incident could also have brought home to him the futility of individual assassinations in the anarchist tradition, by comparison with organisational work among the workers. Since he spent very little time studying while in France, his main French contacts must have been workers who would have taught him the ethics and aspirations of the socialist/communist movement.

Deng appears to have worked at Creusot on the Loire, in Bayeux, Châtillon-sur-Seine, and finally at Billancourt in 1925, where he worked in the Renault factory. He did not attend many classes but must have learnt much about the workers' movement in France and probably picked up spoken French although he never speaks it today. Deng associated with the future Marshal Nie Rongzhen and Zhou Enlai, as well as with other young Chinese who later became prominent in the Communist movement — including the future economic planner Li Fuchun, foreign minister Marshal Chen Yi, and the leader of the women's movement, Cai Chang.

When Deng first arrived in France the Communist Party had not yet been founded, but leftist Chinese students in France had formed a movement called the Socialistes which Deng joined in 1922. Its twice-monthly journal for Chinese leftists in Europe was called *Chi Guang* (*Red Light*). Zhou Enlai was editorial writer and Deng Xiaoping was so good at duplicating this journal and other political notices and flysheets that he was nicknamed the 'doctor of mimeography'. Some of the most active Chinese students were deported by the French authorities for staging a sit-in demanding cheap accommodation at Lyons. After Zhou left France in July 1924, Deng succeeded in becoming the leading figure in the Paris branch of the Chinese Communist Party.

Like most revolutionaries, the Chinese in Paris quarrelled frequently among themselves. The rival Youth Party wanted to lay the stress on nationalism for the new China, disclaiming the value of Marxism-Leninism. Once, in 1924, Deng organised a reconciliation meeting but the participants started throwing chairs at one another while he sat quietly on the rostrum looking on.

After speaking at a meeting in Billancourt — a suburb of Paris — in early 1924, the French police raided Deng's hotel room and found primitive printing equipment, pamphlets and books about communism and the Nationalists. The number of Chinese students in France had risen from 400 in 1919 to more than 1,500 by 1921. Unknown to themselves, the French bourgeoisie, academics, and industrialists had brought along a generation of young Chinese radicals whose activities would contribute to the destruction of French interests in East Asia two or three decades later.

In 1926, Deng left France and travelled to Moscow via Berlin before returning to China.

Chapter 2

THE YOUNG COMMISSAR

T he China to which Deng returned in 1926 was undergoing violent internal upheavals. In July of that year, Chiang Kai-shek, the military right-hand man of the revolutionary leader Dr Sun Yat-sen, had launched the Northern Expedition against the old-style warlords from Canton. Winning a succession of quick victories, the Nationalist armies seized Wuhan, the most important city of central China, which was at the junction of the north–south and east–west arterial transport systems. Leaving it in the hands of the left-wing Nationalist and Communist elements of the expeditionary force, Chiang turned eastwards down the Yangzi River to subdue the armies of the Nanjing warlord, Sun Chuan-fang.

Under agreements previously reached between Chiang and the Communist leaders at the urging of the Moscow-based Comintern (the Communist International or foreign political wing of the Soviet Communist Party, also called the Third International), and despite the growing ideological gap, Chinese Communists were permitted to join the Nationalist Party in 1923 on condition that they recognise its primacy in the revolutionary movement and submit to its authority. This marked the beginning of the so-called first period of co-operation between the Communists and the Nationalists. The Party Secretary-General, the intellectual Chen Duxiu, accepted this move with reluctance and events justified his misgivings. Considering the extent to which Chiang Kai-shek mistrusted the Communists, it seems strange that he left them in control of a place as strategic as Wuhan.

In 1926, before returning to China, Deng Xiaoping had gone to Moscow and, like some other young Chinese leftists of the time, spent several months studying at the Sun Yat-sen University which had been established in the Soviet capital in 1925. The purpose of the university was to inculcate in the minds of Chinese students the ideas of Marx and Lenin and to train them to be obedient to the instructions of the Comintern, which supplied aid and advice to developing Communist parties. The students studied four hours of Russian each day, together with other European languages. Chinese students were taught through interpreters and, although Deng had no strong academic bent, he was decisive and determined to accomplish anything he attempted. The students also received military training and met some of the Soviet leaders including Bukharin and the ill-starred Trotsky.

After eight months' training in Moscow, Deng agreed to proceed to China in the company of the Christian warlord Feng Yuxiang who had been visiting the Soviet Union at the invitation of Stalin and was interested in Soviet military aid and advisers. Feng, a huge man who dressed like a peasant or common soldier, was famous for his adherence to the traditions of 'muscular Christianity'. He insisted that his men be baptised and follow rigid moral and ethical rules. They were forbidden to drink, smoke, gamble, or frequent whores, they were enjoined to respect the common people wherever they were billeted, and to eschew looting — all of which was highly unusual in a warlord army.

However, Feng's politics were less clear-cut than his religious beliefs. An anti-Communist by temperament, he nonetheless saw the advantages of having the aid and resources of the Soviet Union at his disposal. He brought 98 Soviet advisers back with him from his visit, together with some young Chinese radicals, including Deng, who had been studying and working abroad. In return for this aid the Russians stipulated that Feng should join Chiang Kai-shek's Northern Expedition against the other warlords. Taking part in the campaign would at least give Feng the chance to exact his revenge on Zhang Zuolin, the Manchurian despot who had once betrayed him on the field of battle, and perhaps the opportunity to capture Peking.

Even in the hands of the so-called Anhui, or Anfu, military clique which represented itself as the legitimate government of all China, power over domestic affairs was negligible. Since Moscow was still supporting Chiang as a militant, anti-imperialist revolutionary and was not over-concerned about his primarily anti-leftist views, Feng sought to please the Russians by declaring that he would apply to join the Nationalists. However, widespread civil war broke out before he could put this proposal into effect and upon his arrival in Xi'an, Deng and Feng were plunged into the military and political intrigues which were now dominating the life of China.

Deng helped the well-known communist leader Li Dazhao to set up a military and political academy at Xi'an in the hope that it would become the 'Whampoa of the northwest' to rival the Whampoa Military Academy in Canton. Deng was made head of the political department and, for a while, chief of education. The academy was named after Sun Yat-sen and was controlled almost exclusively by Communists who were permitted, at that time, to belong concurrently to the Nationalist Party. The Xi'an school trained officers for battalion, company, and platoon-level commands. Among the introductory lectures were 'Essentials of Socialism', 'The ABCs of Communism', 'The State and the Revolution', and 'The Three New People's Principles', as well as other courses in political theory propagating Marxism-Leninism among the young officer cadets. Under the Sun Yat-sen Military Academy's leftist influence, other military schools were set up and controlled by the Communists at Wuyuan, Baotou, and Yinchuan.

On 12 April 1927, Chiang Kai-shek suddenly had all known Communists and left-wing activists in Nanjing and Shanghai murdered by roving execution squads in an anti-Communist purge later labelled the 'Shanghai Massacre'. Similar purges were carried out in Canton and other parts of south China and Feng Yuxiang sided with Chiang in his attempt to wipe out all Communist influence. After Deng and other leftists were expelled from the academy they proceeded to Wuhan where, although its political influence in other parts of China had been undermined by the massacres, the main military force of the Communists was still intact.

In Wuhan, Deng was admitted to the Communist Party's Central Committee at the early age of 23. In August 1927, he sat and took notes in one of the most important meetings, where it was decided to expel the veteran Marxist Chen Duxiu from the Party leadership. In charge of policy-making and its implementation, Chen was accused of 'opportunism' and leaning too far towards the Nationalists.

The Communist Party secretly moved its Central Committee headquarters to Shanghai. Deng followed and worked with Zhou Enlai in the Shanghai underground under the title of Secretary of the Central Committee. It was during this time that he married his first wife, Zhang Qianyuan, a county secretary in Jiangxi province. She was pregnant when Deng was despatched to Guangxi and both wife and child died in labour. Early in 1932, Deng went back to Shanghai to see to the funeral. In the same year, the Central Committee moved headquarters from Shanghai to the Jiangxi guerilla base area.

Having wintered in Nanjing, Chiang Kai-shek resumed the Northern Expedition in the spring of 1927, pushing up to the strategic city of Xuzhou in northern Jiangsu province, then turning west to attack the warlord Wu Peifu in Henan. Feng too came down from his northwestern lair to attack Wu and linked up with Chiang Kai-shek's forces in Henan, forcing Wu to retreat further up the railway towards Peking.

In 1928, the Northern Expedition was brought to a successful conclusion with the capture of Peking. But still the Nationalists could not totally unify China, due to their weakness in mountainous southwest Guangxi. However, early in 1929, Chiang Kai-shek succeeded in defeating the Guangxi warlord Li Zongren who was later to become Vice President of the

Nationalist Party. Chiang drove out the troops who had been occupying Guangxi, and General Li Mingrui was appointed Pacification Commissioner for the region.

Guangxi has a large ethnic minority group, the Zhuang, among whom a Communist peasant leader Wei Baqun had established a base of popular support for the Party. Some high officials were also sympathetic to the Communists, so the Party decided to step up its underground work there and Deng Xiaoping was sent to Nanning. He suggested to Li Mingrui that they set up an elementary military training brigade to be supervised by a pro-Communist officer, Zhang Yunyi. Li consented and soon the Fifth (Training) Brigade was formed, consisting of three battalions or nine companies, the instructors recruited from squad and platoon leaders from the Nanning garrison. The brigade was heavily infiltrated with pro-Communists, but with no more than 1,000 men it was decidedly below strength, even for China. Li Mingrui, who wanted to train more troops, recruited bandits and demobilised soldiers whose loyalty to the Nationalists was only notional. He put the Fourth and Fifth Brigades at Zhang's disposal, and their commanders began to plot the defection of the troops.

In September, Deng Xiaoping organised a Communist Party congress in Nanning at which a resolution was passed to arm the local peasantry in preparation for an uprising. This was the formal setting up of the Red Army, which would include industrial workers as well as peasants. The Guangxi Communist leaders sent cadres to the upper reaches of the Youjiang (You River), north of Nanning, to conduct agitation in the villages and to form a militia force of several hundred peasants from the Donglan area.

In late September 1929, Li Mingrui decided to mount an offensive against Chiang Kai-shek's armies in neighbouring provinces. The Communist leaders managed to persuade him to keep the Fourth and Fifth Brigades in Nanning on the grounds that they were not yet sufficiently trained for the field. No sooner had Li left than Deng, Zhang Yunyi, and

15

other commanders went into action. Yuan Renyuan, a veteran revolutionary, recalled in his memoirs:

'We immediately sent the two brigades to the You (Right) and Zuo (Left) Rivers to begin their activity. Zhang Yunyi assumed command of the Nanning arsenal which had six or seven thousand rifles as well as mountain cannon, pursuit guns, machine guns, mines and plenty of ammunition. The Communists prepared to load these arms on boats and carry them away.'

Meanwhile, Li Mingrui was beaten by the Nationalist troops he had encountered and after escaping the field of battle, he openly went over to the Communists. The arms, ammunition, and guards were loaded on to a steamboat commanded by Deng, while Zhang Yunyi led the remaining men on foot. They rendezvoused at Pingma and eventually set up a base at the county seat of Baise in northwestern Guangxi. The area was mountainous and heavily forested, ideal country for guerilla warfare. With Deng as Secretary, the Party leaders held a congress concerning future military tactics before beginning operations.

Thanks to the efforts of the ethnic Zhuang leader Wei Baqun, militias and peasants' associations were established in Baise and there had already been some skirmishes with troops from the Nanning garrison. Baise commanded communications in the border areas of Guangxi, Guizhou, and Yunnan. The Communists now decided on their plan of action with four salient points: a 'mass movement' was to be initiated among the troops and the local people; soldiers were to be 'rectified' or disciplined, the ranks filled out, and a military committee consisting of both officers and rank-and-file was to be set up; through its underground organisations, the Party was to issue firearms to peasants and an anti-gentry and anti-landlord movement would be started; and non-Communists were to be expelled from the ranks and supervision of firepower was to be made more rigorous.

Although these measures were to prove extremely successful in the few Communist-dominated parts of China as Deng
and his associates set about gathering taxes, they gave the
impression that they were themselves warlords setting up a
safe base area. As bandit groups controlled large parts of the
rural areas and often resembled out-of-work soldiers, the rich
families near the Youjiang panicked and fled.

In November 1929, Deng asked the Party leadership in
Shanghai for instructions from the Party and a plan for an
armed uprising in southern China was approved. Deng and
Zhang decided that on 11 December — the anniversary of the
unsuccessful Canton uprising — they would stage another
coup close to home. At 8 a.m. on that day, Deng and Zhang's
troops assembled in drizzle in the main street of Baise,
proclaimed the setting up of the Seventh Army of the Workers' and Peasants' Red Army, and called on them to pick up
their working tools and demonstrate in the streets. At the
same time, the First Congress of the Workers' and Peasants'
Army was being held with Yu Zuoyu as Commander-in-Chief
and Political Commissar. On 2 February 1930, Deng organised the Zuojiang (Left River) uprising at Longchuan and
proclaimed the formation of the Eighth Red Army.

The factional strife in the Nationalists' Nanning units had
distracted their attention from the activities of the Communists in the You and Zuo river areas. Following the Longchuan
uprising, the Nationalist command in Nanning assembled its
forces and attacked the Eighth Army on the Zuojiang. Deng,
meanwhile, had gone to Shanghai to report and receive
further instructions and, on his return in the summer of 1930,
found stronger and more self-confident Communist troops
returning to their Youjiang base after the campaign. Apparently, in imitation of Mao in Jiangxi, whose activities he would
have learnt about at Shanghai, Deng set up an experimental
centre for land reform at Donglan in Guangxi.

Mao Zedong, born in 1893 into a well-to-do peasant family
in Hunan province, had left home in his teens, partly as a
result of friction with his father. He attended military college

for a while in Changsha, the capital of Hunan, and later went for long treks in the countryside to investigate the situation of the peasants who were bitterly oppressed by landlords and the undisciplined soldiers of the warlord. He became attracted to modern Western ideas of society and revolution.

Mao worked in the Peking University library in 1918 where he came into slight contact with other intellectual leaders of the revolutionary movement in China. Later he returned to Changsha to teach and organise agitation among the workers. In the early 1920s, he was officially a member of the Nationalists which was seen as a leftist influence in Chinese politics. After leading the abortive Autumn Harvest uprising in 1927, Mao escaped capture and established a revolutionary armed base at Jinggangshan, in the mountainous borderlands of Jiangxi and Hunan provinces.

From 1928, Mao supervised the expansion of the Jinggangshan base into a 'soviet area' and survived repeated attempts by the Nationalists to suppress his growing forces. But with the help of brilliant young officers like Zhu De and Lin Biao, the Red Army was able to maintain this base until 1934. Even though the Communist soldiers seized the arms of Nationalist troops sent out against them, they gradually ran short of supplies and were in danger of being encircled and overwhelmed by Chiang's forces.

Mao's ideas on peasant revolution brought him into conflict with the Party leadership in Shanghai and the clandestine branch committee in Changsha, which sent him instructions so inept that they could wipe out his entire force if he had attempted to implement them. By the time Deng Xiaoping arrived with his battered remnants from Guangxi, Mao was being increasingly criticised by the 'orthodox' Communists who had studied in Moscow and worked in the labour movement in Shanghai. He was overruled in his policy of holding one base area firmly and eschewing military adventures. Zhu De was sent out to campaign against the Nationalist units in the summer of 1928 and, as his forces were badly mauled before they returned to Jinggangshan, Mao and

Zhu reasserted their authority over other leaders who were pushing the Shanghai line.

When the Chinese Communist Party held its Sixth Congress in Moscow in mid-1928, the well-known Marxist theorist and agitator, Li Lisan, achieved effective leadership over the Party organisation in Shanghai and other cities. Li saw the proletariat as the main driving force of the revolution but he was out of touch with the reality of the peasant revolution espoused by Mao. He and the other pro-Moscow leaders failed to control Mao and his forces who were preoccupied with their own attempt to stage uprisings in different parts of south China. When these failed, the Nationalists counter-attacked with encirclement campaigns against the Communist base area. By the spring of 1929, Mao had formulated his famous theory of revolutionary warfare: 'The enemy advances, we retreat; the enemy halts, we harass; the enemy tires, we attack; the enemy retreats, we pursue.'

Early in 1930, at a conference held at Gutian in Jiangxi, Mao again attacked the Li Lisan line. Mao was all for gradual development of the situation, consolidation of territory held, and good discipline rather than what he called 'revolutionary impetuosity'. Because Mao himself was guilty of fatal impetuosity from 1958 on, it is easy to forget that in his formative years as a leader he advocated a cautious and prudent strategy.

In August 1930, Mao, Zhu De, and another future famous commander, Peng Dehuai, attempted to storm the city of Changsha. Deng Xiaoping and Zhang Yunyi had incorporated their two regiments into the Third Army Corps under the command of Peng and they succeeded in capturing Changsha for ten days before the Nationalist armies forced their men out. Eventually the Communists withdrew to their bases in Jiangxi and despite the defeat at the battle for Changsha, their reputation as fighting men was enhanced. More importantly, however, the authority of Li Lisan had been effectively undermined.

By 1930, Li Lisan had gained control in the Party Centre. In 1928, for security reasons, the Sixth Party Congress was held in Moscow and the following were appointed members of the Politburo: Xiang Zhongfa (Secretary), Li Lisan (Head of Propaganda), Zhou Enlai (Head of Military Affairs), together with Xiang Ying, Qiu Qubai, Zhang Guotao, and Cai Hesen. Qu Qiubai was accused of 'adventurist' errors and later he and Zhang Guotao were posted to Moscow as representatives of the Chinese Party at the Third International. This would appear to be a strange choice, especially since Zhang was regarded by Stalin as a 'rightist'. Although Stalin had turned against the leftist Trotsky, the world Communist system was considered basically a 'left' movement and 'rightist' was a derogatory label. The label of rightist was also attached to Cai Hesen by Li Lisan. In 1929, Cai was stripped of his Politburo membership and sent to Moscow 'to study'. His office was taken up by Li Lisan, then an alternate member of the Politburo but was promoted to its Standing Committee at the same time. So, in reality, the Politburo in Shanghai was controlled by Li Lisan, Xiang Zhongfa (who was arrested by the Nationalist police and executed on 24 June 1931), and Zhou Enlai.

On 1 June 1930, the Politburo passed a resolution on current tasks, proclaiming that a new revolutionary tide was fast approaching and that Communist victories should be scored in one or more provinces. In August, Li Lisan's representatives went to the Youjiang base to transmit orders to attack the cities of Liuzhou and Guizhou. A new base was to be set up in northern Guangdong with the aim of bottling up the Nationalist forces in the south of the province. Canton was to be attacked, followed by the 'completion of the revolution' in south China.

With these ambitious goals, Zhang and Deng moved their troops out after the Mid-Autumn Festival. The dry south China winter provided good campaigning weather and in early October the troops mustered at Hechi and the Seventh Red Army convened a Party conference. It was decided to rename the three columns under Zhang and Deng as 'divisions'. From intelligence reports they knew that the much-feared Guangxi commander, General Bai Zhongxi, was moving out of Liuzhou with reinforcements, forcing the Communists to abandon their plan to attack the town. The Front Committee studied the situation and decided instead to turn eastwards, towards the Guangxi–Hunan border.

By now the troop strength of the Seventh Red Army had been considerably reduced and Deng and Zhang Yunyi merged the three divisions into two regiments to be called the 55th and the 58th. At the beginning of 1930, they began moving into northern Guangdong and, after traversing several counties, they decided to cross the Lechang River and set up another base in Guangxi. Mo Wenhua, a Communist officer, recalls:

'The Lechang is deep and swift. There are white horses on its surface. It looked unfordable. On the bank, which twists and turns exceedingly, there were only two small boats on the shore and these were the only means of crossing the river. Deng stood on a high spot on the bank and examined the situation for a while. Then he came down to discuss things with Zhang Yunyi. At 3 p.m. the 55th Regiment led by Deng crossed the river. After establishing a beachhead, they could see nothing of the enemy. More than two hours later most of the armed units of the 58th Regiment had also crossed and it was quiet on both banks. There only remained a company of Zhang's garrison troops, two companies of infantry and a medical brigade with a recreation company — about 500–600 people who had still not crossed the river. Suddenly concentrated firing was heard. A large force of Nationalist troops from the strategic Shao Pass were coming quickly down the road towards the river. Deng and Zhang were separated. In this engagement Deng showed himself to be a forceful commander who also knew how to conserve ammunition.'

Both regiments escaped the ambush and met up later at Yongxing in Jiangxi. Towards the end of March 1931, the

21

Seventh Red Army convened its second Party congress at Yongxing and made up its troop strength to some extent. It arrived in Jiangxi reduced from its original strength of 20,000 men to 6,000. Deng was sent secretly to Shanghai to talk to the Party Centre and receive orders regarding his own future.

At this time the Party Centre in Shanghai was dominated by the Moscow-trained Twenty-eight Bolsheviks, led by the Communists Wang Ming and Bo Gu (Qin Bangxian) who had recently come home from training in Soviet Russia. The 24-year-old Wang, whose real name was Chen Shaoyu, had ousted Li Lisan's protégé Xiang Zhongfa from the post of Secretary-General. Bo Gu, who later became Secretary-General for a brief period, was an ideological enemy of Mao, particularly critical of Mao's belief in the peasantry as the most useful working material for revolution.

On the orders of the Party, Deng returned to the town of Ruijin in Jiangxi, where he was made Secretary of Ruijin district's Party Committee and subsequently promoted to Secretary of the Jiangxi Provincial Committee. Whilst in Ruijin, Deng became closely acquainted with Mao Zedong and his dismissal of directives from Shanghai in favour of his own practice of rural before urban revolution. There was little the Shanghai Party headquarters could do about this, but as the Centre gradually moved from Shanghai to the Central Soviet in Jiangxi from April 1931 to early 1933 to escape persecution by the Nationalist secret police they came into direct conflict with Mao.

In 1934, Deng was entrusted with the editorship of the Red Army's political journal *Red Star*. He continued as its editor throughout the Long March, a journey that would bring the Communists to Yan'an in northwest China, where they would remain for the duration of the Anti-Japanese War and World War II.

Deng, who had more experience of real conditions than the Twenty-eight Bolsheviks, sided with Mao. However, the Shanghai group succeeded in removing Mao from his post as Chief Commissar of the Communist troops in Jiangxi and replaced him with Zhou Enlai. It seems that a strong friendship between Mao and Deng soon sprang up despite a gap of roughly ten years in age.

The mutiny in the Red Army units stationed at Donggu in central Jiangxi in 1931 has been variously described as 'political rascals organised by Chiang Kai-shek' and 'Nationalist secret agents'. Mao and Zhu De dispatched a strong force to put down the mutiny and several thousand men were executed in what Jerome Ch'en in his book *Mao and the Chinese Revolution* has called 'the bloodiest purge in the entire history of the Chinese Communist Party'.

Deng was appointed to be Secretary of three core Jiangxi soviet counties. He was already known as a strong supporter of Mao at Ruijin in 1932, and because of this became a target of the personal and political attacks made on Mao and his supporters by the Moscow-trained Bolsheviks, Bo Gu and Luo Fu. When the attacks appeared in print, Deng was moved to another and less important post — Head of Propaganda for Jiangxi province.

The Communists had a way of demoting or marking down for investigation any leading figure who came under suspicion of political deviance. They were often moved sideways to different types of work, presumably to cut them off from any useful political ties and alliances they might have initiated in their previous post. The same musical-chairs tradition has lasted into the 1980s, but Deng was not to get off so lightly for having crossed swords with the Bolsheviks. The struggle against him was led by one Luo Mai. The accusation against Deng was the same as had been levelled in the past against Mao, although there is no evidence that Mao was 'struggled against' by his accusers. Like Mao, Deng wanted to pursue a lenient policy towards relatively well-off peasants and farmers, in the interests of making them allies in the land reform program.

Deng made a self-criticism; but beyond a certain point he would not go: 'I cannot say more. What I wrote is true,' he insisted. He was detained for interrogation and despite being underfed while in detention, he survived due to his strong constitution. When Deng was released he was under suspicion of wanting to defect to the Nationalists. Astonishingly, he was appointed Secretary-General of the Red Army General Political Department, a post which in later decades became one of the most important in the Party. He asked to be transferred to a lowlier job after a few months; the reason for this is not known.

In 1933, Deng had his next taste of political disgrace when he was censured, along with Mao, for having sided with the Party leader of Fujian province, Luo Ming, who had incurred the wrath of the Party Centre. Luo Ming was a Cantonese revolutionary, closely associated with Li Lisan, who had entered western Fujian province to take over the post of Secretary of the Fujian–Guangdong–Jiangxi region where the Communists were active. He had been trained in Marxist theory and was the author of a book called *Party Construction*. However, Bo Gu, a prominent member of the Twenty-eight Bolsheviks group, had accused him in a 1933 report of dampening the enthusiasm of the masses in the border area through passivity and pessimism. Reference was made to a report Luo had written, in which he said:

'It is very difficult to assemble the masses in this border area for rallies or to mobilise them for military action, as they lead an erratic life, sometimes going to the mountains, sometimes at peace, and sometimes thrown into panic.... Some people here have complained about the dismal life caused by repeated enemy attacks. But the authorities still ask them to prepare for a prolonged war. What will become of them? . . . Many people say they have been sufficiently hard pressed to seek a temporary compromise, even though in their hearts they are still red, believe in the victory of the whole revolution, and cherish the hope of victory for the Red Army.'

Bo Gu ridiculed Luo Ming by saying that if Chairman Mao, Stalin, or Lenin went to harangue the peasants of western

Fujian, even they would fail to arouse revolutionary fervour according to Luo's thinking. Zhang Wentian also criticised Luo severely, accusing him of relying only on the Red Army regulars to fight the Nationalist troops who invaded the 'soviet' areas. The problem was that Luo's pessimism was only one reflection of the mood of the Red Army following reversals suffered in the Nationalists' Fourth Encirclement Campaign in 1933. These attitudes were attacked by the Party Centre as the 'Luo Ming Line', and one of those criticised was Deng Xiaoping, then Secretary of the Jiangxi provincial Party organisation. Mao's third brother, Mao Zetan, who was with him in Jiangxi, together with Gu Bo and Xie Weijun, were also the objects of attacks. Mao Zetan was accused of having based his guerilla tactics on stories in the famous old novel *San Guo Zhi Yan Yi (Romance of the Three Kingdoms)*, which generations of Chinese generals and revolutionaries have consulted in search of inspiration. Deng Xiaoping was accused of having belonged to the group which included Mao Zetan and strongly supported Mao Zedong. Deng was dismissed from his post and replaced by Li Fuchun who later became a famous economic planner. The 'deviants' were accused of 'opportunistic vacillation'.

It was stated in the Party organ *Douzheng (Struggle)* cited in Kuo *Analytical History*, that

'Most of these people are petty-bourgeois, manifesting the residual mentality of landlords and rich peasants. They have defied the official Party line due to their pessimistic and negative sentiments. . . .'

Also implicated were Mao's secretary, Gu Bo and Tan Zhenlin, Commander of the Fujian–Guangdong–Guangxi Red Army units and a future expert in the People's Republic:

'In particular, Comrade Tan Zhenlin actually joined with Deng Xiaoping in proposing the opportunist slogan of preparing for a fourth war at the convocation of the Party in Soviet areas. This was an attempt at anti-Party activities. Recently, after his opportunist errors had been repeatedly pointed out by the Central Bureau and the Provincial Committee, he ignored warnings to reform, insisting on his own ideas.'

Another prominent victim of the 'Luo Ming Line' affair was the theorist Lu Dingyi, who lost his Party membership even though he made at least two confessions to errors. The accusations against Lu went back to his period in Moscow when he had acquiesced in Qu Qubai's 'opportunist theory' instead of opposing it. Lu's error was particularly grave because he was the Director of the Propaganda Department of the Communist Youth League, a mass organisation which prepared young people for Party membership and nurtured their sense of ideology. When eventually rehabilitated, Lu Dingyi made an important contribution to the Party propaganda machine. Nevertheless, a crueller fate was reserved for him than his denunciation in the Jiangxi period. After being co-opted for a few months into the conspiratorial Cultural Revolution group in 1966, he fell victim to the Red Guards and was maltreated, incarcerated, and eventually died.

In October 1933 when Deng was lecturing in politics, Luo Mai, Director of the Party's Central Organisation Department, specifically identified Deng Xiaoping as the leader of the 'Luo Ming Line' group. In January 1934, at the Fifth Plenum of the Sixth Central Committee, Deng was denounced for engaging in 'anti-Party factionalism' and it was proposed that disciplinary measures be taken against him. He was removed from his post of Ruijin Party Secretary but retained the editorship of *Red Star*. Following the Zunyi Conference, in January 1935, his backing of Mao in Jiangxi was rewarded when Mao assumed the unchallenged leading role of the Party and the Red Army.

Chapter 3

THE ZUNYI CONFERENCE

The story of the Communists' Long March from Jiangxi to northwest China in 1934–35 has been told many times by Chinese writers and foreign authors such as Edgar Snow, Agnes Smedley, Harrison Salisbury, and Dick Wilson, so there is no need to rehearse it in detail here. Deng's activities during the March, apart from his attendance at a key Party conference and his full rehabilitation from political limbo, are hardly mentioned in the source materials available.

By the latter half of 1934, Chiang Kai-shek's Fifth Encirclement Campaign against the Communists in Jiangxi was imposing intolerable strains on the Nationalist troops. Formulated on the advice of Chiang's German military adviser, General Hans von Seeckt, the Nationalists besieged the Communists' mountain strongholds with concrete blockhouses, keeping them short of food, especially salt. The ring of blockhouses was tightened and the Communists' mobile guerilla warfare became less and less successful, forcing them to leave.

In October, the Red Army marched out of Jiangxi with 80,000 men and a handful of women, an enormous baggage train, ammunition and mortar shells, books and documents, a printing press, and even theatre props for propaganda shows. Most of this impedimenta was shed as the March progressed, initially in a westerly direction, then later north, with frequent twisting, turning, and backtracking. The winter was quite severe in the mountains and many of the men were badly clothed and poorly shod. Better-equipped Nationalist units pursued them and provincial armies blocked their way, forcing them to keep to the mountains and difficult low-lying swamps.

The leaders did not know exactly where the March would lead them. After a fierce battle was fought to cross the Xiang River in northwestern Guangxi, they decided to head for Sichuan province where it was hoped the powerful pro-Communist commander, Zhang Guotao, would welcome them.

In January 1935, at the small town of Zunyi in Guizhou province, the Communists paused to hold an important conference. Harrison Salisbury interviewed a number of Long March veterans in Peking in 1984, and in his book, *The Long March*, he reconstructs the scene thus:

'The room was bare except for a kerosene lantern swinging overhead, a rather battered heavy table in the center, possibly twenty-five chairs of different shapes and sizes in a rough semi-circle, a small iron stove (the temperature was January-raw), a few strategically placed white-and-pink enamel spittoons and some ashtrays. Occasionally, body-guards brought in hot water and tea.'

Twenty men gathered on several consecutive evenings for sessions, which often lasted until midnight, that were full of exhausting rhetoric and bitter accusations. The full members of the Politburo attending the conference, according to official Chinese material published in 1984, were Mao Zedong, Zhu De, Chen Yun, Zhou Enlai, Zhang Wentian (alias Luo Fu), and Bo Gu. Alternate members of the Politburo present at the conference were Wang Jiaxiang, Deng Fa, Liu Shaoqi, and He Kequan. The central military leaders Liu Bocheng and Li Fuchun attended. Lin Biao, Nie Rongzhen, Peng Dehuai, Yang Shangkun, and Li Zhuoran represented as army corps leaders. There was also Otto Braun (alias Li De), the German military adviser from the Comintern with his

28

interpreter, Wu Xiuqian, and Deng Xiaoping, then head of the general office of the Central Committee and no longer tainted by the 'deviance' he had shown over the 'Luo Ming' affair.

After the strategic destination of the Red Army and the location of the new soviet area had been discussed, Bo Gu, as the chairman of the conference, gave an explanation of the Red Army's failure to deal with the Nationalists' Fifth Encirclement Campaign in Jiangxi. Zhang Wentian gave a counter report and Zhou Enlai made a supplementary report. Mao gave a detailed critique of the military errors that had forced them to leave Jiangxi. This was a direct attack on the policies pursued by Bo Gu and Braun. Other military leaders also had their say, but Braun, who smoked heavily in a corner, sulked for the rest of the conference. He said he was only an adviser and if the Chinese wanted to go their own way militarily, there was nothing for him to say about it. As Wu Xiuqian described it:

'He had a square frame and he usually sat like a rock until ready to speak. Now he showed his anger in the changing colour of his face. It grew red as he listened to Bo Gu and turned white when Mao began to attack him. At no point did he lose physical control, but he smoked cigarette after cigarette . . . digging deep into the stock he had gotten from the newly confiscated stores of Zunyi. He looked more and more depressed and gloomy.' (Harrison Salisbury, *The Long March*)

The resolution of the conference apportioned the blame for the Communist defeats on the Nationalists' Fifth Encirclement Campaign which had forced them to abandon the Jiangxi soviets in the first place. However, Bo Gu argued that it was physically impossible to defeat the strong Nationalist force whose concrete blockhouses had encircled them. The resolution rejected this argument, saying that Bo Gu had failed to realise that the Communists had greatly enlarged their military forces and could have defeated the enemy. He was also said to have underestimated the failures in political work within the soviet areas and had pursued an erroneous line in military affairs. The resolution said:

'Under these circumstances [the blockhouse policy], our strategic line should have been decisive battles for defence (an offensive type of defence) concentrating superior forces, selecting the enemy strength [when we had] the confidence [to do so]. But in the campaign against the Fourth "Encirclement", [we] adopted a pure defence line (of defence of positions only), rather than decisive battles for defence, coupled with the so-called tactics of "short swift thrusts" as advised by Braun. This enabled the enemy's strategy and tactics of a protracted war and the principle of blockhouses to achieve their aims and to inflict partial losses on the main force of the Red Army, forcing [us] to leave the Central Soviet. It must be pointed out that this line runs counter to the basic principles of the strategy and tactics which had helped the Red Army to victory.'

The resolution argued that 'pure defence' was impractical when the Communist forces were so short of heavy equipment, such as artillery, and had no aeroplanes.

'Only by developing from defence to counter-offensive (both in campaigns and strategically) and then to offence, by winning decisive engagements, and by whittling down the enemy's strength, can we pulverize the enemy, defend our soviets and develop the soviet revolutionary movement.'

These criticisms of Bo Gu and Braun echoed the thinking of Mao and his supporters, including Deng who listened in silence to the debates around the table. It became clear that most of the experienced battle commanders supported Mao to some degree and were tired of the dogmatism of Bo Gu and the crude manners of Braun.

The final resolution recommended mobile warfare using both guerilla tactics and main-force units according to the circumstances; it formulated the principle of 'people's war', claimed in the 1960s to be the brainchild of Mao and Marshal Lin Biao. The resolution pointed out that the blockhouses were not invincible. They 'made the enemy's units tired, dispersed his strength, and nursed his reliance on them — leading to a loss of confidence in victory once he leaves them. He must come out of them when he advances towards us; he cannot build them all over the country in order to restrict our operations.'

The resolution added that the failure of the strategy supported by Bo Gu and Braun had been demonstrated at the battle of Guangchang in April 1934, when the Communists suffered near-disastrous losses in a positional conflict with the Nationalist forces. Mao and his supporters were determined that no such losses should ever be risked again over the issue of a single battle. They favoured 'a protracted war and swift battles', which was not the same as the policy of 'short, swift thrusts'. They knew from experience the need for soldiers to eat, rest, and train — factors which the internationalists did not appreciate. They held that it was permissible to let some soviet areas be overrun by the enemy since they could be restored after the enemy was lured into the trap and destroyed. Bo Gu and Braun had merely aimed at defending every inch of the soviet areas without going all out to defeat the enemy.

Characteristically, Zhou Enlai broke the impasse at Zunyi with a diplomatic manoeuvre over a period of time: he surrendered to Mao his role as Chief Military Commissar and Head of the Military Affairs Committee. Mao gradually shared the power of military decisions in his new capacity as a member of the Standing Committee of the Politburo and later as one of the 'team or group of three' in charge of strategic command. The functions of the Military Affairs Committee had been suspended with the creation of the former 'group of three' — Braun, Bo Gu, and Zhou Enlai — just before the beginning of the Long March and were not revived until the summer of 1935 when Mao and his company met with Zhang Guotao.

The main arguments had centred round the Communists' response to the Nationalists' Fifth Encirclement Campaign between 1933 and 1934. The resolution accused Bo Gu of considering the defeat of the encirclement campaign as 'an objective impossibility'. There had not been a shortage of personnel on the Communist side, as more than 100,000 workers and peasants were mobilised and armed, but political work had been neglected and, it was said, 'we have concealed the bad effects of the erroneous line'. The Nationalists' forces adopted the strategy and tactics of a protracted war on the principle of blockhouses, the resolution added. 'Their attempt was to wear out our human and material resources, to reduce the size of the soviet and finally to destroy us by engaging our main forces.' The resolution added that the Red Army should have been conducting a strategic line of

'. . . decisive battles for defence — not pure defence, but seeking decisive engagements in order to turn them into a counter-offensive type of defence. . . . For victory, we must not refuse to give up temporarily our main forces for the sake of the soviet.'

The 'pure defence' proponents did not even pay attention to a telegram from the Third International in Moscow, criticising their line. The military leadership, the resolution stated, had been too prodigal with its manpower.

'For triumphant combats, the Red Army must make necessary heroic sacrifices. This is the characteristic of the armed forces of (our) class; this is the basis of our revolutionary military victories. If the *quid pro quo* for the sacrifices is victory, they are worthwhile. But this does not apply to the worthless "dare-to-die" type of fighting. We must know that only by preserving our personnel can we preserve our Soviet.'

As to the vexing question of whether Deng Xiaoping attended the Zunyi Conference, the weight of evidence indicates that he did, but only as an observer (possibly as a notetaker and as editor of *Red Star*). There is no evidence that he spoke. A Red Guard publication in 1967 accused Deng of being a proponent of the 'goulash communism' ascribed to Soviet leader Nikita Khrushchev, who was also interested in a consumer reform in the Soviet Union. For instance, Deng is quoted by the Red Guards as having said to the townspeople of Zunyi during a return visit there in the 1950s:

'Communism means there must be residential points, each with at least 25,000 people. Your residential point [Zunyi] must have all the things to be found in Peking and Guiyang [capital of Guizhou province]. In the future it will be permissible to have high-heeled shoes, lipsticks and TV sets. Don't we want to eliminate the differences between town and countryside? Well, this is how.

When communism comes, everybody will have a sewing machine, with which to make the kind of clothes one likes. Full freedom of choice in clothing is permissible. One may wear whatever dress one likes. The same applies to shoes. Those who like shoes made of cloth will wear shoes made of cloth. Those who like rubber shoes will wear rubber shoes. Those who like grass sandals will wear grass sandals to their hearts' content. With the money saved, they may buy a pair of leather shoes. There will be a combination of high-class and low-class things. Complete uniformity is to be avoided.

There should be spaces for recreation. One sports ground for several hundred families is not enough. . . . I propose that China become a country of bicycles, with everybody owning one bicycle. Bicycle riding is good for the body. Farming implements are to be drawn by motor vehicles.

What kind of work will be the most important in the future? Taking care of babies will be the most important. In the whole nation, 20 million people are needed to do this job. An important part of the work is to educate and train child care personnel. They should be paid higher salaries than university professors. Another important job is cooking. In future everyone will have 60 catties [30 kilograms] of pork to eat each year, and drink two ounces of *baiganr* spirit.'

The Red Guard publication added the following gloss to its list of Deng's 'revisionist' statements:

'Such was the "communism" in the mind of Deng. It was an unqualified return of capitalism and pseudo-communism. Instead of struggling for communism, people were to struggle for lipstick, TV sets and high-heeled shoes, for pork, liquor and bicycles. Strengthening of proletarian dictatorship, elimination of class and class differences, revolutionization of the thought of man and raising high the Great Red Banner of the Thought of Mao Zedong ... all these vanished into the air! In Deng Xiaoping's own words, the five things were food, clothing, housing, transport, and recreation. How is this kind of communism different from Khrushchev's "goulash" communism?'

After the Zunyi Conference and the arrival of the Red Army in Shanxi province, although Deng's activities in 1936 are obscure, Mao's new ascendancy obviously worked in Deng's favour. After the outbreak of the war with Japan in July 1937, a further redesignation of the various armies was implemented. The First and Fifth Front Armies were combined to make the 115th Division, under the command of Lin Biao. The Second Front Army became the 120th Division, commanded by He Long, and the Fourth Front Army became the 129th Division, commanded by Liu Bocheng. Barely a year and a half later, in January 1938, Deng was promoted on the death of the 129th Division's commissar and was made Political Commissar of the 129th and nominally Deputy Commander of an important army division which eventually grew to embrace nearly 50 regiments. Even with the low manning levels which persisted in the Red Army's component units, this was an impressive posting for a man still in his mid-thirties.

Liu Bocheng was born in Sichuan and having failed the lowest grade of the Imperial examinations, he attended a military school and served as a junior officer with a warlord in Sichuan, where he became acquainted with Zhu De, the opium-addicted warlord commander who subsequently rose to be Commander-in-Chief of the Red Army. At the age of 45, Liu commanded the 129th Division.

Politically, Liu hovered between the Communists and the Nationalists, but after the decisive split between them in 1927 he went to the Soviet Union for extra study and training. On returning to China and working briefly for the Communist leader Li Lisan in Shanghai, he made his way to the soviet areas in Jiangxi. He undertook high-level instruction and training activities and in 1932 became Chief of Staff of the Central Revolutionary Council. He took part in the Long March and his knowledge of Sichuan and its hostile ethnic minorities enabled him to render valuable service to the Red Army. It was Liu's men who captured Zunyi. Their chief task from then on would be to fight the Japanese rather than the Nationalists.

In the autumn of 1937, Liu marched the 129th Division into southern Shanxi province where they took up positions in the Taihang mountain range which straddles the Shanxi–Hebei border. In September, his men launched a daring night raid on a nearby Japanese airfield at Yangming-bao and reported that they had destroyed 24 aircraft. They claimed that by November they had killed 1,000 Japanese.

Because they were nominally in a period of 'co-operation' with the Nationalists, the Communists had to decide how much of their energy to devote to fighting the Japanese and how much to the covert struggle with Chiang Kai-shek. In August 1938, Mao Zedong called a meeting at Luochuan, a small town in the Shanxi panhandle, which Zhu De, Liu Bocheng, and other important commanders attended. It is not clear whether Deng was present, but he was probably briefed on its conclusions when Liu Bocheng returned to his base.

Mao proposed that the Communist armies should not weaken themselves by engaging in too much combat with the Japanese. Zhang Guotao, Zhou Enlai, Peng Dehuai, and other military commanders were shocked by this cynicism. Mao compromised by agreeing to an all-out effort against the Japanese, although he insisted on putting the emphasis on guerilla warfare. From then on, Zhu De installed his Eighth Army headquarters alongside the 129th Division in the Taihang Mountains, so he was probably in frequent contact with both Liu Bocheng and Deng Xiaoping. The patience with which Deng had built his career was now paying off as he was commissar of a major field unit in the proximity of the commander-in-chief.

The Communists were shaping up for their first big head-on clash with the Japanese, and Mao's policy of retaining overall guerilla warfare was not thoroughly implemented. From August 1940 onwards, the Communists began disrupting rail communications in north China, severely hampering the mobility of the Japanese. The 129th Division alone committed 47 regiments to the plan for a major confrontation in north China and organised impressive logistical support in the countryside, but as the winter clamped down the Japanese struck back with a scorched-earth policy. By the summer of 1941, Zhu De, Liu Bocheng, and Deng found themselves bottled up in the Taihang Mountains, a situation not dissimilar to that in Jiangxi in the early 1930s. It was only in December that the Communist high command showed signs of realising the value of Mao's guerilla tactics and reverted to them in an attempt to deny the Japanese control of the rural areas.

This decision coincided with the Japanese attack on Pearl Harbor which brought the United States into the war. Tokyo was forced to divert troops to the Pacific, leaving the commanders in China with the increasingly difficult task of achieving genuine control of the eastern half of the country. The western provinces were able to hold out because the great difficulties of the terrain hampered invasion. Protected by the surrounding mountains and the problems of navigation on the middle Yangzi River, Chiang Kai-shek made Chongqing in Sichuan his wartime headquarters.

Chapter 4

THE STRATEGIST

The atomic bombing of Japan in August 1945 was followed soon afterwards by Japan's surrender to the Allies. The Communists were piqued that the Americans only flew in Nationalist officers to accept the surrender. The Chinese civil war resumed in 1946 despite attempts by the Americans to arrange a reconciliation between the two Chinese factions. During the anti-Japanese war, Deng had been mostly in Yan'an or in the field, but sources on his activity at this time are very inadequate. Zhou Enlai had spent the anti-Japanese war in Chongqing where Chiang Kai-shek had moved his headquarters when the Japanese had conquered east China.

By the end of the war the Chinese economy was in ruins. Following the explosion of the atom bombs over Hiroshima and Nagasaki, the Soviet Union declared war on Japan and most of the industrial plant installed in Manchuria by the Japanese was carried off to Russia. Food was short and inflation was rampant.

The Japanese Imperial Army had spread its domination of China as far south as Hong Kong and east to Shanghai and Nanjing and had been in control of the large Chinese island of Taiwan since 1895. Some of the strongest opposition the Japanese had met was in Shanxi province where the socialistic warlord Yan Xishan sometimes collaborated with Communist troops. The only provinces free of Japanese occupation were

Sichuan, Yunnan, Guizhou, and parts of Guangxi, as well as Tibet and the boundless deserts and oases of Xinjiang, which was virtually independent.

On 1 July 1947, Liu Bocheng and Deng led their troops, by now known as the *Dajun* (Grand Army), southwards across the Yellow River. Taking a disused schoolroom as their headquarters, they assembled the senior officers to discuss the situation. Referring to a map on the wall, Deng is reported to have said:

'At present the enemy's main strong points are Shandong and Northern Shaanxi (to be distinguished from the neighbouring province of Shanxi). In Shandong the enemy has 60 brigades, totalling 450,000 men. In northern Shaanxi he has 15 brigades totalling about 140,000 men. His strategy is that of the dumbbell. If he has put the two weights in northern Shaanxi and Shandong, what we've got to do is break the bar, and take the war into the territory controlled by the Guomindang.'

General Liu Bocheng then gave a report on the military situation. The parity between the Nationalists and the Communists, he said, had shifted to the Communists' advantage and they might soon go over to an offensive instead of a defensive stance. Pointing to the map, Liu said:

'Look at the Dabie (Great Divide) Mountains here. They are shaped like a child's stomacher (ie roughly triangular, with the apex at the bottom). They are a salient at the point where the Yangzi turns south. When we cross the Dabie Mountains, we can threaten Nanjing in the east and put pressure on Wuhan in the west. As for the enemy in the north, we can suck some of his forces in and lighten somewhat their weight in Shandong and northern Shaanxi and other battle areas. Our men will be able to destroy the enemy at will. Of course, things may get tougher as time goes by . . . . Revolution is a difficult matter. Everyone must make his own psychological and organisational preparations. This is a bold plan, but it is not foolhardy . . . . '

Deng then explained Mao's view on the matter:

'The move to the Dabie Mountains has three possible outcomes. One is that having paid the price [in casualties and lost equipment], we can't find a place to stand firmly, and will have to retreat. The second is that we won't find such a place, and will have to fight resolutely when surrounded. The third possible outcome is that, having paid the price, we will gain a firm foothold.'

Deng was in favour of the plan to seize a secure base. Like Mao, he wanted a rapid advance into the Dabie Mountains, because from there they could attack the Nationalist forces in the Central Plains and build up a solid position. He said:

'Eventually we will make the Central Plains our base and with another advance we can cross the Yangzi and liberate the whole country . . . . If we don't break out now, what will happen? Of course we can continue to kill a few of the enemy in a civil war, but the people and resources of the liberated areas will be slowly reduced until they are exhausted, and we will find it very hard to continue. Chiang Kai-shek wants to pursue the war in the liberated areas to achieve his goal of our complete liquidation. So if we break out, we will sabotage his plan.'

Deng then listed the lessons of historical experience:

'In the period of the Five Battles of Encirclement in Jiangxi in the 1920s and early '30s, Mao Zedong wanted to break out with the Red Army to exterior lines, but at that time the dogmatists would not permit this course of action, and as a result we had to move house on a big scale — by the Long March.'

Chiang, for his part, was not wasting time. Six Nationalist brigades comprising three divisions defending the Long-Hai railway (which linked Shaanxi with Jiangsu) were to manoeuvre northwards with the aim of turning the Communists' flank. But Liu and Deng laid a trap for them and claimed to have destroyed two of their brigades with minimal losses for themselves. They laid ambushes for advancing Nationalist forces and the enemy troops rushed into a pocket-shaped gap in their own lines only to find themselves 'in the bag'. Despite initial successes, however, the Communists were feeling the damage of the fierce fighting and were not really in shape to pursue the remaining Nationalist units. As well as guarding numerous prisoners who did not elect to change sides, their morale was low, compounded by inadequate preparation on the ground. If the Nationalists had counter-attacked them in southwestern Shandong, they would have been in a tight corner.

Sensing the Communists' problems, Chiang Kai-shek flew to Kaifeng, the ancient Chinese capital in Henan province. Since he believed that they wanted to move north he put them in the uncomfortable position of fighting with their backs to the river. Deng allegedly remarked:

'The enemy is using the "restaurant strategy" — making you eat a little bit at a time, till you burst! . . . Of course Chiang Kai-shek has many other strategies, such as destroying the Yellow River dykes and causing a flood to drown the [Communist] Grand Army in southern Shandong [in 1938]. He doesn't care about the 100 million peasants living on the south bank of the river. If it rains heavily for a few days, the Yellow River will be swollen and the Nationalist planes will continually bomb the dykes. Whichever way you look at it, the situation is bad.'

Mao and other central leaders at Yan'an wanted a rapid advance by the Grand Army. Apart from rooting out small

Nationalist units and anti-Communist village militias along the way, they were to avoid big battles with the enemy and dispense with a rearguard. The aim was to reach the Dabie Mountains within a couple of weeks. There they would have a tactical advantage and could draw the Nationalist troops into ambushes and guerilla fighting as they had done in Jiangxi. The Party leadership also wanted General Chen Yi's East China Field Army to break out of Shandong where it had been bottled up, and the Hunan-born General Chen Geng's Central Plains Field Army to leave southern Shaanxi and attack Nationalist forces in Henan. On 7 August 1947, Liu and Deng's forces marched roughly southwards in the direction of the Dabie Mountains. In the huge Central Plains they found hardly any Nationalist soldiers and the anti-Communist village militias offered no resistance.

Chiang Kai-shek was taken aback by this move. He believed the Communists wanted to recross the Yellow River northwards and engage his forces in the northwest and the northeast. It had been raining steadily for several days, and Chiang made the error of declaring that the Communists 'are like drowning rats as they are washed south'. Indeed, the obstacles in the Communists' southward path were formidable, including two medium-sized rivers and miles of mud created by the previous destruction of the dykes.

Liu and Deng saw the campaign as very risky but were determined to pursue it, continuing southwards until Chiang Kai-shek realised they were heading for the Dabie Mountains. By that time, Chiang had lost the advantage and began to see his strategy fall apart. He despatched 200,000 troops to catch up with the Communists and annihilate them, but for too long he had been misled about the Communists' true goals, for his armies any longer to make close contact with them.

The difficulties faced by the Communists were certainly severe and the Nationalist forces were pursuing them closely. There were times when Chiang's army and the Grand Army's rear were almost within artillery range of each other. The

Nationalist air force was harassing the Communists, a tactic the soldiers particularly feared and hated. The men were soaked to the skin and knee-deep in mud as they plodded on through the night, and when they bivouacked they barely had time to cook a meal and dry their uniforms. Deng reminded the officer corps and the rank and file:

'One can't take pity on soldiers. The hunger and exhaustion of some of the men is the price of the hot food and safety of the others. The difficulties and dangers of this time and place are the price of the victory and happiness of the whole country in the future. We must get used to thinking big and not look for easy ways out.'

On the evening of 17 August, the Grand Army reached the area previously flooded by the Yellow River. It varied from 27 to 33 miles wide. In the nine years since Chiang Kai-shek had changed the river's course to hamper the Japanese invaders, the area had become a huge lake and more than 300,000 people had lost their lives or farmland, swallowed up by the river. After the outbreak of the new civil war in 1946, Chiang again bombed the dykes to restore the river to approximately its former course.

The Huang Fan Qu (the area formerly flooded by the Yellow River) was still thick with mud and it took the Communists nearly three days to cross, with soldiers clinging to each other for safety. Liu and Deng and other officers walked their horses through the quagmire. Trucks and heavy artillery pieces had to be dismantled and in many cases abandoned.

After the passage of the Huang Fan, they reached the north bank of the Sha River and made a successful crossing. When word of this reached Chiang Kai-shek, he became fully aware of his erroneous interpretation of the Communists' strategy and saw that they were advancing towards the Dabie Mountains in a purposeful manner. The nightmare of another succession of encirclement campaigns and anti-guerilla warfare rose before the Nationalist leaders. Chiang ordered two divisions totalling some 30,000 men to rush to the south bank of the Ru River and stop the Grand Army from crossing.

The Grand Army reached the north bank of the Ru River on 23 August. On the south bank, at a town called Runanbu, all the boats had been taken away and smashed by the Nationalist troops, making it impossible for Liu and Deng's men to cross. The next day the Nationalist emergency forces were deployed along a front more than 10 miles wide on the south bank of the Ru. By clinging to bundles of sorghum stalks and pieces of wood for buoyancy, the Communists forced a crossing and established a bridgehead. This manoeuvre drove a wedge into the Nationalist lines on the south bank. The Communists rounded up whatever boats could still be found in the vicinity and set up a pontoon bridge, enabling the main-force unit to cross the river and begin a see-saw battle with the Nationalist troops.

Liu and Deng came up close to the front lines. Deng asked Chief of Staff Li Da to brief them. Li explained the position in a few words: 'It can be seen that the enemy's plan is to stop our main forces, to fight a decisive battle on the Ru and disrupt our plan to reach the Dabie Mountains.' As enemy shells fell nearby, Deng reportedly said: 'That's it, then. Apart from fighting our way across the river, there's no way out. If we don't cross the Ru today, the enemy will come on us from behind. If we can't get across, we'll have to split up and wage guerilla warfare, or turn back.' General Liu added: 'When two armies meet, the braver one wins. From now on, by day or by night, regardless of the enemy's heavy artillery and his aeroplanes, we shall use an offensive strategy. We shall create a river of blood from here!'

The three Nationalist divisions behind them had already made contact with the Communists' rear. After fierce fighting, the main force of the two leading Communist brigades quickly crossed to the south bank and occupied several small villages, punching a hole in the Nationalists' hastily-formed

45

line. The Communist soldiers took as their slogan: 'We can only advance, we cannot retreat.' The Nationalist troops, not expecting to encounter such resistance, were forced on to the defensive. Liu and Deng accompanied the infantry on foot. Liu was a man of nearly sixty and his health was not very good, but he reputedly walked more than 10 miles with the men. A little after one in the afternoon they reached their assembly point at Pengdian. Deng assembled the senior officers and told them:

'We still have a very difficult obstacle to pass on our way to the Dabie Mountains — the river Huai. You had better take a rest. Tomorrow we must send some troops out to seize the crossing point at Xixian, get ready the lumber we used in crossing the Ru, and get to the Dabie Mountains quickly.'

Apparently there was a freak snowfall, but a legend to the effect that the Huai froze over and some of the men crossed it on foot seems implausible. However, having crossed the river, the Grand Army took a tortuous path through the foothills and entered the Dabie Mountains. At that time Chiang Kai-shek, counting on Liu and Deng's inability to establish a foothold quickly and fight in their own rear, had 33 brigades at his disposal. Liu and Deng convened a conference at a small town in Xin county. Placing special emphasis on fighting spirit, Deng explained to the officers the meaning of their move southwards, adding that their suffering had not been wasted. Some officers had allegedly developed 'rightist' defeatist inclinations and were unwilling to face further combat without a rest. However, morale soon improved and the Dabie Mountains base was successfully established.

The Communists were now a direct threat to the big city of Wuhan and the entire lower Yangzi. They had easy access to the Central Plains and were being reinforced by the East China Field Army's troop concentrations hitherto bottled up in Shandong. They now needed a decisive battle to force the

Nationalists on to the defensive, once and for all.

From August 1947 until the spring of 1948, Liu and Deng devoted their greatest efforts to rebuilding the Grand Army's ranks with fresh recruits drawn from the local towns and villages. The arrival of seasoned troops from Shandong and east Hebei also helped to strengthen numbers. During this time they fought several significant actions with the Nationalist forces, seizing control of a good 100 miles on the north bank of the Yangzi.

When Chiang Kai-shek surrounded the Dabie Mountains base in the spring of 1948, the Communist forces comprised five separate columns, a 40 per cent increase in strength over the previous year. This accretion of forces clearly strengthened Deng's status as the Red Army's overall Commissar, or political adviser. The Grand Army had pushed back the Nationalists to the extent that it gained effective control of the Central Plains from Shandong to the Yangzi, and as far south as northern Anhui province. From a desperate, mud-soaked rout, the Communists had established themselves as a formidable and disciplined modern army. The artillery lost in the Huang Fan crossing could easily be replaced with guns captured from the Nationalists.

The battle of which Deng was most proud was the Huai-Hai campaign of 1949, which Whitson calls 'the greatest battle of the twentieth century on the Chinese mainland'. Deng Xiaoping was appointed to head a new Huai-Hai Front Committee, and his organisational talent showed in the way he recruited the support of about two million peasants in transporting supplies.

While members of the Nationalist high command failed to co-operate with each other and played leap-frog amongst themselves, Liu and Deng succeeded in pinning down a large contingent of Nationalist forces at Xuzhou. Trenches were dug by the peasant support forces, as in an old-fashioned siege, and only about four per cent of the Nationalist Seventh Army are said to have escaped death or capture.

The 129th had dominated the fight for north central China, taking as its area of operations the ancient heartland which includes southeast Shanxi, northern Henan, Hebei, and western Shandong. This region was known to the Communist armies as the Jin-Ji-Yu-Lu after the ancient names of those provinces, although geographically they are only approximations of the modern provincial boundaries. The 129th became known as the Jin-Ji-Yu-Lu Army.

Liu and Deng had deployed their troops in southeastern Shanxi to prevent the Nationalists from seizing the Peking–Hangzhou railway. The Communists, under Liu and Deng together with Shanxi warlord Yan Xishan who had sent a relief column, laid siege to the area historically called Shangdang. Shangdang is now known as Changzhi after the county seat. Summarising the situation, Liu Bocheng said:

'The purpose of Yan Xishan's relief force is to lift our siege of Changzhi. But he's really just going to fall into our trap. Besieging the town is really just our way of confusing the enemy. The enemy is like a big pig: you can't eat him up in one mouthful but if you cut him up into pieces you can swallow him bit by bit.'

Pointing out the advantages and disadvantages of the situation, Deng Xiaoping said:

'Just put the meat close to our lips, and we'll soon see how to eat it . . . . If our commanders at all levels will just make use of the strong points of our army, expanding and exploiting the enemy's shortcomings, we'll be able to wipe him out neatly and completely.'

This final part of the Chinese civil war, which lasted from 1946 until 1949, is extremely complex and repetitive in the narration, and is of interest mainly to military historians. It is not the purpose of this book to describe it in detail, but an extract from a narrative by Deng Guozhong, one of the senior officers serving beneath Liu Bocheng and Deng Xiaoping in the 129th Division, gives some idea of what was involved. Deng Guozhong writes:

'Our troops were given the task of attacking two hilltops — the Mopan and the Laoye, which are connected by a saddle. Yan Xishan's troops had had a tough time of it, advancing on us through heavy rain and thick mud and eventually taking up positions on the Mopan whose name means "grinding platform", and on the Laoye "grandfather". On October 2 the big battle began.

Two of our regiments were detailed off to put up a show of attacking Changzhi. The last of the 129th Division, accompanied by local militia, marched northwards to meet Yan's relief column. The people of southeast Shanxi hated Yan because of the number of people his troops had killed there. The bad weather hampered Yan Xishan's relief force, and they were continually being attacked by our local militias. In every village they passed through, the grain stocks had been removed and the non-combatants evacuated. The enemy troops by now had holes in their uniforms and their shoes gaped open. They had little to eat and their morale was declining.

The enemy left the road at Chixian, about fifty miles from Changzhi, hoping to cross the saddle between the Mopan and the Laoye and fall on our besieging troops. But we were waiting for them and turned both their flanks. They were forced uphill onto the two mountains to establish a foothold and work out another plan. Our men were given the task of attacking the hilltops, and heavy fighting broke out on October 2.

The Mopan is described by its name. The summit is a small piece of flat land. The slopes consist of layer upon layer of 25 foot high terraces, and the hill stands about 1,000 feet above the surrounding country. Half way up there is a village with only eight or nine households. Yan Xishan's troops, who were strong in defence, set up earthworks and crescent-shaped outer defences. Following the step-like ridges, they had dug out trenches and communications ditches as fine as a spider's web. Two of the houses in the village were taken over as an HQ; the window frames and doors were all taken down and put on top to improve the cover. The enemy was counting on the fact that he had many machine-guns and his artillery was strong, and he planned to hold this hilltop firmly till he could break out and relieve Changzhi. They were unaware that the trenches they had dug would simply turn into their graves.

Before attacking the enemy, I summoned several regimental commanders and we analysed the enemy's position together. Everybody agreed that in order to destroy the enemy on the Mopan it would be necessary to penetrate and hold his outer defences, and do our best to squeeze him before making a massed assault. While penetrating the strongpoints, we would attack step by step to draw them forward.

At dawn on October 3, the Resolute Ninth Regiment, the 31st and the 13th made determined attacks separately on the south and southeast sides of the Mopan, and began to fight for control of the outer defences. We started bombarding the enemy positions. Under cover of the heavy fire, we used hand grenades, bayonets and other weapons of close combat and seized useful terrain, pushing the enemy back step by step and fighting till dawn on October 4. On the day before the attack, at a meeting of the officers of the Resolute Ninth, Fu Yusan, the commanding officer of the Ninth, took out some 15 Yuan of military scrip and said: "To protect the fruits of victory and prevent the reactionaries from attacking us, all our company must resolutely conquer the Mopan. If I should be sacrificed, here is my last payment of Party dues!" By dawn the 2nd Battalion had reached the small plateau on top of the mountain. Fu Yusan was badly wounded, and when he heard the victory bugle he smiled and died.

The enemy made a massed counter-attack, most inhumanely (*sic*) throwing incendiary grenades, so that the uniforms of some of our men caught fire. They rushed forward and used their burning clothing against the enemy. There was a mêlée on the plateau. One of our men had been with the Nationalist forces until nine months previously, when he was captured and joined the Communist army. He had not yet even been issued a Communist uniform, but he fought fiercely.

Our casualties were very heavy and the 2nd Battalion only had 60–70 men left. Of the officers, only two platoon commanders were left. Just as we were reinforcing, the enemy charged down the slope, firing light machine guns. Our retreat was cut off, so we scrambled down a mountain stream. We had fought in guerilla warfare before and were experienced in following streams. The enemy gave up the pursuit.

The battle had been going on for two nights and two days and the enemy's casualties were heavier than ours. He was reduced to holding this isolated mountain-top position. The provisions he had brought he had already eaten. Most of the troops on the summit had no food or water; they only found a few unripe corncobs, beans, herbs and some wild-birds' eggs. To draw water they had to risk death from our snipers.

The next day we managed to lure the enemy out to counter-attack us. But his line wavered and broke and our troops gave chase. They were caught like a turtle in a jar. While we pursued them, even our clerks and grooms and odd-job men flung themselves into the battle. By the next day they were guarding prisoners and gathering armfuls of rifles, gleefully returning to HQ. In this battle alone we captured over 5,000 men and about 200 machine guns, and towed away several heavy artillery pieces, as well as much ammunition and equipment.

The enemy commander in Changzhi, meanwhile, had been trying to follow the orders in Yan Xishan's radio message which read: "Shangdang must be fought for, Changzhi must be held, the relief troops must get through, and the rebel army must be destroyed . . . ." But they abandoned the town and fled westwards. They kept running into our troops on the road, who wiped them out. Only 3,000 survived out of 20,000 who had been sent to the Shangdang area.'

The Communists' occupation of the Dabie Mountains provided them with a secure base area from which they could threaten, and eventually capture, the traditional heartland of Chinese civilisation — the Central Plains on either side of the Yellow River. Deng's plan paid off, but there was heavy fighting ahead before north China was finally cleared of Chiang Kai-shek's army.

Deng had likened the Nationalists' military posture in north China to a dumb-bell, with the two weights in northern Shaanxi and southwestern Shandong and the bar bisecting the Central Plains. It was this 'bar' that Deng and Liu now proposed to snap in two, separating the weights.

Chen Yi's East China Field Army broke out of Shandong where it had been bottled up by Nationalist forces and positioned itself in eastern Henan, in the vicinity of the former Northern Song dynasty capital of Kaifeng. A 20,000-man division of the former Shanxi–Shandong–Hebei–Henan Army took up a position in western Henan, blocking the advance of Chiang Kai-shek's force in Shaanxi. Liu Bocheng and Deng Xiaoping remained in their Dabie Mountains' stronghold, forming the bottom corner of an inverted triangle ready to assault the enemy on the plains.

The importance of Deng's work was recognised when Mao Zedong, and the other Communist leaders, decided to put him in charge of a new co-ordinating committee for the forthcoming offensive, which would be named the Huai-Hai campaign. The Huai is a large river which rises in Henan province and flows through Hubei and Anhui before debouching into Lake Huzi in Jiangsu. Hai ('sea') refers to the coastal plain in east Jiangsu.

Commissars like Deng were responsible for organising the huge logistical effort in preparation for what William Whitson has called 'the greatest battle of the twentieth century on the Chinese mainland'. According to Whitson's calculations, more than two million peasants were mobilised to supply field rations, ammunition, and gasoline for the forces. Deng was the secretary of the Chinese Communist Party Front Committee created on 16 November 1948 to command the Huai-Hai campaign. Other members of the committee were Liu Bocheng, Chen Yi, Su Yu, and Tan Zhenlin. Meanwhile in Manchuria, Lin Biao's Northeast Field Army had captured Shenyang and occupied the surrounding province of Liaoning. By the end of October, the Communist Central Plains and East China Field Armies occupied Kaifeng and Zhengzhou, a vital rail junction controlling both the east–west and north–south arterial lines of communication from Beiping (the Nationalist name for Peking) in the north to Wuhan on the Yangzi, and from Nanjing and Shanghai in the east to Xi'an in the west.

The Huai-Hai campaign was fought mainly around the strategically placed city of Xuzhou in northern Jiangsu. Xuzhou dominated the intersection of the Long-Hai east–west railway linking Xi'an with the east coast, and the Tianjin–Pukou railway which linked Nanjing with Hebei and Shandong. The Communists committed some 600,000 men to the battle around Xuzhou. The Nationalists had mustered 63 divisions, but they were considerably below strength and totalled not many more than half a million men.

In mid-November, Liu and Deng succeeded in encircling, and badly mauling, six out of seven of the Nationalist armies committed to the field. The Nationalist commanders mistrusted each other and failed to co-ordinate their actions, enabling the Communists to capture huge amounts of up-to-date American material which was of great use to them. Chen Yi succeeded in preventing many of the enemy forces from escaping southwards or to the west, and only a minority of the survivors succeeded in taking refuge in Xuzhou with its 300,000-strong garrison defenders. Particularly fine service was rendered by the Communist commander Wei Guoqing, who was to play an important political role in China in the 1970s.

By late November, Liu and Deng had laid a trap for the Nationalist 12th Army, which had so far escaped a severe attack. Even though a sortie was sent from the garrison at Xuzhou, the army could not be saved and its commander, Huang Wei, committed suicide. The battle was fought desperately day and night on both sides, the Communists using their time-honoured tactics of hand-to-hand combat with grenades and bayonets. The beleaguered Nationalists, however, were receiving supplies by air-drop and fighting a more-or-less conventional war. The winter frosts vindicated Liu and Deng in their mobilisation of the peasantry whose hastily-dug trenches and earthworks prevented Nationalist relief columns from getting through. The Nationalists' overall commander for the Huai-Hai battle, Du Yuming, was trapped with his men with rapidly dwindling food supplies behind a slowly diminishing perimeter. The old Nationalist tactic of encirclement of the enemy had been efficiently turned against it by Liu and Deng. The Communists were also playing their old game of besieging an enemy force to lure in relief columns which were then trapped and annihilated. This was the most humiliating defeat the Nationalist armies had ever suffered, and despite vanishing chances of survival they showed enormous courage.

In late December 1948 through to early January of the following year, in an attempt to persuade them to surrender, the Communists relaxed the pressure on the trapped Nationalists. On 6 January 1949, the Nationalists attempted to break out in a disorganised fashion and were destroyed as an effective fighting force in less than a week.

The Communists had shown the tactical mastery and determination that was always their *forte* in difficult conditions. Now they were ready to receive the mantle of nationwide power. Although Chiang had lost some 400,000 of his best troops, he was not yet finished. The Communists still had to cross to the south bank of the Yangzi and carry the fight into the difficult terrain of southern and southwest China which, for the past two decades, had been the source of most of the Nationalists' support and manpower.

The real beneficiary of this epic battle was Deng Xiaoping. At the early age of 44, under Mao's overall command, he had shown himself one of the most effective military leaders in the whole country. Liu Bocheng was a fine soldier, but he was growing old, and most people knew the real achievement belonged to Deng. As it became evident that Chiang Kai-shek would soon be defeated, Party leadership must, of necessity, think about peacetime recovery and reconstruction. This was partially to be made possible by Deng himself in the 1949 campaign to reconquer his native province, Sichuan, and to carry to a successful conclusion the 'liberation' of Yunnan, Guizhou, and Guangxi.

In the course of 1949 the Communist armies were, yet again, redesignated and reorganised. In Deng's case this meant a change of title from Chief Political Commissar of the Central Plains Field Army to that of the Second Field Army. Concurrently, Chen Yi's East China Field Army was renamed the Third Field Army, and Lin Biao's Northeast Field Army became the Fourth Field Army. Much has since been made of the alliances forged in the top commands of these redesignated armies in terms of their effect on the subsequent course of Chinese domestic politics.

It is interesting to observe how many top military commanders in Deng's Second Field Army were still active in politics in the 1960s and 1970s, when China was racked by internal conflicts and power struggles. These men included Li Da, who was one of the two deputy commanders of the Second Field Army and its Chief-of-Staff. In 1950, he became Chief-of-Staff of the Chinese 'volunteer' intervention force in Korea. Later he held mainly ceremonial posts and in the Cultural Revolution he disappeared until 1972, when he was rehabilitated as Deputy Chief-of-Staff of the People's Liberation Army (PLA). Song Renqiong also survived. Born in 1909 in Hunan province, he was a professional soldier who gravitated towards political work and was one of the three deputy commissars of the Second Field Army, evidently a favourite of Peking, to take up a wide variety of important military and political posts. In 1967, during the Cultural Revolution, he was denounced as a 'renegade, traitor and follower of the capitalist road'. He disappeared in 1968, but resurfaced in 1974 and was appointed to head the Seventh Ministry of Machine Building, responsible for development and production of military aircraft and missiles.

After the Communist victory in north China, Mao was opposed to peace talks with Chiang Kai-shek. Mao said, 'The enemy won't destroy himself,' and he was determined to cross the Yangzi and conquer all of south China. Chiang wanted to negotiate, but Mao had laid down impossible conditions. He wanted all Nationalist 'war criminals', presumably including Chiang, to be put on trial, and he demanded that the existing state constitution be abolished along with the Nationalist judiciary. The Nationalist armies were to be 'democratically re-assigned', land reform was to be carried out, and a Political Consultative Committee 'with no reactionary elements' should set up a 'democratic' coalition government.

By now Chiang had made up his mind to retreat to Taiwan, and by the spring the movement of men and equipment across the Strait had begun. The Communists, meanwhile, were preparing to force a southward crossing of the Yangzi along a 300-mile front. They found the river only lightly defended and the Second Field Army was able to occupy

Nanjing on 23 April 1949, while the Third Field Army took Shanghai. The First Field Army, commanded by Peng Dehuai, set out to occupy northwest China including the huge desert region of Xinjiang, while Lin Biao's Fourth Field Army came south to evict the Nationalists' most able commander, Bai Chongxi, from Wuhan. The Communist forces rolling southward now numbered about a million men, including many Nationalist turncoats. Deng, Liu Bocheng, and Chen Yi were still acting in concert with their Second and Third Armies. The Front Committee remained in existence with Deng as its leading member. The other members were Liu Bocheng, Chen Yi, Su Yu, and Tan Zhenlin.

Mao was determined, in his own words, 'to pursue the revolution to the end'. If the Nationalists wanted to surrender, well and good, but he set the surrender terms at a level which he knew Chiang Kai-shek could not accept. He said, 'The enemy won't destroy itself . . . whether they are Chinese reactionaries or American aggressive forces in China, they won't retire from the stage of history voluntarily.' He considered that people who favoured peace talks were 'practising appeasement and splitting the revolution'.

Mao believed that only by thoroughly smashing the Chinese reactionaries and expelling American aggressive forces from China would China ever achieve independence and have democracy and peace. On 14 January 1949, Mao laid down his terms for the surrender of the Nationalists:

1.   War criminals would be tried (probably including most of the Nationalists' senior commanders);
2.   The 'puppet constitution' was to be abolished;
3.   The 'puppet judiciary' was to be abolished;
4.   Reassignment of all 'reactionary' troops according to democratic principles and confiscation of the funds of the Nationalist bureaucracy;
5.   Land reform;
6.   Dropping of 'treasonable conditions';

7. Convocation of a Political Consultative Conference with no 'reactionary elements' participating and the setting-up of a democratic coalition government; and
8. Take-over of all the authority of the Nanjing 'reactionary' government at all levels.

These eight preconditions for peace talks spelt the unconditional surrender of the Nationalists. Chiang Kai-shek refused the terms offered by Mao. He said he would retire to his home in Zhejiang province, while secretly contemplating a full-scale evacuation of the Nationalist forces to Taiwan.

Li Zongren, the former warlord from Guangxi and Vice-President of the Nationalist regime, now took the stage and became President, declaring his willingness to accept the eight conditions and offering to start negotiations in Peking on 1 April. Chiang sent two top aides and a team of negotiators to begin talks. On the eve of their departure he confided in one of the aides that he did not believe the peace talks could succeed, and he was planning to take refuge in Taiwan.

The peace talks duly began on 1 April in Peking, with Zhou Enlai heading the Communist delegation. The armistice they offered was even stiffer in its terms than the eight conditions set by Mao, and President Li could not accept them. The Nationalist negotiators were detained in Peking. Three weeks later, Mao and Zhu De proclaimed a new offensive and nearly a million Communist soldiers began crossing the Yangzi along a 300-mile front.

In February 1949, the Red Army carried out yet another round of reorganisation and redesignation of its units. The Northwest Field Army was redesignated the First Field Army, commanded by Peng Dehuai. The Central Plains Field Army of Liu Bocheng and Deng Xiaoping became the Second Field Army under their command, and the East China Field Army was redesignated the Third Field Army under the command of Chen Yi, with first deputy political commissar Tan Zhenlin and deputy commanding officer Su Yu. The Northeast Field

Army was redesignated the Fourth Field Army, with Lin Biao as commander and Luo Konghuan as first commissar and Deng Zihui as second commissar. The North China Field Army commanded by Nie Rongzhen was disbanded and absorbed into the First Field Army.

At that time, the First Field Army's goal was to establish full control of the northern and northwestern provinces of Shaanxi, Gansu, Liaoning, Suiyuan, and Xinjiang. The aim of the Fourth Field Army's offensive was to control Hubei, Hunan, Guangdong, and Guangxi. The Second and Third Field Armies' tasks were to destroy the Nationalists' 'thousand miles of water defences' and the Third Army was to take Shanghai, where there were still garrisons of foreign powers. The Second Army under Liu and Deng was to capture the Nationalists' capital of Nanjing. The Communists proclaimed that their 'army of a million heroes' was coming south. The Nationalists' defences on the Yangzi proved to be laughable. The Communist general, Qin Jiwei, recalls:

'On the south bank of the Yangzi, the enemy directly opposite from us were the Sixth and Eight Nationalist Armies . . . . They were not even up to strength in second-class troops. The commanders' morale was gone. All it took was for us to show up on the other bank and they ran as fast as they could, messing their pants.'

Liu and Deng's Second Field Army crossed the Yangzi in a pincer movement to the east and west of Nanjing, which they attacked and captured. The next day, the Nationalists' Second Fleet mutinied on the river northeast of Nanjing and the Nationalist Fourth Division surrendered near Yangshan. 'The enemy's engineering works were useless,' said Qin Jiwei. 'However strong they were, the defenders would all have been killed. The men in charge were just stragglers.'

The Nationalist forces were falling apart and running in all directions. In pursuit, the Fourth Army captured the triple city of Wuhan on 17 May. The First Field Army under Peng Dehuai captured the ancient capital of Xi'an and the Third Field Army liberated Shanghai. In July, the First Field Army captured the important northwestern cities of Lanzhou, Xining, and Yinchuan. The Fourth Field Army captured the southern provinces of Hunan and Guangdong without encountering opposition, while the Third Field Army attacked maritime Fujian province in southeast China and, in August, captured the main city of Fuzhou.

Liu and Deng's Second Field Army advanced on a westerly course up the Yangzi and took the cities of Chongqing, Chengdu, and Guiyang. In December, it occupied Yunnan province and the now defunct province of Xikang, adjacent to Tibet. The roles of Deng and Liu were now reversed, for the Party named Deng First Secretary of the new Southwest Military Administrative Region with Liu as his deputy. Deng had come full circle, via Shanghai, Paris, Moscow, Xi'an, Guangxi, Jiangxi, the Long March, Yan'an, the Dabie Mountains, and Nanjing. His career to date was certainly impressive and he was still only 45 years old.

Chapter 5

FROM SICHUAN TO PEKING

T he end of the Chinese Civil War brought a great change to Deng Xiaoping's life. Hitherto his main preoccupation had been with war; now he was to show how well he would perform in peacetime. As a native of Sichuan it was logical for the other Communist leaders to appoint him head of the new government in southwest China. This region was defined by the provinces of Sichuan, Guizhou, Yunnan, Xikang (now western Sichuan), and later it included Tibet. The capital of the southwest region was Chengdu in Sichuan. Now, Chengdu is the capital of only that province. Five other military administrative regions covered north China, the northeast, the northwest, east China, and the central-south region. In each region there was an authoritative bureau of the Communist Party and a regional military authority. The six regions were revived briefly from 1977 to 1978 when Deng and his supporters were preparing for political and economic reform throughout China.

Southwest China is notoriously difficult to rule from the northern part of the country. It is mountainous and heavily forested and has borders with several other countries. It is inhabited by about 30 ethnic minorities who settled there over the centuries because of population pressure and warfare or famine in northern and central China. There has never been any love lost between the Hans (ethnic Chinese) and the minorities, who have generally been pushed into the mountains while the Hans occupied the fertile valleys. During the Long March, the Communists had passed through parts of the southwest and often encountered hostility and even physical attack from members of the minorities who are skilful archers and hunters.

From July 1950, Deng headed the Party organisation, Liu Bocheng the Military Affairs Commission, and war-hero He Long was in charge of the military Regional Authority in the new Southwest Military and Administrative Committee (MAC). Deng had now attained the rank of Regional Party First Secretary which put him within grasping distance of membership of the Politburo in Peking. He only became a member of the Central Committee at the Seventh Party Congress in 1945. His performance in the Civil War since 1945 had been remarkable and his gift for leadership was now recognised in his appointment as the number one person in the administration of southwest China. Politically he also leap-frogged his old commander, Liu Bocheng, who became Second Secretary of the Southwest Bureau, while Deng became Vice-Chairman of the Military Administrative Committee headed by Liu. This political move was topped by the later appointment of Deng to the posts of Chairman of the Southwest MAC, Political Commissar of the Military Region, and Mayor of Chongqing. At this time he restored links with his family whom he had not seen for three decades. Dorothy J. Solinger, in her book *Regional Government and Political Integrations in Southwest China*, points out:

'The fact that military control was paramount in the initial conception of these governments meant that generally speaking, each area was made the territory of one of the five Field Armies of the People's Liberation Army (PLA). Thus many of the rulers at this level were revolutionary generals used to independent command. Further, each area had its particular political, economic and cultural traits. These called for an adaptation of the general policies emanating from Peking. Finally, the chaotic nature of the takeover called for improvisation and expediency. This situation unavoidably led to the delegation of a greater measure of autonomy to the Field Army staffs than might have been desirable otherwise. All these factors may have meant that the regions were ruled somewhat independently especially at first.'

The tenure of Deng Xiaoping and Liu Bocheng as political and military bosses of the southwest region was of limited duration, the Politburo requiring their talents in other capacities. In 1951, Liu became Chairman of the PLA Military Academy in Nanjing and, in August 1952, Deng became Vice-Premier of the Government Administrative Council (subsequently the State Council) in Peking, an office he retained until the Cultural Revolution. Deng was named a Vice-Premier together with the Moscow-trained economist Chen Yun, the leading literary figure Guo Moruo, Huang Yanpei, a prominent expert on education, Dong Biwu, a founder member of the Party and experienced administrator, and others. In 1953, Deng was also appointed to the Standing Committee of the first Chinese People's Political Consultative Conference (CPPCC), a body whose main task was to supervise the drafting of a state constitution. The actual drafting was done by a committee headed by Mao to which Deng was also appointed.

In 1954, the constitution was promulgated and abolished the Military Administrative Regions. It emphasised that China was 'a people's democratic state led by the working class and based on the alliance of workers and peasants'. It concentrated on the rights and duties of citizens, and the guiding role of the Communist Party in national affairs was barely mentioned, this doubtless being assumed. The constitution also aligned China with the global peace movement. Three subsequent constitutions in 1975, 1978, and 1982 reflected changes in the political philosophy of the leadership.

Deng also took part in the work of committees that drafted an electoral law and drew up rules for the 'election' of delegates to the National People's Congress which was, theoretically, the supreme legislative power. Before 1977, little formal legislation was drafted in China as the leaders relied mainly on temporary or emergency regulations which were often not published. Deng, however, came to believe in clear-cut rules and regulations if they facilitated rational control of public affairs.

In 1952, when Deng was transferred from Chengdu to the national government and Party centre in Peking, China was in the grip of important transformations and international events. At Panmunjom, armistice talks were in progress to negotiate an end to the Korean War in which Chinese volunteers had played a major role in fighting the United Nations' forces led by the Americans. One of Mao Zedong's sons, Mao Anying, had been killed in Korea in May. He was 29 years old and the offspring of Mao's marriage with Yang Kaihui who was executed by the Nationalists in 1930.

The Party and government were engaged in the so-called Five Antis, a determined campaign to root out corruption in industry and commerce, tax evasion, theft of state property, breaching of government contracts, and stealing of information in the interests of economic speculation. Some culprits had already been shot.

In 1952, Li Jingquan was appointed Chairman of the Provincial People's Government in Deng's native province of Sichuan. This replaced the Southwest Military and Administrative Committee and symbolised the end of the predominantly military rule put into effect at the close of the Civil War. Tibet was declared a military region following its occupation by Chinese troops in 1951.

The government organs were adjusted in 1954 with the introduction of a constitution. Deng was made a Vice-Premier of the State Council, the leading organ of administration. The

Regional Committees were abolished and the provinces came under the rule of governors and Communist Party first secretaries. Unfortunately, this system perpetuated traditional provincialist feelings in different parts of China. During the Cultural Revolution, Li Jingquan, who took over the role of Chief Administrator of Sichuan from Deng, was accused of having created 'an independent kingdom' in Sichuan.

In May 1954, real power at the national level came to Deng with his appointment to the post of Secretary-General of the Communist Party. When the Party was growing up in the 1920s and '30s, this post was literally that of a secretary. It involved shuffling documents, taking notes at important meetings, and general organisational work. Stalin had shown how such a job could be transformed into the very seat of power in Russia, as it was in the nature of the post that the person holding it controlled the central archives. Knowledge of other people's backgrounds, especially their past errors, is one of the keys to power in Communist countries. Assisting Deng as Party Secretaries were: Yang Shangkun, a Moscow-trained member of the returned students' group who became Chief Political Commissar in the First Field Army commanded by Lin Biao and who, at time of writing, is President of the People's Republic of China; Liu Lantao, a political activist and specialist on north China affairs who still held prestigious but not crucial Party posts in 1986; Song Renqiong, a former Nationalist officer who defected to the Red Army in 1931 and who, during the anti-Japanese war, served as a senior political commissar under Deng; and Tan Zhenlin, veteran revolutionary and political commissar and expert on agriculture and east China affairs who, in 1987, was still Vice-Chairman of the Party's Central Advisory Commission headed by Deng. All four of these men shared with Deng a talent for politics and organisation. In addition, Deng's new assistants had been born within two years of his own birth date of 1904, which suggests that he felt easiest in the company of people who had shared his experiences of revolution.

When Soviet leader Nikita Khrushchev visited China in 1954, he reached agreement on three important points in the Sino–Soviet relationship. The Russians agreed to give China economic aid, to withdraw their troops from Port Arthur which they had captured in 1945 from the Japanese, and to liquidate joint stock companies in Xinjiang related to the mining business.

The internal politics of post-war China are thought, by some historians, to have been influenced decisively by the system of loyalties and friendships built up among the revolutionary military leaders in the 1920s, '30s, and '40s. Certainly a great many of the most prominent civilian leaders of the post-1949 period had their origins in the Red Army, whether as officers of the line or as political commissars. William F. Whitson points out that not only were Deng's main military associations with the New Fourth Army in the period of the anti-Japanese war (1937–45), but also went as far back as the late 1920s and the days of the Second and Third Armies in Guangxi.

In the mid-1950s, Party unity was marred by the purge of Generals Gao Gang and Rao Shushi. Gao Gang was commander of the Northeast (Manchurian) Military Administrative Region — the same position Deng had held in the southwest. Born in Shaanxi, Gao was highly praised by Mao at Yan'an for his knowledge of the province's affairs. In 1952, Gao was appointed to head the newly established State Planning Commission which drew up the first Five Year Plan (1953–58) for economic development. However, Gao's approach to management of the country's industrial economy was apparently in conflict with that of Mao, Deng, Liu Shaoqi, and other top leaders. In the early 1950s, planning was based on the Soviet model and reflected some of the inner contradictions and tensions of that mode. Gao Gang, whose region adjoined the Soviet Union and had historically been under strong Russian influence, evidently favoured the Soviet system of letting single managers run industrial plants without referring every detail of operation to the plant's Party Committee. According to denunciations of him, which became more and more specific between 1953 and 1955, this matched his alleged attempts to set up an 'independent kingdom' in Manchuria.

Ironically, Deng's opposition to the system of 'one-man management', as promoted by Gao Gang, was reversed when Deng returned to national pre-eminence in the late 1970s. Deng has tried to induce factory managers to assume more personal responsibility for their operations. He has also instructed Party cadres to reduce the level of their interference in day-to-day management decision-making and to act solely in a guiding capacity to implement policy decisions from on high.

Rao Shushi, a native of Jiangxi province, served as a Political Commissar with the Red Army in East China, becoming head of the East Military and Administrative Committee in 1950. Two years later he was appointed to Vice-Chairman of the State Planning Commission, together with Deng Xiaoping, Chen Yun, Lin Biao, Peng Zhen, Peng Dehuai, and nine other prominent personalities. Like Gao Gang in Manchuria, Rao Shushi's personal influence in east China, including big industrial Shanghai, was considerable and he may have had disagreements with the other members of the Planning Commission. However, this does not really explain the vehemence with which Deng, in a speech in 1955 about the alleged anti-Party plot concocted by Gang and Rao, attacked both men.

'The basic characteristic of the anti-Party alliance of Gao Gang and Rao Shushi is that they carried on widespread conspiratorial activities in order to seize supreme power in the Party and State. This alliance took over control of some regions and operational branches and used them as "capital" for opposing the Central Committee and carrying out acts of robbery, and with the same objective carried on agitation against the Central Committee in every region and in the People's Liberation Army. Their conspiratorial activities went against the interests of the Party and people and served only the interests of the enemies of the Chinese people.'

Obscure though the Gao–Rao purge was, its effect was widespread. Several other quite prominent figures in Manchuria and east China were implicated and disappeared from view. Mao, Liu Shaoqi, Deng Xiaoping, and Peng Zhen had demonstrated their ability to stand firmly together against any internal challenge. Their prestige was approaching its collective apogee.

In 1955, Deng was appointed to the Politburo. Speaking on behalf of the Central Committee, Deng announced that Gao Gang had been condemned for having endeavoured to make Manchuria 'the independent kingdom of Gao Gang', of being 'an agent of imperialism', and of having engaged in 'anti-Party conspiratorial activities' designed to seize the leadership. He was expelled from the Party Central Committee and committed suicide. Rao Shushi was likewise expelled from the party and was reportedly subjected to 'disciplinary action'. He dropped from sight.

One of the Red Guards' accusations made against Deng in 1967 was that when he had been in Chengdu he had extended protection to his own family, especially his younger brother Deng Shuping, born in 1913. According to a Peking publication, *Red Guard*, issue No. 2 of 1967, Deng Shuping was 'a counter-revolutionary element guilty of numerous crimes, a local despot and landlord . . . thoroughly evil and cannot be forgiven'. During the 10 years preceding the Communist victory,

'[he was] successively chief of the Nationalists' (local) joint security system, secret society boss, chief of the county requisition office, chief of stores, civil administration section chief and manager of the Nationalists' reactionary newspaper *People's Livelihood Daily* . . . all of which were reactionary positions. He indulged in killing, arson, rape, plunder, fine food, wine, women, and gambling. He left no evil undone.'

The Red Guard report was said to have been prepared by the *zhengfa* (judiciary) commune of the College of Law and Political Science in Peking which claimed to have sent out teams to investigate Deng's former activities in southwest China. It quoted the local people as saying in 1967, 'Immediately after the Liberation, had not Deng Shuping fled, he would have been the first to face the firing squad.' Instead, according to the report, Deng Xiaoping helped his brother to become a Vice-Mayor and Deputy County Chief. The Red Guard report went on:

'He knew very well that his younger brother would be suppressed by our People's government, and that other members of his family would be struggled against. Out of his counter-revolutionary class nature, and reactionary class stand . . . he impatiently summoned to Chongqing this Deng Shuping, who was then the Nationalist's civil administration section chief in Fengjie county. Giving him confidential verbal instructions, he asked the latter to hurry back at once to their home town Guang'an and take to Chongqing as fugitives all the landlord and counter-revolutionary elements of the Deng family. As Deng Shuping was leaving, Deng Xiaoping gave him a family group photo and told him that it was a safe-conduct in and out of the premises of the Southwest Military Administration Committee. Accordingly, in the spring of 1950, on the eve of the great land reform and movement for suppression of counter-revolution, the counter-revolutionary element Deng Shuping brought Xia Bogen (a fugitive landlord element, Deng Xiaoping's step-mother), Deng Xianlie (a fugitive landlord element, Deng Xiaoping's elder sister), ... Xie Jinbi (a fugitive landlord element, Deng Xiaoping's younger brother's wife), and a large group of children of landlords and local despots to Chongqing as fugitives. They hid in the Southwest Military Administration Committee. In order to safeguard the life of the counter-revolutionary element Deng Shuping, Deng Xiaoping specially arranged for them to live in the same building in which he himself lived. Not only did they live in the same building, they also ate at the same table. These demons and freaks lived in the same guesthouse, had meals cooked by a special kitchen and drove around in cars. They had all the luxuries in the world.'

Deng Xiaoping realised that his other brother, Deng Gen, might be subjected to attack if he remained longer in Chongqing. In the first half of 1966, according to the Red Guards, Deng had him transferred to Wuhan as a deputy mayor of the big triple city of Hubei province in central China. They added that in Wuhan he sat around 'taking things easy and drinking chicken soup' whilst the flames of land reform were engulfing Sichuan. He committed suicide in the Cultural Revolution.

What is one to make of Deng's alleged protection of his 'counter-revolutionary' family? Were they oppressive land-lords by the standards of the time? The Red Guards cited no specific incidents of 'murder, rape, arson, looting and plun-dering', crimes that were routinely attributed to the landlord class by the Communists. Landowners above a certain finan-cial level were routinely denounced and shot during the land reform. Perhaps Deng could have shown more political fer-vour if he had left his family and friends to the anger ascribed by the Red Guards to the masses in Guang'an county. But how much does the revolution demand of a single person in terms of eliminating human feeling in the interests of overthrowing the ruling class? Whichever way one looks at it, it is clear that

Deng could not bring himself to see his relatives harmed, something which in the West would be thought at least understandable.

Chapter 6

CHANGE OF EMPHASIS

By 1956 the Chinese Communist Party had not held a full congress for eleven years. The Seventh Congress in 1945 had taken stock of the achievements of the Party and the Red Army in the war and it provided a forum at which to centralise the leadership's thinking and impose a degree of political discipline that was difficult to sustain in wartime. The Civil War had made it impracticable to call all the top leaders to one place from their active military commands and posts as senior commissars, and when the war was over they were preoccupied with the urgent tasks of imposing civil order and winning people over to socialism. Nonetheless, the delay in holding the Eighth Congress must have reflected some disparity of political views among the Party's most prominent activists.

The long-term leadership of the Party was, however, relatively stable. A large proportion of office-bearers listed at the Seventh Congress were still in power in 1978, and some continued to play effective roles in 1987!

By 1956 and at the Eighth Congress, the Party's role and function had changed considerably. The Party was now the ruling body of the biggest human polity that had ever existed. It was actively involved in the struggle against 'imperialism', especially that ascribed to the United States. Until six or seven months before the Congress, China's relations with the Soviet Union appeared sunny and fraternal. With Soviet-made arms, the Chinese Army had fought a sizeable war in the early 1950s against the Americans and other UN forces in Korea, and she had astonished the world by holding her own and reinforcing the Communist state in North Korea.

With food supplies stabilised, industry reviving, and culture and the arts well patronised, popular enthusiasm for the Communist rulers in China was at its height. The general air of progress and hope for the future was not dampened by the fact that the island province of Taiwan was still occupied by the Nationalists who had strong American military, naval, and air support. On the contrary, it provided a rallying point for patriotic Chinese in many countries and colonial territories. Many either returned to help their motherland recover its lost status in the world or engaged in anti-colonial struggles in Southeast Asia. For this the Communists could claim the greatest share of the credit. The Eighth Congress in 1956 was designed to solidify achievements to date and to demonstrate the Party's unity in the face of further challenges. Nobody, it seems, realised that the Ninth Congress would not be held for another thirteen years. During this time there would be terrible suffering and confusion, famine, anarchy, destruction of Chinese culture, economic decline, and the break-up of the educational system. Most people in mainland China would have regarded such predictions as Nationalist propaganda cooked up in Taiwan. The most politically significant act of the Seventh Congress in 1945 had been to enshrine the 'Thought of Mao Zedong' as an essential feature of the Party's future role. Article 2 of the new draft, presented by Deng Xiaoping, included the following admonition to Party members:

'The Communist Party of China guides its entire work by the teachings which unite the theories of Marxism–Leninism with the actual practice of the Chinese Revolution — the Thought of Mao Zedong — and the fight against any dogmatic or empiricist deviations.'

Article 2a said, 'It is the duty of Party members to understand the fundamentals of Marxism–Leninism and Mao Zedong Thought.'

The Chinese delegation to the Twentieth Congress of the Soviet Communist Party held in Moscow in February 1956 was led by Deng and Marshal Zhu. The Chinese leaders had only six or seven months in which to mull over the implications of Khrushchev's anti-Stalin speech if they were to hold their own congress on schedule. They saw the denunciation of Stalin as evidence of both the Russians' unreliability and of their arrogant assumption that they should give the lead to all ruling Communist parties in the shaping of global strategy. The Russians considered the Chinese Communist Party was most definitely a younger brother. The Chinese knew of Stalin's purges in the 1930s, but they were not sensitive about wiping out 'class enemies' and made no criticism; what is more, they did not think de-Stalinisation necessary.

The characteristic Chinese reaction to such a slight was to save face by not complaining or reproaching the Russians, thus gaining time to work out a unified approach to the Stalin question before their own Party congress. The month after Deng had delivered his speech on the Party statutes, the Hungarian uprising broke out and popular unrest became a problem in Poland and East Germany. This showed what could happen when any ruling Communist party relaxed its political and social control even slightly. Deng's speech in September 1956 was clearly intended to establish a compromise, showing tolerance towards the views of people not in the Party and at the same time avoiding the dogmatic attitudes within the Party ranks. He said: 'The help they [people outside the Party] can give us can only increase steadily. So our task is to hold fast to [the policy of] co-operating with them, and to induce them to be of more use in our struggle against bureaucracy and in our country's struggles of all kinds.'

Deng also delivered the report on the amendment of the Party statutes of eleven years before, and many of his comments are indicative of the dilemma that was growing in his own political thinking and which must have influenced the new rules. Hitherto a loyal and strong supporter of Mao, Deng was, at the least, instrumental in removing the references to 'Mao Thought' from the Party statutes as revised at the Eighth Congress in 1956. The theme of the new statutes was to play down class struggle and to affirm that the bourgeoisie had ceased to present a serious threat to the Party or to the stability of the country as a whole. Intellectuals were to consider themselves as belonging to the ranks of the working class. The Soviet personality cult, which had led to the virtual deification of Stalin in his lifetime, was specifically rejected and condemned.

Certainly not for the first or last time in his career, Deng was skating on thin ice as far as his relations with Mao were concerned. He dwelt at length on the evils of personality cults and, to anyone with ears to hear, the only candidate in China for such a cult was Mao. Was Deng becoming disillusioned with Mao after supporting him on most matters for more than three decades? Did he want to warn Mao indirectly that he should not attempt to create a personality cult and, at the same time, alert other top leaders to this danger? Did he genuinely deplore the Stalin cult or was he, as he made out in his speech, sincerely concerned about the whole issue of personality cults without specifically pointing the finger at his old patron? These are still unanswered questions. However, Deng formulated several important principles in his 1956 speech which omitted mention of Mao:

'The Chinese Communist Party takes Marxism–Leninism as its guide to action.'

'A Party member's duty is to make efforts to study Marxism–Leninism and raise the level of one's own awareness.'

'The cult of the individual is a phenomenon with a long history and cannot but be reflected in our Party life and our social life . . . . Our Party rejects the deification of the individual.'

More than a decade later, in 1967, these seemingly unexceptionable guidelines were condemned by Cultural Revolution activists and held up as evidence that Deng paid no attention to the key role of Mao Zedong and did not even recommend the study of his works.

Deng went on to describe what he considered to be signs of 'leftist' deviation in the Party although, in Chinese terms, they could just as easily be regarded as 'rightist' errors. He said in his speech:

'Squandering the Party's authority to run things on one's own, arrogance, imperiousness, rashness, considering oneself clever, not discussing things with the masses, imposing one's own opinion on people and upholding errors for the sake of one's own authority are absolutely incompatible with the Party's mass line.' (There could hardly have been a better description of Mao's behaviour over the next two decades, to which Deng was to fall victim twice, in 1967 and 1976. But it is not certain that Deng originally aimed it at Mao.)

Deng criticised the Party's performance on many counts. 'It suffered,' he said, from an 'inappropriately excessive concentration of power' and added that the practice of 'masking the reality of personal monopolisation under the cover of collective leadership must be resisted.' He said that high-sounding phrases like 'arduous struggle for communism' were useless because illiterate peasants, who composed a large proportion of the Party membership, would simply not understand them.

To Deng's critics in 1966 and 1967, this was evidence of his belief in 'peaceful transition to socialism'. Indeed, Deng had said that the Party had 'basically completed the socialist phase', which meant that it was on the brink of implementing full communism. If the Soviet Union had declared the disappearance of its bourgeoisie in the 1930s, why should China not claim the same achievement now? By the time Deng was rehabilitated for the third time in 1977, it was evident that China did not have the material basis for true socialism, let alone the ability to strike out for early transition to communism. In classic Marxism, socialism is a condition in which every able-bodied person 'works according to his or her ability and receives according to his or her work'. Communism is a condition in which 'everyone works according to his or her ability and receives according to his or her needs'. The problem is how to define a person's needs. Years of political activity followed by years of solitude and exile from 1967 until 1973 apparently brought Deng to the conclusion that communism cannot be built amidst poverty and that socialism is as much an economic as a political condition, which was something denied by the leftists. Evidently in 1956, Deng thought there had already been such political progress and that a classless society had been all but achieved. In his speech introducing the new Party statutes, he said:

'Quite recently the situation has undergone a fundamental change. Workers and administrative staff are now only one part of a single social class. The poor peasants and middle peasants have become members of agricultural production cooperatives. The bourgeoisie has already been put in the position of a class which is being eliminated. The differences between them will soon have merely historical significance and the vast majority of the intellectuals are on the side of the workers.'

This was almost primitive utopianism: not even Mao ever came close to proclaiming the existence of a classless China.

He continued to believe in the prolonged class struggle which Deng had mentally abolished. In place of the struggle with the dying bourgeoisie, Deng said the government had entered into a joint venture with them, and given them an economic and political role in society. In theory the old democratic parties still existed under the protection of the Communist Party, and this fiction was revived under Deng in the mid-1980s. Their capitalist tendency towards corruption had been corrected, and most of them had realised that there was no point in resisting the 'advance of the proletariat'.

In 1957, only a year after his proclamation of the submission or conversion of the bourgeoisie in his report on the Anti-Rightist Campaign, Deng was called upon to make a catalogue of the political sins of the intelligentsia who were considered by far the most dangerous sector. Nearly two decades later he was attacked by the ultra-leftist Gang of Four supporting Mao's widow, Jiang Qing, who claimed that the bourgeoisie continued to exist in the very leadership of the Party, that is in Deng and his policies. Nonetheless, in 1956 Deng laid it on the line that only the unity of the Party and its close relations with the masses had enabled it to gain victory. 'There is no doubting that if our Party had not been united, we would not have been able to lead the people in such a short period of time to carry out this complex task.'

As Mao was later to recall, Deng and his allies 'divided the Standing Committee of the Political Bureau into a "first" and "second" line, and set up the Party Secretariat.' 'I retreated to the second line,' Mao added. 'Liu Shaoqi and Deng Xiaoping were in the first line. Liu, as Vice-Chairman, managed a portion of the important meetings, and Deng handled everyday affairs.' But Deng, as Mao's supporters were later to charge, consistently monopolised power, made arbitrary decisions and, perhaps most unforgivable of all, 'met Chairman Mao on equal terms and without ceremony'.

Mao himself later complained, 'Deng Xiaoping is deaf but when we had a meeting he always sat in the place farthest away from me. Since 1959 he has not briefed me on the work of the Central Committee Secretariat.' Deng and Liu Shaoqi, Mao asserted, had tried to pigeonhole him. They had 'treated me as if I were their dead parent at a funeral' (*South China Morning Post,* 5 September 1967). Many of Deng's past political pronouncements, both written and verbal, are taken from flysheets and brochures disseminated by the Red Guards in the ultra-leftist Cultural Revolution during its height in the period 1966 – 67.

The veracity of such fierce and polemical attacks on the Party veterans whom the Red Guards, instigated by the conspiratorial Cultural Revolution group around Mao, subjected to physical and mental assault is questionable. Can such material be considered reliable when its tone is so prejudiced? Perhaps the answer to the problem of quotations purportedly recording Deng's 'capitalist' or 'revisionist' remarks is that there is little or nothing in them that does not conform to his known opinions and policies both before and after the Cultural Revolution.

Mao seems to have taken umbrage at Deng's attack on personality cults. Throughout the mid-1950s, Deng expressed his thoughts on personality cults of leaders, formalism in Party literature, lack of communication with the masses, and the inevitability of leaders making mistakes. He said many times, perhaps more often than Mao himself liked, that even Chairman Mao was fallible. In November 1956, Deng told a World Youth Delegation in Peking that 'Chairman Mao frequently says that he has often made mistakes, but we know he has made fewer mistakes than we [the rest of the leadership] have.' In February 1957, he commented in a speech to a conference of provincial and municipal Party Secretaries that 'it is impossible that the [Communist] Youth League should never make a mistake; a provincial Party committee cannot avoid making mistakes either, and Chairman Mao has never said that he cannot make mistakes.'

On the conduct of political campaigns, Deng told a

Communist Youth League conference, 'To take the mass line means using all kinds of measures, including shouting our heads off. . . . We don't mind people shouting their heads off, but it must be a *mass* campaign.' Later when the Red Guards accused him of upholding the Party, and not Chairman Mao personally, as the true arbiter of mistakes, he replied, 'There is only one key question — the Party. If you stand firm on that, though you should make ten thousand mistakes, you'll be basically correct . . . . If the Youth League hasn't got out of its rut [of political errors], the mistake is also the Party's.' In October 1955, when discussing the convening of the Eighth Party Congress in the succeeding year, Deng also said, 'Party manuals should be more accessible, and they shouldn't quote Chairman Mao's words, otherwise they will become textbook words' (that is, formalistic slogans not necessarily relevant to the actual situation).

The question of 'mistakes' in Chinese Communist thinking is extremely important. When a cadre makes a mistake, it can be used to justify two different courses of action. If the person who makes the mistake is otherwise on good terms with his or her superiors and has a good record of ideological loyalty and docility, depending to some extent on the seriousness of the mistake as assessed from above, he or she may get off with a reprimand or a change of job.

However, if the person who commits the error has in other ways annoyed the higher levels of the Party on different occasions in the past, a mistake may be treated almost like a criminal offence and be severely dealt with by demotion, imprisonment, exile or even capital punishment. The leniency or severity of punishment also depends on the predominant political atmosphere of the day. For instance, during a politically tense period, if someone maltreated a newspaper picture of Chairman Mao they could easily be imprisoned, forced to do menial work or, in extreme cases, shot. However, during a period of political let-up as in 1986, a senior provincial official could illegally import thousands of Japanese cars for resale at a profit and get away with no more than an admission of error and a self-criticism.

To have made political or organisational mistakes in the past, and admit to them, can be taken as manly forthrightness. On the other hand, to have been investigated for an error and exonerated by the authorities may mean you will carry around what the Chinese call a 'tail', a burden of persistent suspicion which may affect your advancement. The secret of survival is to gauge correctly the political climate at a given time to determine whether it may be more prudent to admit to past error or try and cover it up. In the 1950s, the leadership was not at the stage when mutual accusations would be thrown around in public — that would begin in 1966.

Stalin died in 1953 and was succeeded by Georgiy Malenkov as leader of the Soviet Union. From 1955 onwards, the real ruler of the Soviet Union was Nikita Sergeyevich Khrushchev, a flamboyant politician who would arouse the lasting hatred of the Chinese Communist leaders.

Stalin had already treated Mao in a high-handed manner. Leaving aside the whole history of the Soviet dictator's mis-reading of the situation in China during the period of revolutionary struggle, he seemed uncharacteristically unsure of how to deal with Mao when the latter visited Moscow in 1950.

Nonetheless, the Soviet Union agreed, at a price, to help modernise and develop China's industries and economic infrastructure. Huge hostels were built in major cities to accommodate Soviet experts and technicians. Nowadays they are still used to house foreign teachers and sub-editors or have been converted to hotels for the growing tourist industry. Thousands of Chinese went to Moscow and other East European capitals to learn Russian and to study technical subjects. Undoubtedly some of them were covertly recruited by the Soviet security and espionage services to serve as watchdogs and agents of Soviet interests in China. As their respective temperaments are totally different, it is somewhat surprising that many of the Chinese trainees acquired a lasting affection for Russia and her people and have welcomed, since the death of Mao, the modest revival of Russian studies in China.

If the Chinese side of the Sino–Soviet dispute from the late 1950s was based on Mao's dislike of the Russians and his historical resentment of their attitude towards the Chinese Communist Party, there seems to have been no such emotional rejection of the Soviet leadership on the part of Deng Xiaoping. He had sided strongly with Mao over the so-called 'Luo Ming Line' in Jiangxi in the early 1930s, which placed him on the nationalistic side of Party policy and against the 'internationalist' faction of the other former Chinese students in Moscow, the Twenty-eight Bolsheviks. At the 1935 Zunyi Conference, he watched as Mao was raised to supreme leadership, and the chief spokesmen of the Bolsheviks, Bo Gu and Otto Braun, were attacked and humiliated. As the Soviet star sank in China, Deng's rose, regardless of whether he had any personal grudge against the Kremlin's rulers.

In the decade from 1956 to 1966, however, Deng was the most closely involved of all the Chinese leaders in the dispute with Moscow. On several occasions he headed delegations to the Soviet capital to seek a solution to the widening ideological rift between the two countries, although the arguments and polemics bore the mark of Mao's mind rather than Deng's or Zhou Enlai's.

Until the Cultural Revolution began in 1966, it was impossible to discern clearly any divergence of views in the Chinese leadership with regard to foreign policy. China was intransigently anti-American and anti-imperialist in international strategy, equally intransigently anti-Soviet in her evolving 'Third World' ideology. As the split widened, there began to appear a racist streak in the Russians' dislike of the Chinese. For their part, the Chinese had reason to regard their northern neighbours as crude, even semi-barbaric encroachers on their territory.

The importance of the Sino–Soviet split for international developments in China from the late 1950s onwards cannot be overrated. It profoundly affected and reflected the problems of modernisation with which the country had been struggling since the 1840s. Also it presented a serious obstacle to the Soviet rulers' dream of dominating east and south Asia with China's help.

The vindictive withdrawal of Soviet technicians and scientists in 1960 had an immediate effect. It heightened China's need for self-reliant economic development, which Mao thought would enable her to catch up with the West in industrial production in a short space of time. That attempt failed, and was partly instrumental in bringing about the biggest political split the Chinese Communist Party had ever experienced.

On 23 September 1957 at the Third Plenary Session of the Eighth Central Committee, Deng made a report on the 'rectification' campaign which had just been carried out. It was a far cry from his talk on rectification given to Party cadres in 1943. In that speech he talked about the need for cadres to reform themselves and their style of work and ideology. The tone was exhortatory and many of the ideas could have come directly from a Presbyterian sermon, for example the importance of honest self-examination and ridding oneself of slack or evil ways, as well as accepting and learning from the criticism of others.

By contrast, in 1957, Deng was reporting on the progress of the rectification campaign begun in May of that year, which had been carried out 'mainly in organisations of the Party and the government at and above provincial and city levels; in institutions of higher learning, democratic parties, the press and publishing, as well as in scientific and technological, literary, art and medical circles.'

'Since then,' Deng explained, 'the movement has gradually spread to the workers and peasants, to industrial and commercial circles and to primary and secondary schoolteachers and staff. At the same time, the armed forces have also launched the movement. Now the campaign is being broadened to embrace the whole nation.'

The new movement was not concerned exclusively with raising the ideological level of Party work. It was aimed at the whole of society, which the Party ruled through its various control mechanisms. Rectification applied to the Party's policy with respect to both domestic and foreign affairs, and in a famous phrase attributed to Mao Zedong, it was intended to solve the 'two different types of contradiction — those between ourselves and the enemy, and those among the people themselves.' Deng said that the first type were antagonistic, irreconcilable, life-and-death contradictions. These included 'the contradictions between the reactionary bourgeois rightists and the people'. He wrote:

'The contradictions between the people on the one hand, and on the other the counter-revolutionaries in the cities and countryside, the former landlord and rich-peasant elements who are still engaged in destructive activities in the villages, the rogues, hooligans, thieves, murderers, rapists, the criminals who graft and embezzle, those who seriously undermine social order or gravely violate the law or discipline, and those whom the public regard as bad elements — all these are also contradictions between ourselves and the enemy. All contradictions other than those mentioned above are contradictions among the people themselves.'

A large number of activities regarded as contradictory to the revolution were common crimes which are forbidden and punished in every civilised country, but the Marxist hatred of 'reactionary bourgeois rightists' can be used to increase or reduce at will the total number of people considered to be 'enemies of the people'. 'Bourgeois' and other political jargon words can be applied to anybody at any time.

Another group of contradictions are considered to exist 'among the people'. There are 'bourgeois and bourgeois intellectuals' who may accept 'socialist remoulding'. Similarly, 'with petty-bourgeois elements (peasants and workers in city and countryside who work on their own), particularly with the well-to-do middle peasants, the question is also one of enabling them to accept 'socialist remoulding'.

Deng remained an orthodox Marxist–Leninist throughout this period and was known to the outside world as an ally of Mao. Rectification, Deng said, should have the aim of remoulding or improving the attitudes of the bourgeoisie, bourgeois intellectuals, and the well-to-do 'middle' peasants. 'We must make great efforts to unite with and educate the middle elements. Only then can we isolate the rightists and swell the ranks of the left.' Twenty years later, by contrast, Deng was preparing to isolate 'leftists' in the Party and society at large, and ridiculing the term 'rightist' as meaning little more than that 'you are doing your job properly'. The Secretary-General went on to observe that the working class poor and lower-middle peasants were the strongest force in the defence of socialism.

> 'A small number of them, however, still have petty-bourgeois ideas and may succumb to bourgeois influences. But if earnest efforts are made to bring out the facts and set forth the reasons, they will easily understand . . . . [The Communist Party] is in the main healthy, and the vast majority of the Party members who are functionaries are sound . . . . But the great airing of views by the masses has exposed a large number of shortcomings in our work, and our style in work. Some of the shortcomings are serious and it would be dangerous not to have them corrected. Moreover, among Party and Communist Youth League members there are a few rightists, and also some who have shown right-deviationist thinking.'

Deng advised people to put their trust in the masses and the 'mass line'. He also praised 'the great airing of views and general debating, by bringing out facts and reasons, putting up big-character posters, and holding discussions and controversies.' 'Posters in big characters' are officially described as 'posters put upon walls or boards by workers and staff in public organisations, schools, factories, and so on. Written in big Chinese characters, they contain criticisms or suggestions for the improvement of work.' There are also small-character posters, but these are naturally less effective.

Deng said the rectification movement had in general been a success, with a distinct swing to the left in political attitudes. But it must not be abandoned now; rather it should be further widened and deepened, especially in government offices.

He proposed that former capitalist and bourgeois intellectuals should be 'remoulded' until they accepted socialism, but insisted this be done by non-violent means. He also wanted the so-called democratic parties (rump organisations left over from the Nationalist period) to participate in government and to become gradually more favourable to socialism.

Deng then turned to that most vital of all of China's problems — agriculture. In 1957, the 'people's communes' had not yet been launched and the Party's agricultural policy was based on the running of co-operatives to encourage the peasants to give each other mutual aid and share equipment and commerce through state regulation of the supply and marketing of the most important farm products, such as grain and cotton. Individual peasant farmers should be encouraged to join up with co-operatives and there should be no freedom to indulge in 'capitalistic' activities.

How different even this mildly socialistic scheme was from the Dengist policies of the 1980s — when peasant families and even individuals were allotted tracts of land formerly under the ownership of the people's communes, and encouraged to take part in almost any kind of enterprise.

Another contrast between the policies of 1957 and those of the 1980s concerned savings. In that early rectification speech, Deng said peasants should be 'encouraged' to practise economy and thrift. Not quite two decades later, the Party and government smiled on peasants whose entrepreneurial talents turned their families into 'ten thousand *yuan* per year households'. (In 1988, the official rate *yuan* was equal to about US$3.30 — but its real value was about half that.) In the latter period, the peasants were admonished by the leadership: 'Enrich yourselves!' (by all legal means). They were encouraged to buy colour TV sets, refrigerators, and even motor vehicles, by contrast with the 1950s when the most longed-for possessions were a radio, a wristwatch, a bicycle, and a sewing machine.

With regard to the industrial working class, Deng's tone in 1957 showed a certain lack of ease, as though he and the other leaders were gradually feeling their way towards a better understanding of the urban proletariat, thought to be the backbone of any Marxist revolution. Most of the leaders had spent their careers up to 1949 as commanders and commissars, first as guerilla troops mainly of peasant origin and later as regular units of the Red Army. The sea in which they swam was the peasantry who supplied them with food and acted as scouts. The Communists reciprocated by ridding the areas they passed through of landlords, if only temporarily, and gave the local peasantry their first inkling that their miserable condition need not be regarded as fixed or immutable.

Relatively few of the Communist leaders had extensive experience of agitation or revolt in the major industrial cities (Liu Shaoqi was one). Uprisings which they instigated in several cities in the 1920s failed. In the 1935 Long March, they avoided cities which were the strongholds of the Nationalists. The urban workers were mostly illiterate, but they were a good deal more sophisticated than the peasants and some of them were former members of street gangs or secret societies.

In his 'rectification' speech, Deng took an orthodox Leninist line towards China's fifty-odd ethnic minorities, most of whom are located in strategically sensitive border areas. First, he warned the minorities against adopting nationalistic, anti-Han attitudes, and while condemning 'Han chauvinism' (considering only Han to be true Chinese and superior to other ethnic groups) he laid more stress on the unity of all nationalities with each other and with the Han. He admonished local community leaders to guard against the danger of anti-Han tendencies.

This is no small order in China where most of the minorities, big and small, have historically lived in a state of mutual hostility with the Han who often expropriated the territory of the minorities, forcing them out into the mountains, forests, and deserts on the fringes of the country. The Han have also suffered periodic and even national conquest by such warlike races as the Mongols, Jin Tartars, and Manchus.

Those who tried to disrupt Han–minority relations, Deng said, were in violation of the Constitution and were 'anti-socialist rightists'. The only viable solution to the minorities problem was to found strong Communist Party organs amongst themselves. But 'we should guard against hastiness'.

In a statement of caution, the Secretary-General said, 'In the national minority areas where democratic reforms have been completed but socialist transformation has not yet been carried out, *the struggle with the rightists must not be waged among the general public*, but socialist education can be conducted within certain sections and in an appropriate way.'

On the important topic of the People's Liberation Army (PLA), according to Deng, 'a few rightists' had been found, but 'the composition of the armed forces in general is pure'. Existing faults were slack discipline, excessive intake of recruits, and too much attention to technical and military factors as opposed to ideology and politics. By contrast, from 1975 onwards, Deng argued that the PLA paid too *little* attention to technical work and too *much* to ideology!

Even slum-dwelling workers in a place like Shanghai regarded the Red Army's peasants in uniform as country bumpkins. Deng also said in his 1957 speech that 'problems arising from among veteran workers and former servicemen should be handled with particular care.'

The Secretary-General disclosed that in 1957 the Party had 12.27 million members, including 2.8 million probationary members. The Party membership was overwhelmingly rural, and it goes without saying that most of the peasant members were illiterate — many still are. The 1957 figures compare with 41 million Party members in 1987, of whom some 16 million joined during the 1966–76 Cultural Revolution decade, which made them of very dubious stripe to Deng and his followers.

Deng laid much emphasis on the question of rectification of unhealthy tendencies among Party members — still one of his preoccupations at the end of his life. He said, 'The rightists in the Party must be expelled.' Three decades later he tried to expel the 'leftists' — without much success, except at the top-most level.

In regard to intellectuals, Deng said in 1957 that they should have some experience in practical work, even if only toiling alongside the peasants. A change of emphasis occurred in the 1980s, when Deng's supporters called for such veteran intellectuals to be released from menial work and returned to their former place of study and residence to continue teaching and research work. But by then most of them were too old or exhausted by the Cultural Revolution; their jobs often became sinecures, pending the growth of a new academic generation.

As to the general problem of cadres (those who do not perform manual labour, or in the English phrase 'white-collar workers'), Deng said:

'Many of the leading organisations and cadres have seriously divorced themselves from reality and from the masses. Responsible comrades busy themselves with routine, keep too little contact with the masses and do not clearly understand their problems. Many privileges in daily life have facilitated the tendency of the cadres to alienate themselves from the masses. Not a few have become conceited and arrogant, refusing to apply the mass line or consult the masses about problems in work.'

Deng listed three overall measures designed to heal the ills affecting Party life:

'Overcome sectarianism and tendencies towards special privileges, adhere to a rational low-wage system and do our best to ensure a livelihood for everyone. It is essential to persist in using (reform) methods as mild as drizzle and as gentle as a breeze.'

Early in 1957, Deng evidently knew or sensed that the country was heading towards some kind of political upheaval that would be leftist in essence and derive its main impetus from Mao. He was concerned about its effect on the young scientists and technologists who had begun to graduate from China's universities, especially Qinghua University in Peking.

Qinghua had been built with American funds in the 1920s, aiming to give well-to-do young Chinese an understanding of Western culture and a façade of Western behaviour, which would put them at ease in the company of foreigners and encourage them to go to America for further studies. In the 1950s, it became the powerhouse for the modernisation of Chinese science and technology, with teaching carried on frequently by Chinese academics who had patriotically returned from overseas to help their motherland recover from the damage wrought by war and revolution. Many of these would soon be humiliated and even driven to suicide in the anti-Rightist campaign of 1957, or if not then, in the Cultural Revolution ten years later.

In January 1957, Deng gave a speech at Qinghua which foreshadowed the moderate or pragmatic line he was to take after his future disgrace in the Cultural Revolution, his reappearance in 1973, and his overall policies as supreme leader of China in the 1980s.

As though foreseeing the disasters of the Great Leap Forward which would be initiated in 1958, Deng warned his audience of the dangers of trying to go too fast in such a complex business as the modernisation of China. 'Our Chinese donkey is slow,' he said, 'but that has its advantages too. A car goes very fast, but if you crash you'll be killed. The donkey is very slow, but it's safer.'

Deng devoted a considerable part of his speech at Qinghua to discussing the relationship between socialism and democracy. Just a few months before, Hungary had exploded into rebellion against its Soviet masters, and there had been unrest in East Germany and Poland. Premier Zhou had visited Moscow and parts of east Europe and was credited with having exercised a restraining influence on the Russians in their oppressive measures. Doubtless he had discussed his observations with Deng, who now told his academic audience:

'When it comes to dictatorship and democracy and the relationship between them, all countries, each at different times, experience [this relationship] in different forms. We [in China] don't need any more democracy here. They [the Hungarians] had too much democracy, which wasn't good either. Stalin's mistakes in the last period of his life were caused by this problem. When socialism has conquered, the machinery of dictatorship should be softened — but he didn't do this, he emphasised class struggle.'

Deng then turned to the question of democracy in China — which he had said was not required in any greater measure than already existed. Perhaps unwittingly foreseeing the Cultural Revolution, Deng ruled out the introduction of what the Chinese call 'big democracy'. This consists of 'spontaneous' rallies and demonstrations, pasting up of wall-posters with a political content, criticising others, and even physically maltreating high officials and teaching staff.

One of Deng's most important legislative measures after he assumed nationwide leadership in 1978 was to have the permission to use such political tactics written right out of the Constitution of the People's Republic which had incorporated them in 1954. Deng said:

'We are not in favour of "big democracy", because it is not in the interests of the proletariat and the broad masses of labouring people. Problems among the people should not be tackled with "big democracy", and inside the Party itself there are also problems of "big democracy" and "little democracy" [minor differences of opinion]. For struggle within the Party, "little democracy" is good. There was a time when "big democracy" within the Party was effective in overthrowing some people. But then others would rise up. It could be effective [at the time], but in the long run it was disastrous. If you think "big democracy" is so good, "little democracy" would not satisfy you. This kind of thinking is erroneous. Criticism should be gentle.

"Big democracy" is effective in our treatment of the enemy, but it is not in the interests of the people [if conducted among them]. Among the people it's different . . . . From the point of view of the people's internal [interests], "big democracy" isn't a thing you can adopt. It can have the opposite effect [to what is desired], and causes economic and political losses.

At normal times in the past there were no [distinctions among] big-character, medium-character or small-character posters. When a campaign came along, we'd immediately write ten thousand sheets of posters, each person on the average writing eight to ten sheets. But were the results so great? That's doubtful. Big-character posters written this way became a matter of competition.'

But Deng also used his speech to say, 'We have had too much dictatorship in the past. Now we should ease up a bit.'

It is important to understand the Chinese concepts of dictatorship and democracy. Dictatorship is theoretically the dictatorship of the proletariat — *but as expressed and implemented by the Party.* The Party, once in power, really has no time for spontaneous political movements among the workers and peasants. It only needs the enthusiasm of the masses for the policies it formulates in their name, and in any early revolutionary period the enthusiasm of the masses is not hard to stimulate. Demonstrations, rallies, the humiliation or killing of former oppressors, seizure of land and property, are all things to be done under the Party's control. Otherwise they may be regarded as political deviation, sabotage, or mere hooliganism. As time goes on, the dictatorship of the Party on behalf of the proletariat becomes increasingly oppressive and there may be spontaneous revolts even among the proletariat. These must be suppressed by the increasingly sophisticated machinery of the Party dictatorship which maintains itself in power by killing or otherwise getting rid of anyone representing or feared to represent 'reactionary' opposition.

If the dictatorship is so severe as to arouse the resistance of some of the proletariat or the intellectuals in a revolutionary state, the leadership may 'ease up a bit', as Deng put it, and liberalise restraints of a political, economic, or cultural nature. This is called 'democratic centralism', even though there is no genuine participation of the proletariat in the government.

Chapter 7

THE MODERATE

T he rural areas from 1958 to 1961 were dominated by Mao's experiment with 'people's communes', which Deng initially supported. The peasants, however, did not react well to the imposition of mass labour and work-points in lieu of products or cash. They did not like eating in mess-halls or having their children taken care of in nurseries so the women could do more work in the fields. Nor did it appear sensible to do as Mao's supporters did and specify a particular depth for ploughing applicable right across the country! The peasants expressed their lack of enthusiasm for the communes by the age-old tactics of the peasantry — they worked slowly and produced less than before. Within three years, famine caused by mismanagement of the land and its human resources was threatening the country.

The administrative structure of the communes was pyramidal: at the top, commune headquarters were based in the former townships or *xiang*. The 'production brigades' which made up the communes typically consisted of several hundred, sometimes over a thousand, peasants, grouped in their original villages which were referred to now as 'production teams'. Their work-points were based on an assessment, made daily or every few days, of their strength and diligence. Cotton cloth for clothing was strictly rationed and they received most of their income in kind, especially grain and cooking oil. Some of them ran small industrial enterprises even after Mao's institution of 'backyard steel furnaces' had been abandoned because the required quality could not be attained — a part of that rushed experiment called 'the Great Leap Forward', in which China tried to catch up with the industrial nations at record speed.

In July 1962, Deng Xiaoping addressed a conference on domestic and international affairs convened by the Communist Youth League. In his speech, he aired his views on the four-year-old people's communes and the economy in general, both of which were functioning poorly he said.

Unpublished at the time, this was an important statement of his views on the present state of affairs in China. Because it was the function of the Youth League to acquaint its members with the thinking of the top leaders, what he said would have become well known to millions of young people who four years later would be activists in the Cultural Revolution. Deng's audience in 1962 included people who would be fiercely attacking him in 1966–67.

Deng asked the Youth League delegates rhetorically:

'At present, has the domestic situation taken a turn for the better? Some people don't think so. What we mean is the overall situation in politics. Chiang Kai-shek and Khrushchev have correctly assessed our situation. Our people are united, but the economic situation is very difficult. Even holding the line is a big development.'

This was indeed bold talking, but Deng was in favour of that:

'Nowadays it looks as if we don't dare to speak out. Not just the feeling in the League — it's the same thing in the Party. Bad clothing and bad food, inadequate living quarters, work norms are falling. In the past we've said some things too often, we've said them *ad nauseam,* and made much of them, with the result that the People's Communes have been a bit too leftist.'

Foreshadowing his own abolition of the communes in 1979 onwards, in 1962 Deng proposed that they should revert to the status of enlarged districts. 'Nowadays they [the rural cadres and activists] just hang out a couple of slogans or only one [the production brigade's and the commune's] and only occupy themselves with propaganda and trying to get things started. The communes have become meaningless.'

Despite Mao's fierce attachment to the communes which he had master-minded, Deng actually proposed that the name 'commune' should be suppressed and that the rural units should revert to large co-operative ventures without the intense social regimentation and communal labour of the huge new agricultural conglomerations.

In his speech to the Youth League conference, Deng proposed streamlining. He recommended abolishing the production brigades and amalgamating them to form big new villages. 'If there is a village head now, there will be a Party secretary. Where there's a Party secretary, there will be a copy clerk.' In this way, the number of administrative personnel could be reduced, said Deng. In his later policies for agriculture, however, he favoured splitting the brigades up into their original villages and the villages into families, to farm on their own or in small groups for profit. Deng said, 'Reduce the administrative procedures, reduce the number of people eating "leadership meals", and if there's any grain left over, let the peasants eat it. If the peasants can eat a bit more and if they have time to catch their breath, restoring production will be easier.' The economic situation was inflationary because the peasants wanted tools, not banknotes. 'When a peasant in the northeast wanted to buy a sickle which was priced at fifty cents, he threw down five *yuan* (ten times the price) and took the sickle away,' Deng said to illustrate his point. This indicates that the people's communes system was accompanied by nation-wide inflation.

Deng was bold enough to say that many of the peasants wanted to split up the land again to share it out among families

—an idea abhorred by the Maoists. 'Our production is greatly reduced by comparison with 1957,' he said. 'As long as we can bring about a rapid restoration, it doesn't matter how we do it.' It was on this occasion that he made his best-known pronouncement: 'It doesn't matter whether the cat is black or white, as long as it catches mice.' A later leftist commentary on these remarks of Deng's said:

'The "black and white cat" is Deng's large-scale propaganda-making for the policy of dividing the land and letting the peasants become individual producers. It's his most telling confession. At the conference of Central Party Secretaries, and at the Seventh Plenary Session of the Seventh Convocation of the Youth League in 1962, he more than once peddled this revisionist garbage. Towards the end of the League Conference, when he noticed that the atmosphere was tense, he phoned Hu Yaobang [then Chairman of the Youth League] several nights in a row, asking that when his report was published this expression should be omitted, and added several sentences about individual production not being the way out, because he wanted to [cover up] his black countenance.'

Deng also said:

'Some places are practising "guaranteeing grain [production] by the household", assigning tasks to households, and dividing the fields up by households. If they do this, what would the peasants want with private plots? We would be able to reduce all the tedious little formalities, and we would be able to have more people participating in direct production.'

Deng used the Youth League conference in 1962 to criticise Chinese industry.

'Industry is like an overthrown landlord,' he said. 'It's like a factory that can't get started but is still propped up . . . . The amount of goods on the market has shrunk — it's really awful to behold. Things are expensive. The workers aren't eating well. Nowadays it's hard to make a living and people are depressed.'

In the second half of 1961, Deng had paid close attention to the affairs of the Communist Youth League, the equivalent of the Soviet Komsomol. Most young people at that time belonged to the League unless they had a very 'bad' class background or were delinquent in some way. Membership of the League was the stepping stone to membership of the Party and eventually, for the lucky few, the ruling élite.

Deng was not, then or today, especially noted for his work with young people. He does not look down on them or ignore them but he never threw himself into youth work as did former Party Secretary-General Hu Yaobang or Vice-Premier Hu Qili who were at different times chairmen of the League before they were selected for the Politburo. In a speech to the League Congress, Deng boldly attacked the policy of victimising the offspring of landlords, rich peasants, counter-revolutionaries, and 'bad elements'. At about the same time, Deng, Head of State Liu Shaoqi, and Peking Mayor Peng Zhen and their supporters were coalescing into a 'moderate' group. They were devoted to repairing the damage done by the Great Leap Forward and the early phase of the people's communes, which had brought the country to the brink of mass famine. Deng voiced criticisms of some of Mao's cherished policies — especially the hostility towards people with a 'bad' class background. Deng told the congress, 'The League's Central Committee should examine how to rely on young people, how to give hope to the offspring of landlords and rich peasants and bad elements, backward elements and people who don't want to make progress . . . . Exerting influence on them is better than letting them influence other people.'

This was very advanced thinking for the Communist Party after a mere twelve years of the nation-wide exercise of the 'dictatorship of the proletariat'. It was thinking so advanced, in fact, that it was utterly swept aside in the Cultural Revolution and the persecution of offspring of so-called reactionaries and counter-revolutionaries was intensified to a hitherto unknown degree.

Deng's next important speech on youth work had been in October 1961, when he addressed the Senior Secretaries of the League. His approach was one of strict common sense:

'Young people have their own preferences. Some like to work with radio, some like to play ball-games, some like to do scientific experiments and some like reading books on natural science. You must understand that young people have different likes and needs. Organise them on a voluntary basis, then you will be able to exploit their talents.'

Returning to the problem of young people with 'bad' class backgrounds, he said: 'A large part of our work should be devoted to living with them, participating in activities with them, chatting and joking with them, playing chess with them.'

On broader matters of Party principle, Deng condemned formalism in the admission of errors.

'It's not just a question of saying mistakes have been made over the past few years and that's an end of it. We still have big shortcomings. One might say our instruction has been too strict and too intense. The Youth League's historical mistakes were all caused by swollen-headedness.'

The anonymous leftist who in 1967 compiled the anthology of Deng's statements over the years, adds characteristically: 'This is sarcasm and double-talk. In fact Deng wants to make out that those years were a write-off, by attacking the

Party's general line and attacking us on the grounds that we made errors of line.'

Reflecting a life-long dislike of hysteria and bombast, Deng said that 'the easiest type of work is to convene a mass meeting, put out a common slogan, bash gongs and beat the drums and make a lot of noise — it's the most economical form of [political work], but really how good are the results?'

Deng urged the League secretaries (distinct from the Party secretaries) to broaden their minds.

'For the next few years we should pay particular attention to study for cadres . . . . The main content of these studies should be investigation and research, a bit of reading — that is, socialist theory, philosophy, history and natural sciences — general knowledge. Our demands regarding cadres' study should be relatively strict. That way we can reduce the level of blindness and raise our own self-awareness.'

In August 1965, Deng returned to his theme regarding the quality of youth work when he addressed Party secretaries responsible for League activities. He was rash enough to say that 'for young people it's no good to be studying Mao's works year in and year out.' He allegedly told his own children that only the fourth volume of Mao's selected works was of a very high level — so high, he said, that they would not understand it.

Deng also told the League secretaries that political classes after work were excessive.

'There are some units where every day at knocking-off time people have to study and read [political] articles. Even those with babies can't go home and look after them. The results are really very bad. It's a tactic that exhausts the workers. In reality it's social oppression. If you don't study the selected writings of Mao Zedong, you won't get your bonus.'

In the spring of 1961, Deng had told a separate central work conference in Canton:

'[T]he present situation is that the relations of production are strained (*jinzhang*), relations between the Party and the masses are strained. Relations among cadres are strained. For the past three years the economic system has been shattered, our enthusiasm has been shattered. Natural catastrophes are not the important thing — the important things are the disasters brought about by people.'

He compared the economic situation to a horse-race:

'This isn't "one horse taking the lead", as in the past. Now we want "two horses stretching out their necks". We must adjust the usual relationships. Supplies for the coal and steel industries must lift up their heads and carry the rest forwards in gradual development. This kind of development by example is helpful.'

Deng's sensitivity towards the problems of leadership in a huge body, such as the Chinese Communist Party, was illustrated by the 1962 'Conference of the Seven Thousand', a greatly enlarged session of the Central Committee taking in Party members from all the most senior posts. His speech was first published for general release on 6 February 1987, in the overseas edition of the *People's Daily*, which is mainly read by people of Chinese race living in Southeast Asia, local governments permitting, North America, Britain, and other countries with sizeable Chinese populations. For domestic consumption, it was also printed in the 1987 No. 4 issue of *Red Flag*, which was now the name of the theoretical and ideological organ of the Party, replacing *Red Star*. Deng began by referring to previous speeches made before the conference by Liu and Mao with which he declared himself in total agreement. He then turned to matters affecting the Party and especially its strong points. The Secretary-General said the Party had a 'good guiding ideology'. The Chinese revolution had been 'led to victory by Mao Zedong Thought and not by any other thinking'. Deng declared that the Party had a good Central Committee headed by Mao. The Party's history since the Zunyi Conference of 1935 had shown this.

'Some comrades may ask: Doesn't the Party's Central Committee also have shortcomings and make mistakes? Didn't Comrade Liu Shaoqi say in his report that the Party Central Committee is chiefly responsible for the shortcomings and mistakes in our work over the past few years? How should this point be explained? In my opinion, no Central Committee is free from shortcomings and mistakes. The question is whether we solemnly and seriously look at the questions and handle them in the style of seeking truth from facts.'

Deng's next good mark for the Party was the quality of its members and the 'backbone elements', the cadres at county secretary level and above as well as military officers of regimental rank and above who had been 'tempered in the long revolutionary struggle'. Those who had joined the Party after 1949 had already received twelve years of experience in administering post-war China, and Deng quoted Liu as saying that even in making mistakes the 'backbone elements' had become 'immunised' by the experience — by which he meant they had learned from their mistakes. In his next point of praise of the Party, Deng ascribed to Mao the slogan 'seek truth from facts'. Ironically, this later became the watchword of his systematic abolition of many of Mao's social, economic, and political experiments after the latter's death. Deng said that since the 1935 Zunyi Conference, Party work had shown 'a perfect system'. It treated people who erred with persuasion, not violence, 'refraining from overheated struggle and merciless attack'. In view of what would happen to the Party in

1966–67, Deng must have had many later occasions to reflect how wrong he was in expecting such a peaceable mood to prevail and, indeed, by 1962, there had already been plenty of 'overheated struggle'.

The Party's other strong point was identified by Deng as its good relations with the masses. If the Party made errors the masses might think it had 'gone' (ceased to be relevant), but when it corrected those mistakes the masses would say, 'the Communist Party has come back'. A comic image.

Turning to the Party's weak spots, Deng said that 'in recent years many comrades have been busy with specific work and have not discussed Party issues or paid much attention to Party building.' The reason was that many members had not studied enough, particularly Mao's Thought. The result was that 'many slogans are unrealistic, excessive targets and impatient demands are set, and there is also a number of inappropriate "big efforts".' Another weak point was that, especially in recent years, people had become less willing to speak out honestly and report conditions as they really were. The key element in a Party official's behaviour was whether he or she behaved like an official or acted as the servant of the public. Party cadres should strive to avoid being 'contaminated with the airs of officials'.

One important question was that of centralisation and decentralisation of the Party organs. Deng supported centralisation and said that the phenomenon of decentralisation was 'very serious'.

'There are many things that appear in form to be more centralised than in the past, but in fact the phenomena of commandism and of a few people or an individual acting in an arbitrary and despotic fashion are very serious . . . . This conference has proposed that it is necessary to strengthen democratic centralism and bring democracy into play.'

It is around the concept of 'democratic centralism' that the debate concerning civil and political rights and freedom in social and cultural matters has long been discussed in the People's Republic of China. The most commonly encountered type of 'democratic centralism' consists of the Party and government making policy from the top downward while paying attention to criticisms or suggestions from the bottom up. Sometimes, as in the 'Democracy Wall' movement of 1978–79 or the student demonstrations of 1986, the Chinese people's desire for greater participation in government makes itself felt from below.

Even though Deng stated in 1962 that it is centralism that is the most important thing, all too often these movements end in demotion, ostracism, or gaol for the activists who have taken the 'democratic' part of the political slogan too literally. The constitution and Party statutes may lay down what are democratic elections for leading posts in a Chinese Communist framework, but it is not the West's idea of democracy. Sometimes there may be more than one candidate for an area or organ of administration, but in a majority of cases it is Peking's man or the local authorities' favourite who will be elected, and the people simply accept that. On the other hand, as Deng said in his speech, he also feared the growth of commandism — when the higher authorities simply passed policies down without listening to any criticisms or suggestions. Cadres were also timid in offering suggestions, often submitting them in anonymous letters. 'The leaders should be a bit more broad-minded in their attitude. They must tolerate others,' Deng said. But he reserved the right of criticism of the Party for Party committees, the Standing Committee of the Politburo, or his own bailiwick, the General Secretariat.

At this point the record shows that remarks by Liu and Mao were interpolated in the text of Deng's speech without any explanation as to whether they simply made them verbally and interrupted Deng, or whether they were in the form of notes on the text. For instance, Deng talked about Party organs meeting to have 'heart-to-heart talks' on problems arising or mistakes being corrected.

Liu: 'The members of the Party committee at all levels should have a Party Life meeting once a month . . . . '
Deng: 'Not necessarily once a month. Once in three months would be fine.'
Liu: 'Once a quarter or four times a year would also be good for holding Party Life meetings . . . . '
Mao: 'For checking on work, summing up experiences and exchanging views.'

The leaders appeared to be extemporising with their running commentaries on Deng's speech. This is quite unlike their usual behaviour on a conference rostrum. Deng next said Party officials should freely 'vent their air' (express their views).

Mao: 'Do not blame those who have vented their air wrongly.'
Deng: 'They may vent their air as much as they want to.'
Mao: 'You should accept other people's correct criticisms. It is no good either to blame others if their criticisms are wrong.'
Deng: 'Not everyone vents his air correctly. It does not matter if he vents his air wrongly. On the one hand, we should not expect others to agree with us when we have vented our air wrongly. . . . On the other hand, we must not demand of others that they should vent their air correctly every time!'

Deng turned to one of his favourite themes: criticism of excessive emphasis on mass movements such as rallies, parades, criticism sessions, and repetitive speeches. 'Daily involvement with movements is not good,' he said, despite the fact that Mao was known to approve of them and would later use them to destroy his enemies and also many an old ally.

Deng cited the movements of the past to eradicate opium addiction and implement land reform. Those movements, he explained, were successful because they were carried out 'on the basis of thorough-going and painstaking work', with the implication that the more recent ones were not. He criticised the use of mass movements in making accusations against people, resulting in wrong political verdicts being passed. These must be corrected by a full-time committee which would conduct investigations. Xi Zhongxun, a member of the Party Politburo, recommended the speech when it was eventually published in 1987. During a visit to the Zhuhai Special Economic Zone in Guangdong province, he said Deng's speech made 15 years previously 'is of practical and far-reaching significance in guiding our Party building and our work'.

In a speech to another high-level conference in March 1962, Deng had summarised the damage done to the economy by the Great Leap Forward and talked about some of the remedial measures required.

'There are some places that need three to five years [for recovery], some need seven, whether it's in agriculture or industry. We should just go ahead one step at a time .... The main thing in production is to make parts. Tractors must be built first of all from parts. It's important to make things for everyday use, too .... Truly grasp necessities. We can withdraw currency from circulation. You can examine the matter and produce a bit more. Put the prices of goods up by fifty per cent and wages up by fifty per cent, but the key is still [production of] industrial goods .... The basic method is to *reduce* the number of people [in industrial jobs]. The important thing is to slow down the speed of construction. This can't arouse opposition, though it may damage our reputation. The way to solve the difficulties of industry is to dismount many people and reduce their numbers.'

A Red Guard critique of this speech said five years later:

'The Liu and Deng bunch proclaimed with all their might
that we are now in a most unusual situation, an extraordinary situation, and we must take extraordinary measures.
So they "got off their horses all along the front!" After this
conference Liu and Deng officially ordered the establishment of a finance and economy working group to strengthen
their control of overall matters of finance and economy,
and pursue the restoration of capitalism on a big scale.'

These speeches of Deng's showed that he had become
openly critical of Mao's tough, uncompromising policies.
However, he and other leaders continued their outward
deference to him, though this did not save most of them from
the coming storm of the Cultural Revolution.

Chapter 8

RUSSIA AGAIN

A fresh round of Sino–Soviet talks began on 5 July 1963 and, with the Mayor of Peking, Peng Zhen as his deputy, Deng headed the Chinese delegation which went to Moscow. Also included were Kang Sheng (later to be known as the 'evil genius' of the Cultural Revolution) and Yang Shangkun, a distinguished military leader and member of the 'Twenty-eight Bolsheviks'. The Central Committee of the Chinese Communist Party preceded the visit with a statement four days earlier to the effect that the Chinese representatives had been instructed to 'safeguard the unity of the socialist camp and the international Communist movement'. Peking, in other words, was announcing in advance that if the talks failed to restore harmony between the two parties it would be the fault of the Soviets. The Chinese side also chided the Russians for not having published the text of a Chinese letter dated 30 March of that year and for calling the opinions of the Chinese Party 'groundless and slanderous'. It blamed them for taking 'a serious step in further worsening Sino–Soviet relations'.

On 4 July, the Chinese government protested against the Soviet Union's expulsion of five Chinese citizens, three diplomats, a post-graduate student, and an 'institute functionary' for distributing copies of a Chinese official document to Soviet citizens. It added that Soviet personnel in China had been doing the same thing with their own government's statements, often not printed in the Chinese press. Peking said the Soviet Union had 'extended the ideological differences between the parties to the relations between the two countries'. The *Beijing Review* added that the Russians had blocked the Chinese delegate to a meeting of the 'World Congress of Women' — a united front organisation. The hall was packed with Russians who booed and whistled, refusing to let the Chinese delegate take the rostrum. The Indian lady delegate 'even used the congress rostrum to slander and make unwarranted attacks against China'. India had been very hostile towards China since the 1962 border fighting. Only the North Koreans complained about this barracking of China, whilst Albania attacked the Soviet Union's moves towards disarmament agreements with the United States.

The British delegate, Joan Carritt, took the side of the Soviet women in the conference hall manoeuvring which made a nonsense of the entire proceedings of the women's congress. Simultaneously, the North Vietnamese government in Hanoi attacked Yugoslavian leader Tito for his critique of Chinese foreign policy, confirming Tito's status as the Chinese whipping boy in the Sino–Soviet dispute. Tito later became a favourite of the Chinese. For the time being, China left the door open to a reconciliation with Moscow. Foreign Minister Marshal Chen Yi said 'the Tito clique' wanted to sow discord between the two big powers, 'but the Chinese and Soviet people want unity and oppose a split'.

The Chinese delegates returned to Peking on 21 July, and Deng and his colleagues were given a rousing welcome at the airport. Even Mao was among the welcoming party which also included Liu Shaoqi, Zhou Enlai, Zhu De, and Dong Biwu. Colourful banners, drums, and gongs greeted the team in the usual Chinese manner of welcoming VIPs. Deng, grinning broadly, waved his arms to the welcoming party. Mao and the others even welcomed the Soviet aircrews of the two planes that had brought the Chinese delegates home, China having no big airliners at that time.

But the only remotely good news Deng brought home was that he had agreed with the Russians to continue the dialogue, although the time and place for the next encounter were not decided. Coinciding with Deng's return from Moscow, the Chinese Communist Party published an exceptionally long letter to the Soviet Central Committee, essentially expounding five main themes:

- Communists 'blotting out' the class nature of the conflicts with 'imperialist' countries;
- Lack of attention to the class conflicts within capitalist countries, not just between capitalist and socialist ones;
- The false idea that the internal order of capitalist countries may be transformed peacefully or that the clash of interests between 'oppressed nations' and 'imperialist' ones could be solved without revolution;
- The view that 'international agreements among the big monopolies' would enable the capitalist countries to solve their mutual difference of interest; and
- The belief that world peace can be obtained through peaceful co-existence of capitalist and Communist countries.

If Deng was involved in the drafting of this article of about 8,000 words, and it is almost certain he was, one can appreciate how much of his working time was being devoted to the Sino–Soviet dispute. He was also probably concerned in the massive polemic dominating the Chinese media in August 1963, which attacked the tripartite treaty between the Soviet Union, the United States, and Britain agreeing to a nuclear weapons partial test ban. China viewed this as a fraud and insisted that only total destruction and prohibition of nuclear weapons would save mankind from the danger of nuclear war.

Despite his likely background contributions, Deng did not put his name to the Chinese attacks on the Soviet Union at this time. It was enough for him to be chief delegate at the various rounds of talks on ideological matters, but was he totally in agreement with the various heads of dispute with the Russians?

He must have known that China herself would have a nuclear bomb within a year, in which case the Chinese attacks on the test ban treaty would look hypocritical. He had seen the collapse of Mao's economic castle-in-the-air between 1958 and 1961 and was aware that some Soviet criticisms of the people's communes were justified. The *Beijing Review* on 23 August published an article from a Soviet newspaper revealing the extent of inefficiency and dishonesty on the Soviet collective farms, whose basic philosophy was not entirely dissimilar to that of the communes. It would not be the first or last time an article printed in the Chinese press had far wider implications and even hinted at the opposite of what it was ostensibly saying. Speculation it may be, but some high member of the leadership group, such as Deng, might well have reprinted the Soviet article with the idea of covertly attacking the Chinese communes. After all, it was Deng who had helped to dilute the communes in 1962 and who would abolish them in 1979.

Chapter 9

CULTURAL REVOLUTION
AND EXILE

The 'Great Proletarian Cultural Revolution' was a unique event in Chinese history. It has been compared, in some of its aspects, with the short reign of Qin Shi Huang Di, the founder of the Chinese imperial system in the third century BC. This comparison is based mainly on the fact that he had the classical books of the time burned and Confucian scholars buried alive. He ran a militaristic, highly disciplined state in which only the government's interests were taken into account; the common people, if they did not accept this, were subjected to cruel punishments.

The youthful Red Guards of 1966 and 1967 also burned many old or foreign books which they thought were contradictory to Mao's ideology. They 'buried' scholars and academics, not in pits but deep in the rural areas where, for the next decade or so, they would labour with their hands alongside the peasantry. There the similarity with Qin Shi Huang Di ends. Mao's ideal state, which he tried to create in the Cultural Revolution, encompassed no discipline save loyalty to himself, the Great Helmsman. The Red Guards were highly aggressive, but not in a military fashion which could make them effective warriors against real armies. Their enemies, Mao's rivals, were knocked down from their positions of high office and public esteem mainly by force of numbers, fanatical fervour, intimidation, a degree of physical violence, imprisonment in harsh conditions, and forced labour. Some were hounded to death and some committed suicide, which in Chinese culture is an act of high moral purpose designed to vindicate the person performing it and bring misfortune on the one who had committed oppressive acts. The violence of the movement recalled the early Fascist periods in Italy and Germany in the 1930s.

School children and young students could not have achieved such goals without top-level support. The Cultural Revolution group, with which Mao surrounded himself in 1966, issued overt and covert instructions to them, encouraging their activities. In the early stages, the People's Liberation Army was bewildered by events, attempting to obey Mao's instructions to 'support the left' and even handed out firearms to some of those whom they believed to be of the left. But in those days everybody claimed to represent the left and eventually, with Mao's approval, the PLA brought the students under control. The PLA helped ship millions of students off to central Asia and other remote parts of the country when they became too unruly even for Mao's purposes. For several years China was turned into a quasi-military dictatorship ruled by a demi-god, Mao, as well as Lin Biao and their supporters in the army. The main restraining force was Premier Zhou Enlai.

Some of the earliest rumbles of a gathering political storm were heard in the remote southwestern province of Guizhou, where Zunyi is located. In late 1964, the province was caught up in the 'Four Clean-ups' (*si qing*) movement, aimed at eradicating corruption and slackness, which had already been in progress for two years in more advanced parts of the country. Local leftists mounted a political attack on Zhou Lin, a local Party bureaucrat who had worked his way up from the Southwest Military Administration Committee since 1951. According to a Red Guard journal published in 1967, Zhou and his supporters were 'taking the capitalist road and oppressing the people'. The publication stated that Deng and Liu Shaoqi had sent a 'work team', a sort of fact-finding and damage control mission, to clarify the situation and restore order. It was led by a leading member of the Chinese Women's Federation, Qian Ying, and a little-known Party bureaucrat. These investigators set to work uncovering the reasons for the unrest in Guizhou, allegedly to the point of imprisoning and shooting some low-ranking cadres and covering up Zhou Lin's reputed maladministration. In Peking, Deng announced that Zhou's problems would be sorted out by the central authorities and the local people 'need not bother about it'. But the trouble continued and in November 1965, Deng personally visited Guizhou in the company of Li Jingquan, Party boss of neighbouring Sichuan province. However, even after their visit, the province's political problems continued to sputter until 1967, when Deng was directly denounced by Red Guard investigation teams who had travelled from Peking to the three southwestern provinces of Guizhou, Yunnan, and Sichuan. Zhou Lin, like so many other provincial administrators, disappeared from the scene and may have died, as he did not return to prominence after Mao's death at the end of the Cultural Revolution period in 1976. The Red Guard journal stated in 1967: 'We want to tell Deng Xiaoping this solemnly. In Guizhou, there is apparent leftism, but actual rightism. You protected Party persons in authority taking the capitalist road. You struck against the broad revolutionary masses and you resisted the Twenty-three Rules!'

The Twenty-three Rules were drawn up as guidelines for the conduct of the Four Clean-ups and were mainly applicable in the rural areas. They concerned: (1) analysis of the situation; (2) the nature of the current movement; (3) unified expression of views; (4) standards for campaigns; (5) work methods; (6) 'concentrating one's forces to fight a war of annihilation'; (7) 'squatting on the spot' (making a thorough investigation of local conditions); (8) grasping the problem as a whole; (9) problems related to cadres; (10) establishment of poor and lower middle peasants' associations; (11) timing; (12) policy towards the covering up of private land ownership;

(13) imposing the Four Clean-ups in financial and commercial work; (14) choice of members of the work team; (15) giving (culprits) a way out; (16) application of the Four Clean-ups to the construction industry (a common sphere for corrupt practices); (17) settling the size of work-teams; (18) determining the tenure of cadres at grass-roots level; (19) problems of supervision; (20) 'the four great democracies' (great contending, great blooming, big character-posters, and great debates); (21) attitudes towards work; (22) system of thought; (23) application of the above to the Four Clean-ups in the urban as well as rural areas.

The above gives a fair impression of the special style of Red Guard haranguing of political bosses and party machines during the early years of the Cultural Revolution. When local leftists got the bit between their teeth, encouraged by the leftist tone of the national media, the 'moderate' leaders in Peking or the provinces would send out a work-team — a group of investigators invested with the power to analyse and straighten out local problems. These teams consisted of reliable cadres and workers, loyal to the Party's line, who tried to restrain the zeal of the Red Guards from 1966 onwards. By late 1966 they had earned the hatred of the Red Guards, especially at Peking and Qinghua universities, for allegedly suppressing spontaneous political expression. (Qinghua University was a hotbed of factional fighting in the Cultural Revolution.) Nobody has yet explained what turned dedicated young people into screaming fanatics.

Of course, with the wisdom of hindsight we know that these movements were often not as spontaneous as they appeared, although the participants certainly believed that they had real grievances. The movements were frequently manipulated by high-ranking Party officials, who had an interest in starting trouble to remove their seniors and achieve political power. Such were the type of people who made up the Gang of Four. This was the title given to the most radical group who sought to succeed Mao and Zhou at the expense of the moderate group within the Party. The Gang of Four was headed by Mao's wife, Jiang Qing, together with Chief Political Commissar Zhang Chunqiao, Propaganda Chief Yao Wenyuan, youthful aide Wang Hongwen, and their supporters. Above the sea of movements presided Mao himself, making his personal appeal for the help and support of the youth of China.

Deng, as has been the case on other occasions, was too self-confident to believe that he himself might fall victim to the stormy new movements. For several months he was a member of a small group which controlled or exploited the excesses of the Cultural Revolution. By 1964, the Chinese leadership had already shown signs of growing concern at the inefficiency and corruption of rural cadres and had sent large numbers of students and urban officials to check up on conditions in the countryside.

Little could Deng have suspected the results of the next big revolution — the 'reform' of Chinese education. In June 1965, Deng addressed the Ninth Congress of the Communist Youth League in Peking. He called on its members to carry on the movements of class struggle; to struggle for production and scientific experiment; to play the role of 'genuine internationalists' in the struggle to 'root out revisionism and prevent a restoration of capitalism', sins of which Deng himself was later to be accused.

By late 1966, confusion and disorder were mounting, especially in China's cities. The Mao cult got into full swing in the military with the official army newspaper proclaiming 'Turn our Army into a great school of Mao Zedong Thought!' The *Worker's Daily*, official organ of the Chinese trade unions, declared that it was the duty of the working class to imitate the PLA.

'Factories should be turned into great schools for the living study and application of Mao Zedong's Thought . . . . While the main task of the workers is in industry, they should also study military affairs, politics and culture. They should also take part in the socialist education movement, and in the criticism of the bourgeoisie [which Deng had declared virtually defunct nine years before]. Where conditions permit, they should also engage in agricultural production and side occupations, as is done at the Daqing oilfield [in northeast China].'

At 5 a.m. on 18 August, Mao Zedong mounted the rostrum over the Tiananmen Gate in Peking to preside over a mass rally. Deng was ranked fifth in the leadership group. Japanese correspondents in Peking reported that Liu Shaoqi had made a self-criticism in September and Deng had made one a month later. New posters on Tiananmen Square said, 'Liu is a rightist and number one anti-revolutionary in China and he and Deng Xiaoping must be removed from their posts.' A Red Guard journal wrote:

'The so-called problem of Beijing University is the Socialist Education Movement, which was begun there in October 1964 . . . . Deng Xiaoping became the most vicious criminal suppressing the movement. In order to oppose the Great Proletarian Cultural Revolution, he ganged up with Liu Shaoqi, who appointed Peng Zhen to be head of their black gang and of the Cultural Revolution small group . . . . Deng ganged up with Liu Shaoqi to concoct the "February Outline" (a document put out to quell excessive leftist zeal in 1966) and sought to divert the Cultural Revolution onto the road of "purely academic" criticism. On 3 June they produced the Eight Articles of the Party Centre, laying it down that it was "not permitted to go on the streets [to demonstrate]", and that there was "a difference between internal and public matters", besides forbidding the sticking up of wall posters on the streets and warning people to be "careful not to let secrets out", etc. — scheming to bind the masses hand and foot and suppressing the Great Proletarian Cultural Revolution.'

In December 1966, the violent poster campaign subsided somewhat as icy winds blew through the Peking streets. Red Guards from out of town were ordered to return home and reluctantly complied, declaring that the movement would be started up again in the spring. By then the supporters of Mao Zedong and Lin Biao had turned the heat on Liu Shaoqi and Deng, who were being mentioned exclusively in wall-posters attacking 'revisionists'. The Red Guards announced that they had arrested Peng Zhen in the small hours of 4 December and that he had been shaking so much he could barely dress himself. By 1966, Liu was referred to as the 'number one' enemy at the top of the Party; by 1967, Deng was labelled 'number two' enemy.

By mid-December when Liu and Deng disappeared from public view, the attacks on them became a flood as Xinhua News Agency began referring to them as 'the handful of Party persons in authority taking the capitalist road'.

Tao Zhu who had recently been made chief of propaganda was unaware of the similar fate that threatened him. He attacked Deng and Liu publicly as 'bourgeois reactionaries' who 'spread poisonous influence'. They were among the 'handful' of 'revisionist' leaders but 'found themselves in a more and more isolated position'. Harald Munthe-Kaas reported in the *Far Eastern Economic Review* on 22 December 1966 that they were accused of being 'representatives of the bourgeoisie who have wormed their way into the Party, government, army and various circles in the cultural field and are counter-revolutionary revisionists, bad eggs of the Khrushchev type, and time bombs planted within our Party.' They were 'sitting behind the scenes, manipulating the student mass organizations, sowing discord, creating factions, instigating struggle by force, and even employing various illegal means against the revolutionary masses, while they themselves "sit on the mountain top to watch the tigers fight".'

By 1966, China had already developed the fiercest internal power struggle ever to shake the Communist Party which seemed to turn increasingly inwards. In his 1956 speech on the revision of the Party statutes, Deng had ascribed the success of the Chinese revolution to the Party's having 'formed close relations with the masses, and unified the strength of the people' with no mention of Mao, whereas Lin Biao had said, 'all our achievements and all our victories were seized in the brilliant leadership of Chairman Mao, and are all victories of Mao's Thought.'

Deng's daughter, Deng Lin, writing in a big-character poster, described how her sister Mao Mao had opposed the work teams at the Teacher Training Institute where she was studying, and had asked her father if she should debate with them. Deng had allegedly replied: 'Of course! You don't want to have too many people criticising the work teams, but you should have some forces. Have a two-day debate, hold it in a good-natured and civilised manner, and talk rationally, basing yourselves on facts. That won't amount to shifting objectives.' The Red Guards later accused Deng of conspiring with Liu Shaoqi to oppose a directive of Mao's, to the effect that they should 'not be too hasty' when they sent out work teams to the universities. They had demanded that every department of the Central Committee send out work teams to dampen the ardour of the students, and said the Communist Youth League 'should supervise the activities of all middle-school students'. Deng was quoted as saying: 'It's no good just to make a lot of noise. They've also got to sit down and find out the truth, analyse and criticise, so that the campaign is a high-quality one.' On another occasion in June 1966, he said: 'It's not good to let children kick up as much fuss as they like.'

The purge now touched the military. On 16 May, Luo Ruiqing, the famous revolutionary commander, had been replaced as Chief of Staff by Yang Chengwu, another veteran. The sinister Kang Sheng absorbed Luo's concurrent job as Head of National Security and Secret Police. An assault was launched on conventional schooling, entrance examinations to institutions of higher education were abolished, and student enrolments for 1966, and for four years thereafter, were postponed. In July it was disclosed that Chen Boda was to be the leader of the new Cultural Revolution Group 'under' the Central Committee. In reality, the new Cultural Revolution Group soon became more powerful than the entire Central Committee put together. The Second Plenary Session of the Eighth Central Committee, formed in 1956, met to proclaim the dismissal of Liu Shaoqi, ostensibly on grounds of the mistakes he made in sending work teams into Peking University. However, other disclosures, about much greater 'deviations' in his political career, would soon come tumbling out.

On 20 August, groups of Red Guards, mainly educated adolescents, had started their extraordinary campaign to abolish 'bourgeois and feudal remnants' by changing the names of streets and shops to give them a revolutionary tone. They banned what they regarded as luxurious or ostentatious styles of clothing, they burned or confiscated books, *objets d'art*, furniture, and other things thought to be of 'bourgeois' inspiration. To achieve their aim of complete proletarianisation, they looted shops and homes and were soon emulated by destructive young agitators in Shanghai and other big cities. Soon the rampage spread out over almost the entire country.

Reportedly, Premier Zhou Enlai saved many of the temples, palaces, and other ancient buildings by putting them off limits to the Red Guards and placing military guards around them. Gradually, the PLA officers got the message that they should support the most leftist Red Guards, even to the point of giving them weapons. Meanwhile, throughout China, hundreds of publications, periodicals, and new books were being removed from printing presses. The last eight European nuns in China, one so ill and weak that she had to be pushed across the Lowu border bridge on a luggage-trolley, were deported to Hong Kong.

Giving notice of Mao's leftist economic policies and his lack of repentance over their failure, the Party's theoretical journal, *Red Flag*, attacked the economic theories of Sun Yefang, a scholar who had been compared with the brilliant, but unsuccessful, Soviet reformer, Yevsey Liberman. Both advocated management autonomy and greater material incentives for workers.

Despite having joined the Cultural Revolution Group back in May, Deng Xiaoping himself was now an almost open target of attack. Chen Boda had said at the August Plenary Session: 'The problem of Deng is clear and definite. It is important, too. Deng is the spearhead of the erroneous line. The thought and style of Liu and Deng are exactly opposite to those of Chairman Mao. At present, Liu and Deng will not admit their errors, but are still thinking of attempting attacks. Deng is more obstinate than the others.' Mao added on a note of reconciliation. 'We may not,' he said, 'get rid of Liu by a stroke of the pen. They [Liu and Deng] have committed mistakes, but let them correct themselves.' He and Liu had been forced to submit self-criticisms to a central work conference convened in Peking from 3 to 25 October. On the surface, Mao still showed himself to be in a conciliatory mood towards Liu and Deng. He had told the conference:

'Some comrades say their mistakes are not deliberate ones. They are made because of muddle-headedness, and are therefore forgivable. [We] cannot shift all the blame onto Comrade Shaoqi and Comrade Xiaoping. They are to be blamed, [but] so is the Centre [as a whole]. The Centre has not done its job. Because of lack of time and energy, [I] have not prepared [the answers] to the new problems. Political and ideological work which is not done properly will be improved after these seventeen days of conference.'

The conference had reached a crisis on 16 October 1966 when Deng made a report considered 'erroneous' by the Maoists because it embodied a line similar to that of Liu Shaoqi who wanted to keep the Cultural Revolution under Party control. Deng fought back so stubbornly that Chen

Boda was moved to complain: 'To discuss with Deng as equals is more difficult than to put a ladder against heaven.' Liu and Deng went on attending mass rallies in support of the Cultural Revolution, but both seemed withdrawn and unenthusiastic. Nie Yuanzi, a leftist woman lecturer and Red Guard leader who had written a trend-setting poster at Peking University, continued to 'publish' extracts from the August conference in wall posters which showed Mao to be much tougher in his attitude to Liu and Deng than some of his remarks had indicated. Deng was gradually excluded from his high-level work which was taken over by the Cultural Revolution group.

On 25 December, students from Qinghua University paraded through Peking's streets chanting denunciations of Liu and Deng and, on the next day, Mao's birthday, the two men's self-criticisms were published as wall posters. On the 27th, a rally of some 100,000 people was held to subject Liu and Deng to further attack, though they were not present. The Red Guards also accused Deng of having sheltered in the Party since 1956 some high-up 'renegades'. This he allegedly did by classifying their behaviour as 'erroneous', for which there would be no punishment. When asked if 'wrongly amnestied' people would have their verdicts reversed again, Deng allegedly said, 'If it was [just] error [they were guilty of], they won't have their verdicts reversed again. It doesn't matter if a few bad people are left in the Party.'

Deng was by no means entirely passive in the face of the attacks on his political integrity. A 1967 Red Guard fly-sheet quoted him as having said that Liu Shaoqi was not a counter-revolutionary, and demanded that the judgement on his case be reversed. He shouted, 'The PLA is pursuing the bourgeois, reactionary line.' At a black session held in his home, he said, 'I have done nothing wrong in the Party in the past ten years or more.' Red Guard publications in 1967 kept up a steady barrage of accusations and unofficial quotes from Liu Shaoqi, Deng Xiaoping, and Tao Zhu, by then known collectively as Liu–Deng–Tao. In March 1967, Mao Zedong was quoted as having said about Deng: 'This person does not grasp class struggle. He has never referred to this key link. Still he is making reference to "black cat, white cat", making no distinction between imperialism and Marxism.' Deng was also criticised by Red Guard materials for having heretical views of the State Plan:

'Some enterprises associating themselves with the realities of the industrial front have criticised the unrepentant follower of the capitalist road within the Party for his opposition to the policy of self-reliance, and promoting the attitude of being slaves to things foreign and crawling behind other people; for disrupting the good relations between the centre and the local regions; for promoting the idea of "statutory dictatorship" [rules and regulations for industry]; for opposing "walking on two legs" [combining old and new methods]; and for superficially emphasising what is big and what is foreign.'

Mao was also quoted as complaining, 'Deng Xiaoping has never called on me. From 1959 up to now, he has not discussed anything with me . . . . When in Peking, you would hold a six-day meeting, but you did not even want me to hold a meeting for a single day.' On the origins of the Cultural Revolution, Mao said: 'In September and October [1965] the question was asked: should revisionism appear in the Centre, what should the local [Party committees] do? I then felt that Peking did not carry out my suggestions.'

Deng Xiaoping and some other leaders were in favour of rehabilitating Party members who had been suspended or disgraced for past 'errors', and had denounced communism under duress when they had been prisoners of the Nationalists in order to escape being hideously tortured and killed, as indeed many were. A Red Guard document claimed that Liu Shaoqi and Deng Xiaoping were heads of a 'renegade clique' of some 300 people whose origins went back at least as far as the Eighth Party Congress in 1956. It added:

'For a long time past Deng and Liu were cheating Chairman Mao above them, and the masses and Party members below them, covering up for these shameless renegades, putting them into many important leadership posts in the Party and Government, and relying on them to realise their goal of infiltrating the Party and Government and the PLA and pursue their vile campaign to restore capitalism . . . . At the [1956] Eighth Party Congress, Deng and Liu gathered together for a meeting of the responsible persons of all important departments, to deliberate what attitude to take towards [those Party members] who had once made recantations [of communism]. At Liu and Deng's instigation, the conference decided to issue six draft regulations to divide [the deviants] into three groups — those who had wavered, those who had made a clean breast of things, and those who had committed serious betrayal [of the Party]. Those who had been arrested and made confessions in enemy documents, and signed them, did not count as having made a confession but as having "committed erroneous acts in the presence of the enemy". Their posts would not be affected. Those who after arrest [by the Nationalist authorities] had confessed their conversion from communism in enemy newspapers, and openly attacked the Party, or maligned the Party, were not to be designated "renegades", but should pronounce the verdict on themselves, and could be employed again according to the nature of their confession.'

This policy of overlooking the past if people still had contributions to make to the success of the revolution and socialism was, like so many other things, turned against Deng and his colleagues by Mao and his activists. This contributed to the destruction of a good part of the generation which had helped bring China into the twentieth century.

Deng was put in solitary confinement for two years during the Cultural Revolution. Later he was put under house arrest in Jiangxi province. Little is known about this period of exile. Only his wife, Zhuo Lin, and one of his stepmothers, Xia Bogen, accompanied him. At 65, Deng was the most vigorous of the three, so he had to sweep up, cut firewood, and carry water. Xinhua News Agency said in a dispatch on 26 February 1980:

'In the cold winter there were no heating facilities and they had only cold water to bathe in. Deng worked in a factory in the morning and gardened in the afternoon, and spent most evenings reading books . . . . He remained silent as a stone.

Pufang's back had been severely injured when Red Guards forced him out of an upper storey window at Peking University during the Cultural Revolution. Deng Pufang, his eldest son . . . was paralyzed from the waist down. He could not move and lay in bed at a social relief hospital. But he had to earn his living by weaving waste-paper baskets with iron wire. Hearing this, Deng and his wife asked for the transfer of Deng Pufang, and eventually he came to stay with them. So Deng's household duties became heavier because he had to give more help to his crippled son . . . .

Before sunset every day, he used to take a walk around the small yard. His steps were slow but steady and he was lost in thought walking round and round.

At the same time, people started getting acquainted with him. His attitude in labour, his speech and deportment and his behaviour deeply impressed workers around him. Workers often gave him some daily necessities and helped him grind rice flour.

One drizzly morning his younger son, who was allowed to be with him for a short period of time, had to leave him and return to Shanxi. This one small source of joy would soon disappear. Deng suddenly looked pale and broke out in a cold sweat as he was starting work. He couldn't stand, so the workers helped him lie down, and gave him a glass of water with their sugar ration, then sent him home on a tractor.'

Although the Cultural Revolution was not declared officially ended until 1976, it wound down rapidly after military adviser Lin Biao had attempted an assassination plot on Mao in 1971 and tried to instigate a coup. By 1972, Premier Zhou, an advocate of moderation, took over the general running of the country and helped Mao to supervise its normalisation of relations with the United States and other Western countries. Chinese society had apparently found a compromise between violent and peaceable leftism, and many of the policies instituted in the Cultural Revolution were taken to be immutable.

Chapter 10

THE RETURN

In the China of 1973 there was a mood of hope and optimism now that the violent phase of the Cultural Revolution was over. The country was emerging from near-isolation to take its position in the community of nations. Although Japan and the United States continued to maintain relations with Taiwan, a number of countries including Japan, Britain, West Germany, and the United States upgraded their diplomatic relations with China. Foreign airlines were flying to Peking and Shanghai in increasing numbers, trade was booming, and there was a modest let-up in cultural and social policies.

Internally there seemed to be a move towards what Mao called 'stability and unity', as the leftist faction in the leadership was in a state of disarray after the late Marshal Lin Biao's alleged plot to assassinate the Chairman in 1971. While reportedly trying to flee to the Soviet Union after the failure of the coup attempt, Lin, his family, and some close associates died when the Chinese-owned Trident crashed in the Mongolian People's Republic. Some other plotters shot themselves, and a long campaign was launched to denigrate Lin's memory. Other leftists, however, like Mao's wife, Jiang Qing, Yao Wenyuan, and Zhang Chunqiao (later of the Gang of Four), by closely adhering to the movement to denounce Lin Biao, managed to distance themselves from him and were never actually accused of direct participation in the coup attempt. Instead, disaffected military commanders were blamed and sentenced to long gaol terms.

On 12 April 1973, at a banquet in Peking in honour of Prince Norodom Sihanouk of Cambodia, Mao's niece, Wang Hairong, teased Western correspondents for not spotting Deng Xiaoping amid the attending leaders. This was hardly surprising since no picture of Deng had been published since 1966, except derogatory cartoons, and his reappearance after seven years in provincial exile was quite unexpected to most people. Deng was officially mentioned as a Vice-Premier, but no explanation was offered for his reappearance in the official press. Liu Shaoqi had died in November 1969 in a high-security prison in Kaifeng from lack of medical care after Red Guard beatings in 1967, but this was not commonly known. Asked about Liu, Chinese officials would say: 'Anyway he is politically dead.' This turned out to be untrue as later Liu's *Selected Works* were published in Peking.

Deng's rehabilitation was followed by that of thousands of other veteran officials and cultural figures who had been disgraced in the Cultural Revolution. However, a rumour circulated to the effect that Deng had written a letter to the Central Committee in advance of his return promising 'never to reverse verdicts', that is, never to change Chairman Mao's policies.

In 1973, the political horizon was not empty of clouds. There were still prominent leftists in the Politburo, especially Jiang Qing, Hua Guofeng, Ji Dengkui, Zhang Chunqiao, and Yao Wenyuan. Although the official media were still pursuing the campaign against Lin Biao, on 30 May the Peking *Guangming Daily* published a political commentary which said in part:

'We cannot forget how swindlers like Liu Shaoqi frantically vilified the revolutionary movement of young people going to the mountainous and country villages to receive

Deng at age 16

Deng and fellow student,
Hu Lun, in France

Japan's advance into China 1931-39

The Long March

1936 Deng and Red Army colleagues

1937 Deng with Red Army comrades

Deng and army crossing river

1939 Marriage of Deng and Zhuo Lin

1947 Deng in the Dabie Mountains

1950

1951 Deng in Tibet

1953 Deng voting

1959 Deng on a visit

1960 Liu, Zhou and Deng

1962 Mao and Deng

1964 Zhou and Deng

1964 Family photo on Deng's 60th birthday

Mao and Deng

1973 Deng and Zhuo Lin

*1976 Deng at
Zhou's funeral*

1976 Tiananmen incident

1977 Deng and Ye Jianying's birthday

1979 Deng and President Carter

1984 Deng and Margaret Thatcher

1984 Deng's 80th birthday party

Deng playing cards

re-education from the poor and lower-middle peasants, or how they attacked the correct course of cadres going down to the countryside to be tempered by taking part in collective labour production.'

This line did not last long, however. The Tenth Congress of the Chinese Communist Party was held in August 1973 and its resolutions were leftist in tone. It removed from the Party statutes some of the references to 'Mao's Thought' that had been written in to a massive extent at the ultra-leftist Ninth Congress in 1969. The most intriguing aspect of the Tenth Congress was the emergence of the young Wang Hongwen as Mao's new favourite. A man in his thirties, Wang had been a soldier in the Korean War and a security officer at a Shanghai cotton mill. He had come to the attention of the leftist ideologue Zhang Chunqiao and, after the Tenth Congress, several times sat in on visits by foreign dignitaries to Chairman Mao. His career would be curtailed abruptly in October 1976, when he was identified as one of the Gang of Four and arrested. He was put on trial in 1980 and was sentenced to life imprisonment in a labour camp.

The Tenth Congress was held in secret, but Mao addressed it in person — his last such appearance. Wang's report to the Congress had been used by him to proclaim that the Cultural Revolution would be a recurring phenomenon — something Deng was determined to prevent. Most analysts believed Deng had been brought back to office on the insistence of Premier Zhou Enlai. Mao himself continued to harbour some affection and respect for Deng, and perhaps regretted what he had seen as the need to oust him between 1966 and 1967. Later, however, the Gang of Four criticised Deng to Mao and made no bones about their desire to block his further rise after his rehabilitation.

In 1973 it had seemed ridiculous to associate the new movements in the Politburo with opposition to the newly returned Deng Xiaoping but, in retrospect, clearly this had been the case. Testimony at the trial of the Gang of Four between 1980 and 1981 referred to a conspiratorial meeting of Jiang Qing, Zhang Chunqiao, and Yao Wenyuan at the Diao Yu Tai (Fishing Platform Guesthouse), the main VIP residential complex for foreign dignitaries in Peking. Wang Hongwen was quoted as saying in his confession:

'On October 17 1974, the Politburo was having a meeting and Jiang Qing and Deng Xiaoping had a row. When the meeting ended, we went back to the Fishing Platform Guesthouse and Jiang told me, Zhang Chunqiao and Yao Wenyuan to come for a meeting at Building Seventeen to analyse and discuss the reasons for her quarrel with Deng. She said, "Deng Xiaoping was determined to have a row because he's hostile to the great proletarian Cultural Revolution . . . ." Zhang Chunqiao said, "Perhaps the reason why Deng Xiaoping has jumped out [become politically active] is because in discussing the Fourth National People's Congress [to be held early the next year] there've been nominations for chief of the general staff. . . ." He also said, "I have a feeling something's going to happen soon." I realized that the idea of reporting to Chairman Mao was to cast aspersions on Comrade Deng Xiaoping and stop him from working, and certainly prevent him from becoming first Vice-Premier. The trip to Changsha to report to Chairman Mao was deliberately concocted to slander Comrade Deng behind the back of Premier Zhou and the Politburo.'

More testimony was given by the American-educated Nancy Tang Wensheng, former English interpreter and aide to Premier Zhou and Chairman Mao and often seen in the company of Mao's niece, Wang Hairong. Tang said:

'On 17 October 1974, Jiang Qing called me and Comrade Wang Hairong to Guesthouse Seventeen. The four of them were there. Jiang Qing first got Zhang Chunqiao to brief us

132

on so-called problems of the situation. Turning truth on its head, he said that since the campaign to criticise Lin Biao and Confucius [had begun], the domestic budgetary imbalance and the adverse situation in foreign trade had come about because leading comrades worshipped foreign things. He said, with a malicious, sinister air, "Comrade Xiaoping has made a big issue of the M.V. *Feng Qing* affair [the first China-made freighter to make a round-the-world voyage]. This is no coincidence. Before the great proletarian Cultural Revolution, he took the stand that it would be better to buy ships than to build them and better to charter ships than to buy them." Zhang Chunqiao said, with a spiteful look, "The Politburo meeting on the evening of 17 October was like the February Adverse Current." The four of them told us to report these views of theirs to Chairman Mao. In Changsha, we told the Chairman. When he heard what we had to say, he was very angry and said, "The question of M.V. *Feng Qing* is basically a small one, but Jiang Qing is still carrying on about it." To counter the conspiratorial activity of Wang, Zhang and Yao to subvert the party and seize power, *the Chairman proposed* that Comrade Deng Xiaoping be made Vice-Chairman and first Vice-Premier, Vice-Chairman of the Party's Military Affairs Commission, and chief of the general staff. . . .'

In 1974, the leftists used their influence to hamper the restoration of formal education in China. They praised a student at Liaoning University in northeast China for handing in a blank examination paper on the grounds that political zeal was more important than knowledge. A young Peking schoolgirl, Huang Shuai, was held up for emulation because she had quarrelled with her primary-school teacher — an episode that sent chill shivers down the spines of teachers who remembered their mistreatment in the Cultural Revolution by somewhat older children and students.

Deng was opposed to these campaigns which he saw as

harmful to the restoration of the shattered educational system. Deng thought that education must be carefully restored if China were to have a chance in the global race for scientific progress and economic development. He commissioned an in-depth report on the state of affairs in education, especially higher education, which was tabled before the Central Committee in 1975 when his confrontation with the leftists was reaching its height. China's appearance of relative stability as it entered 1975 masked an ever more intense power struggle between Deng Xiaoping and his supporters and the leftists including Jiang Qing. A New Year's message, issued in the name of the Party leadership, gave a deceptive picture of prosperity and unity. 'In our country, the market is brisk, prices remain stable and production and construction are thriving. All this is in striking contrast with the decline in the capitalist world which is facing a profound economic crisis.' Deng must have known this was nonsense. In a few years' time he would be introducing quasi-capitalist methods of management and incentive in industry though without great success, and would give frank assessments of just how poor and backward the nation's economy still was.

In January 1975, Deng Xiaoping resumed his post as Vice-Premier, and was also named a Vice-Chairman of the Communist Party and a member of the Politburo's Standing Committee. The Vice-Chairmanship is one of the only true positions of power in China; the other is the Military Affairs Commission, whose chairmanship Deng still holds.

The leftists continued cranking up their behind-the-scenes campaign against him, but he did not lower his profile; indeed, he showed increased self-confidence. He was entrusted by Mao with the routine affairs of the Politburo and this restored him, in actual practice, to the leadership of the Party. But he did not yet have a completely free hand because of the presence of leftists on the Politburo and in the Central Committee. As long as Mao lived, however senile, his presence protected the leftists and they, once more, started whipping up opposition to Deng through obscure media debates about Chinese traditional literature and history. The new State Constitution, promulgated at the Congress, was a considerably slimmed-down version of the existing one which had been drafted in 1954, and made more references to political matters and less to administrative affairs. The leftist Chief Military Commissar, Zhang Chunqiao, was made a Vice-Premier, and the Ministry of Public Security (police and secret police) was taken over by a relative unknown with leftist leanings, Hua Guofeng.

Hua, born in Shanxi province, had spent much of his working life administering the part of Hunan province where Mao was born. He had come to the latter's attention when he transformed the house of the Chairman's family into a political shrine to which millions of visitors flocked. He was soon to become Deng's strongest rival for total power, though in 1975 he was only 56 years old while Deng was 71 years old.

The Constitution also enshrined the 'four big freedoms' which Deng saw as a source of anarchy. These are defined as: to put up wall posters; to hold big debates; to bloom; and to contend.

On 29 January 1975, it was disclosed that Deng had been appointed chief of the general staff of the People's Liberation Army (PLA). From a political point of view this put him in competition with Zhang Chunqiao as Chief Commissar of the General Political Department of the armed forces. This looked like a compromise between the leftists and those who supported Deng, possibly thought up by Mao or more likely by Zhou Enlai. At any rate, foreign observers now looked at Zhang as a potential candidate for the premiership. What was also clear was that, after Mao and Zhou, Deng was now the most powerful man in China. He was also regarded as the number one Vice-Premier and number one Vice-Chairman of the Party, which was a massive comeback.

March saw the appearance of a signed article from the leftist Yao Wenyuan in the Party press regarding the dangers of 'bourgeois' and 'revisionist' tendencies in the Party. He expounded his theory that such deviations occurred not just in the ranks, but at the very top of the Party when the policies of Chairman Mao were not properly implemented. He gave a warning against 'people like Lin Biao', which was actually a covert attack on Deng Xiaoping and Zhou Enlai — especially Deng. He proposed the banning of bonus payments to workers on the grounds that it would turn them into 'capitalists'. In that same month, Mao failed to receive three successive visiting statesmen from the Third World, thus intensifying rumours that he was very ill. In April, Generalissimo Chiang Kai-shek died in Taiwan, raising Peking's hopes of a more conciliatory attitude towards the mainland on the part of his son and successor, Chiang Chingkuo.

In the autumn of 1975 an extraordinary debate about 'capitulationism' was started. This took the form of numerous articles in the press denigrating Song Jiang. Song Jiang is a sort of Chinese Robin Hood of mediaeval times, and is read and loved by almost every literate Chinese child. His exploits were recorded in the novel *Water Margin* (*Shui Hu Chuan*), also translated as *All Men are Brothers* and *The Men of the Marsh*. The new debate was centred on Song Jiang's eventual surrender and entry into the service of the emperor of the Northern Song Dynasty in the twelfth century. The most intricate literary arguments were spun to prove Song Jiang's 'capitulationism', though few people in China dared to interpret it openly as the symbol of yet another contemporary political struggle. But, in the end, that was what it turned out to be — another attack on Deng Xiaoping. The allegation of Deng's 'capitulationism' evidently referred to his policies which could be interpreted as 'surrender' to the forces of capitalism. Silly though it was, the *Water Margin* debate soon had people speculating again on the nature of the struggle behind the scenes. The late Liu Shaoqi was attacked for having wanted to 'capitulate' to the Soviet Union, a sin of which Deng could not plausibly be accused. Deng's name was so closely linked with

Liu's in the early party of the Cultural Revolution that such specific criticism of the latter naturally aroused speculation about another 'line struggle'.

The Chinese leaders were still in their anti-Soviet mood. The American Secretary of State, Henry Kissinger, visited Peking in October 1975 to prepare for a visit by President Ford. Western press reports said that his talks with Deng had been a bumpy ride. Infuriated, Kissinger told newsmen that 'our two countries are too self-reliant to need reassurance and too experienced to confuse words with reality or tactics with strategy.' To rub in Peking's view of *détente*, a Chinese official told correspondents that the recent Helsinki conference on *détente* and civil rights was similar to the 1939 Munich talks between the former British Prime Minister, Neville Chamberlain and Adolf Hitler and that the Soviet leader, Leonid Brezhnev, had assumed the role of Hitler.

The next prominent statesman to visit Peking was the West German Chancellor, Helmut Schmidt. He tried to avoid too much talk of *détente* in his discussions with Deng Xiaoping, but he could not prevent the latter from severely criticising the Soviet Union as 'the superpower most seriously praising *détente* and disarmament'. The USSR, Deng added, was 'maintaining an offensive posture far exceeding its defence needs and posing a threat to the people of Europe and the whole world.'

On 1 December, when President Ford arrived in Peking for an official visit, he said in a banquet-speech: 'Rhetoric about *détente* cannot cover up the stark reality of the growing danger of war.' Suspicions that the talks with Deng had been tough seemed confirmed when neither side issued a communiqué.

The next internal political campaign against Deng was commenced in late November 1975, when students at Peking University started putting up wall posters denouncing Zhou Rongxin, the Minister of Education, who died shortly thereafter. The campaign was publicised by the Chinese leadership which had foreign diplomats and correspondents bussed out to look at the posters.

Zhou Enlai died on 8 January 1976 at the age of 78. This brought Deng closer to supreme power, but not before some lurid incidents took place which marked the year 1976 and set the country on a new course. In fact, five years later, it would be alleged at the trial of the Gang of Four that by banning sets of commemorative photographs, they tried to minimise public mourning for Zhou, and many Chinese felt that Jiang Qing, in a dark Western-style head-scarf, was improperly dressed for the funeral. However, the general public showed its grief. Thousands of people holding paper wreaths and weeping openly congregated around the Monument to the Martyrs of the Revolution on Tiananmen Square.

Later, in January, it became known that Deng Xiaoping was to be elevated to the position of First Vice-Chairman of the Communist Party. This sudden growth in his power, together with his role as First Vice-Premier of the State Council and his position as Chief of the General Staff of the PLA must have severely alarmed the leftists. The power stuggle intensified as students at Peking University and Qinghua University disclosed that their poster attacks were specifically aimed at Deng.

Deng did not secure the premiership after Zhou's death. Instead, the title went in acting capacity to the left-leaning Hua Guofeng, who was replaced as Minister of Public Security. Meanwhile, students at Fudan University in Shanghai were putting up more and more posters attacking 'rightists', by which they meant Deng and his supporters. He was also referred to as 'the top Party person in authority taking the capitalist road' and 'China's second Khrushchev', the first being Liu Shaoqi. Hua Guofeng began to take over diplomatic duties, such as receiving foreign dignitaries, which Deng had handled during Zhou Enlai's illness. He gave a warm welcome to Richard Nixon, the Chinese leadership's best-liked American, who had facilitated the restoration of US–Chinese diplomatic links and other exchanges in 1971.

As Nixon toured south China in 1976, clearer evidence came to light that Jiang Qing was active in the anti-Deng propaganda campaign. The Chairman's wife had been setting up stage shows and political evening classes in a small village, Xiao Jin Zhuang, near Tianjin in north China. A report of this village's politicisation through culture appeared in the *People's Daily*. Deng and his supporters were accused of denigrating the attempts to make it a model for Chinese villages everywhere. They wanted evening classes to teach the peasants to read and write, not to make them study political ideology.

By 1976, a violent note was creeping into the wall posters attacking Deng (although still not usually by name). 'When we knock him off his horse, we will kick him hard,' one poster said. The confrontation between Deng and Jiang Qing grew sharper, and it was rumoured that Deng had said of her revolutionary stage-works, 'I can't watch that stuff.' On 29 February, the *People's Daily* accused him of trying to 'emasculate' Mao's policies. He was called a 'three-headed monster' — the other two heads reputedly being Lin Biao and Liu Shaoqi. The *People's Daily* published a recent aphorism of Chairman Mao's: 'reversing verdicts will not win people over.' In other words, Mao was supposed to be accusing Deng of having gone back on his 1972 promise to the Central Committee that he would 'never reverse verdicts' on the Cultural Revolution if he were restored to office.

On 22 February, the leftist, Yao Wenyuan, published an article in the *People's Daily* in which he complained that the 'people following the capitalist road' had opposed the policy of appointing young people, workers, and peasants to important posts. They had also criticised the revolutionary stage-works and the 'barefoot doctors'. The barefoot doctors were Mao's remedy for the shortage of trained medical personnel in the Chinese countryside. They were not literally barefoot, but were lightly-trained medical and hygiene workers who were credited with great achievements in public health. Deng once said of them that they should progress 'to straw sandals, then to rubber shoes' — his way of saying they should be better trained.

Deng must have experienced a sense of *déjà vu* as the new campaign against him unfolded. But this was not 1966. Now, in 1976, he was near the top and, with his usual self-assurance, he pushed ahead with his plans to rationalise the Chinese economy, restore formal education, reform the PLA, and provide more consumer goods and links with the outside world.

But now, with Mao's blessing, Hua Guofeng also had leapfrogged Deng to become acting Premier. The *People's Daily*, controlled by leftists, accused 'unrepentant followers of the capitalist road' of having taken Mao's 1974 admonition to 'settle down and unite' as an excuse to practise 'revisionism'. It condemned 'Khrushchev's goulash communism' and said the rightists had 'unscrupulously split the Party Central Committee headed by Chairman Mao'. This was strong meat and everyone knew it was aimed at Deng. His supporters were accused of having 'subverted certain leading departments, given tremendous promotion to unreformed bourgeois intellectuals, and recklessly schemed to let them run roughshod over the Party committees.'

On 21 March, the leftists signalled to Deng that if he abandoned his present course he need no longer be so directly attacked. In a front-page article it said that the 'historic experience' of the Communist Party was Mao's dictum, 'learn from past mistakes to avoid future ones and treat the illness to cure the patient.' The Party organ went on: 'At this time, will the follower of the capitalist road who is trying to reverse verdicts change his bourgeois stand under the renewed criticism of the people of the whole country and with their help?' Deng showed no obvious reaction to these pressures, but the big showdown was just around the corner.

On Sunday, 4 April 1976, tens of thousands of people came to Tiananmen Square to commemorate the death of Premier Zhou Enlai. April is traditionally the month when the ancient

Qing Ming Chinese festival of cleaning the ancestors' graves is performed. In modern Peking, with its compulsory cremations, this is not the custom, although some older graves remain in the outskirts. The throngs of mourners brought white-and-coloured paper wreaths, many of them in the name of individual factories and institutes. They raggedly sang the 'Internationale' and stuck small pieces of paper to the Monument to the Martyrs of the Revolution in the centre of the square. Many of the pieces of paper contained poems in honour of Zhou whom they had liked for his modesty, dignity, and concern for raising living standards.

On Monday morning, people cycling to work saw that all the wreaths had been removed from the square and clean-up squads had scrubbed off the written tributes. Furious, they converged on the square in protest. It was estimated that, by mid-morning, there were about 100,000 people demonstrating and shouting pro-Zhou slogans. A student who said something critical of Zhou was beaten bloody on the steps of the monument. The demonstrators tried to storm the Great Hall of the People. Yao Wenyuan wanted the security forces to shoot some of the demonstrators. At his 1980 trial, the judge asked Yao whether it was true that he had said 'some of them should be shot'. Yao: 'Only some of them, some of them! I mean *some* of the masses! That was just my feeling, what flashed into my mind! It didn't become one of my concepts!'

Most of the demonstrators' activity on the square consisted of milling around and shouting pro-Zhou slogans. Towards midday the mood became uglier and cars were overturned near the Historical Museum on the east side of the square. Pine trees were ignited as petrol tanks exploded. Firemen who arrived were forced out of their engines and could not stop the flames. A small police station in the southeast corner of the square was set alight and gutted, but no policemen appeared to be hurt. As the cold afternoon wore on, people began to go home and, in the ensuing dark, hundreds of plain-clothed troops of militia formed a human cordon around the square.

It was rumoured later that a large number of rioters had been taken to a nearby park and summarily shot.

None of the Western correspondents in Peking, including the author, saw evidence of demonstrators being shot, but these rumours were very persistent among the common people. The Communist Party has never made a clear and detailed statement on the affair, although later they did refer to it off-handedly as a great expression of public feeling.

This sealed Deng's fate for the time being. Although he was not directly blamed for the riot, it was implied in a Party and government statement that his actions had somehow led up to it. According to officials, and allegedly on Mao's orders, he was suspended from his official posts but allowed to keep his Party membership 'to see how he behaves'. Hua Guofeng was named First Vice-Chairman of the Party, a new appellation, and acting Premier to replace the late Zhou Enlai. In an officially inspired demonstration, hundreds of thousands of workers, students, and schoolchildren marched the streets or rode on the backs of lorries. They thumped big red drums and clashed brass cymbals to show support.

The media campaign against Deng was raised to fever pitch over the next few months. According to *The Times* of 19 May 1976, his supporters were denounced as capitalists, reactionary literati supporting the old landlords, class infiltrators of the Party, secret agents, and 'social scum'. Because Jiang Qing hoped to become the Chairman, Mao was deliberately shown, in press photographs, to be sinking physically when receiving several foreign dignitaries.

An insight into Deng's economic policies, which had aroused so much indignation among the leftists, was given by a trade union study group. They said Deng wanted to reverse the policies of the Cultural Revolution by keeping trade unions out of politics, by leaving politics to the local Party committees, and by entrusting control of production to managers and not to Party officials. The *Guangming Daily* went so far as to call him an adherent of Taoism, an ancient Chinese religion which taught inaction and harmony with nature — hardly an appropriate insult.

On 7 July, another significant event occurred. Zhu De died, thus ending a chapter in the annals of the PLA and the revolutionary struggle. The atmosphere in Peking was tense as though the people were waiting for another big event. It occurred in the small hours of 28 July in the form of an earthquake in the industrial city of Tangshan, 60 miles east of Peking. Tangshan was reduced to rubble within quarter of an hour, and many houses also collapsed or were damaged in the capital. The casualty toll was put at roughly 500,000. This earthquake seemed to confirm the superstitious belief that great political events in China are heralded by abnormal natural phenomena. The superstitious Chinese were made anxious by these 'portents', as the classical word for the death of an emperor means literally 'landslide'. On 9 September, at ten minutes past midnight, Mao Zedong died. He was 82 years old, and his death precipitated a power struggle that would transform the face of Chinese communism.

As the shock of Mao's death subsided, it was clear that it affected people less deeply than the death of Zhou Enlai. The media turned their attention to Deng Xiaoping against whom, it was stated, Mao himself had ordered a campaign of criticism.

On 12 October, it was suddenly announced that the Gang of Four, consisting of Jiang Qing, Zhang Chunqiao, Yao Wenyuan, and Wang Hongwen, had been arrested on the orders of the Politburo. An armed uprising, plotted by leftists in Shanghai, fizzled. According to widespread rumours, Jiang Qing screamed abuse at the security squad which came to arrest her, but her attendants cursed her and spat at her as she was hauled off. Zhang Chunqiao said nothing and remained almost completely silent, refusing to talk even at his trial. Yao Wenyuan, it was said, was flabbergasted and simply handed over a copy of an article he had been writing. Wang Hongwen tried to resist but was overpowered.

The scene was now almost set for Deng Xiaoping's return to power. Deng had spent the last few months in the southern city of Guangzhou under the protection of his old friend, General Xu Shiyou, commander of the Guangzhou Military Region. With that peculiar momentum of Chinese politics, the other leaders and the media continued the campaign to 'criticise' Deng, although it was soon buried in the torrent of abuse which the media were now launching at the Gang of Four. Meanwhile, Hua Guofeng was made Chairman of the Party by the Politburo in succession to Mao who was officially quoted as telling Hua: 'With you in charge, my heart is at ease.' An official oil painting of this scene was printed and distributed widely to factories, shops, and offices.

The vilification of Jiang Qing was carried out, to a large extent, in political cartoons which were also popular in the Cultural Revolution. She was accused of wanting to rule China as the Empress Dowager Ci Xi had in the nineteeth century. She was portrayed as a snake, a fox, and a vain woman wearing Western clothing and dripping with jewels. The general public were much more interested in Jiang Qing's luxurious life-style than in criticisms of her politics. Members of a state farm providing employment for returned Overseas Chinese on the large southern island of Hainan were quoted by Radio Guangzhou as saying:

'When Jiang Qing sneaked into our farm on a visit, she was very fussy about clothing, food, quarters and means of travelling. She was not satisfied with the bed and bed-sheets after they were changed several times. She demanded that within the range of one kilometre from her residence there must be no noise. Motor vehicles delivering things to her had to switch off the engine one kilometre away and then be pushed by more than 20 strong young militiamen. Nominally she was a guest in workers' homes. However, when a bench was offered to her, she was loath to sit on it. . . . She stayed at our farm for two days, and disturbed the peace of the entire place.'

At a seaside resort, in case of sharks, she required a cordon of soldiers to stand around her in the water when she swam. In posters, the Guangzhou police said that she had imported 'obscene films' from Hong Kong. It was reported in *The Times* of 16 November 1976 that:

'Jiang Qing was more cruel than a landlord's wife and she tortured the working personnel maliciously. One cold winter night, a worker did not put an electric heater in her bedroom early enough. When she found out, Jiang Qing scolded him mercilessly, and immediately punished the worker by making him stand outside in his bare feet in the cold for more than an hour.'

She was also quoted as having said: 'The man must abdicate and let the woman take over. A woman, too, can be the monarch. Even under communism there can still be an empress.'

Deng Xiaoping must have enjoyed the torrent of accusations against his old enemy and perhaps contributed some morsels of his own. Meanwhile, the matter of his latest rehabilitation was being considered as the slogans criticising him gradually dried up.

Among those most likely to gain from the fall of the Gang of Four were the top army generals who had stemmed the flood of the Cultural Revolution and lent their support to the October coup. It is not certain which security detachment actually carried it out, but all the top military men in the Politburo seem to have backed it. It was reported in *The Times* of 7 January 1977 that posters in Peking on 6 January claimed that Jiang Qing and her supporters had organised the Tiananmen Square riot to discredit Deng. Three days later there were posters on the square calling for the appointment of Deng Xiaoping to the Premiership and denouncing

Wu De, the mayor, who had unwisely been the last senior official to criticise Deng publicly. Hua's appointment to the acting Premiership caused astonishment in the diplomatic corps because they were expecting Deng to receive the post.

In May 1976, Deng went to Guangzhou for his own safety. Unofficial reports said he had laid down three conditions for his own rehabilitation, which were that the Tiananmen Square riots should be thoroughly investigated, that he should be reinstated to posts at least as senior as those he had held before, and that the reinstatement should be legitimised by holding a National People's Congress and a Congress of the Communist Party. With the exception of the 'thorough investigation' his demands were met.

The political tide turned for Deng in the early summer of 1977 when leading newspapers referred to him as 'Comrade Deng'. He was popular among the common people. It became common knowledge that Hua Guofeng, from his newly elevated position, had said that Deng had no part in the fomenting of the 5 April riot of the previous year. A political manoeuvre and a purge was begun in the ranks of the Central Committee to expel those thought to have been most favourable to Jiang Qing and the other members of the Gang of Four. The left-leaning Party secretaries of Anhui and Gansu provinces were replaced. Three prominent leftists were denounced at a rally in Kunming, the capital of Yunnan province in the southwest. The Gang of Four were expelled from the Communist Party, which was a symbolic measure heralding their later trial.

In July, Deng's return from his third period of political disgrace was forecast by wall posters in Peking. This was officially confirmed by an announcement which also said that the Eleventh Party Congress would be held soon and the Party statutes would again be revised. Deng appeared publicly at a football match in the Peking stadium. Flanked by Chairman Hua Guofeng and the ageing, irrascible Defence Minister, Marshal Ye Jianying, he appeared at a reception in the Great

Hall of the People.

The leadership team backing Deng in 1977 was quite mixed and included an old Red Army comrade, General Xu Shiyou. He had sheltered Deng in Guangzhou during the period of his second exile from Peking and was, at that time, commander of the Guangzhou Military Region. Xu's protection of him was doubtless due largely to the Guangzhou commander's dislike of the Gang of Four. He and Wei Guoqing were the only Politburo members who did not attend the National Agricultural Conference in December 1976 over which Hua Guofeng presided. Liu Bocheng was not there either as he had been in a near-vegetable state for years and was only still listed on the Politburo as a mark of honour. Xu and Wei may have refused to go to Peking because they feared arrest or detention for protecting Deng even though the Gang of Four were already in gaol. In the following year, the most numerous posters supporting Deng's return to power were spotted in Guangzhou.

Other old commanders favourable to Deng were Marshal Nie Rongzhen, Marshal Xu Xiangqian, and Marshal Ye Jianying. Together they made up a formidable caucus capable of handling any military threat to Deng's southern stronghold from the north. Around this time there was much talk of a north–south split in Chinese politics and military alignment and, although it never came to a showdown, it was certainly in line with Chinese historical tradition. Time and again the country has been politically divided by the Yangzi River or by other natural barriers and has split into two or more regions that warred with each other. Nowadays, with tanks, aeroplanes, and military communications controlled by Peking, there is little likelihood of another major civil war in China, but there are times when the views of the regional commanders may differ sharply from those held by the politicians in Peking.

Political leaders who had served under Deng and Liu Bocheng in the 129th Division included Qin Jiwei, Hu Yaobang, and Yang Yong who later became a senior member of the Military Affairs Commission, and they all supported him now, according to information filtering down in Peking at the time. Yu Qiuli, an experienced soldier-administrator, state planner, and political commissar was also counted among Deng's supporters, even though he had survived the Cultural Revolution, which was not usually the best qualification to be a friend of Deng's. One of Deng's biggest enemies was Wu De, Mayor of Peking, being the last prominent person to stop publicly criticising his old patron. To make this more glaring, in July 1977, with Deng back in power, he praised him publicly when the Eleventh Party Congress opened:

'Comrade Deng Xiaoping is one of the leaders of the Party, State and army who has undergone the greatest tests, and has rich experience of revolutionary struggle. Our great leader and teacher Chairman Mao made a clear and all-round assessment of Comrade Deng. When the Gang of Four were running wild, Comrade Deng carried on a firm struggle with them. This meeting has decided to restore Comrade Deng's previous positions, and the whole Party is happy about this, and so are the people of the whole country.'

A pun circulated in Peking to the effect that Wu De's name meant 'shameless'. His recantation was not enough to save his political career and Deng fired him a few months later. Although Deng usually let his political opponents down rather lightly when he eliminated them from power with his salami-slicing tactics, he bore quite a grudge towards Hua Guofeng, the political non-entity who, by becoming a personal favourite of Mao's, leapt into the position of Chairman and Premier after Mao's death. Hua's lack of political judgement was demonstrated by his speech at the conference on agriculture in 1976, where he not only recommended a pace of mechanisation quite impossible to achieve and quite unnecessary in view of the surplus of rural labour resources, but also called for continuing criticism of Deng. Hua said on that occasion:

'At this meeting we have talked very little about criticising Deng Xiaoping, and some people have doubted whether to continue with the criticism of the rightist wind of reversing verdicts, as during Chairman Mao's lifetime. Even if they don't say this, they think it. Deng and the anti-Party clique of the Gang of Four, although they had some sharp contradictions, have the same revisionist nature — they all have an anti-Party, anti-socialist, anti-Mao's Thought tendency. Our overthrow of the Gang of Four is not the same as letting Deng loose.'

Hua would have cause to repent bitterly these words. Deng returned to work in tandem with him from 1977 on, and it would be only a few years before he was pushed slowly but inexorably into a political corner and destroyed as a political force. This was yet another astonishing feat of Deng's manipulative skills.

The Eleventh Congress was held in the second half of August. The new Politburo line-up was heavily weighted with veteran military commanders, perhaps as a reward for their role in the 1976 coup. Many of the Central Committee members of the leftist Tenth Congress of 1973 were removed. The new Party statutes condemned 'dogmatism' but accorded due praise to Mao Zedong Thought. Hua Guofeng in his speech laid the emphasis on making China a 'powerful modern socialist country' by the end of the century.

Deng publicly laid down his goals for the development of the Party and the whole country. As reported by Xinhua News Agency, Deng called for 'less empty talk and more hard work'. He said: 'We have such a wonderful people and such wonderful Party members and cadres. They are industrious, brave, and high in political consciousness. They take a deep interest in state affairs and have boundless faith in our Party.' It can be said that this high estimate of the quality of Party cadres would be borne out by statements Deng made after he had been back in power a while longer. In his August pronouncement, he criticised the 'serious loss and wastage in the economy' caused by recent political conflicts. He followed this up with a weighty though unsigned analysis in the *People's Daily* of things that had gone wrong with the Chinese economy. He said that all industries should show profits and that these should be used to boost workers' welfare. It was a herald of his attempt to reform Chinese industry which would prove to be one of his greatest headaches in the 1980s.

At the same time as he was assessing the internal state of the country, a turning point was reached in the International Communist Movement when, in September 1977, President Tito of Yugoslavia was warmly welcomed as an honoured visitor to Peking. China had long since stopped using Yugoslavia as its whipping boy for the ideological dispute with Moscow, and she had even shown interest in what she had previously called Yugoslavia's 'revisionist' economic system which gave workers a share in management.

A fresh political challenge to Deng's authority was sensed in September 1978, when General Wang Dongxing, commander of the 8341 Guards detachment, which had acted as Chairman Mao's bodyguard and controlled the archives of the Central Committee, published an article in the *People's Daily* glorifying the role of his unit and his own close relations with Mao. It was probably the 8341 leadership guard detachment that organised, or at least stood guard for, the purge of the Gang of Four. This self-glorification would be Wang's undoing.

For one thing, Wang's apparent challenge to Deng was the origin of the fierce struggle over 'the two whatevers'. This was a doctrine to the effect that whatever Mao recommended should be done and whatever Mao did not promote should not be practised. The theoretical journal *Red Flag*, now once more in the hands of Deng and his supporters, hit back with the statement that 'Chairman Mao was not superstitious about the wisdom of a single person, but relied on the wisdom of classes and masses. Individual wisdom is restricted, the wisdom of the masses is infinite.'

In December, wall posters disclosed the return of Hu Yaobang to an important job. Hu had been head of the Communist Youth League and an old protégé of Deng's. At 64, he was in good shape to take over the Party's powerful Organisation Department, and he was also known as one of Deng's favourite bridge partners. He had been living in obscurity since being denounced by Red Guards in 1967.

Meanwhile, Deng had been having talks with the visiting American Secretary of State, Cyrus Vance, that concentrated on the problem of Taiwan. Because the United States had not downgraded its official relations with Taiwan or curtailed arms supplies to the Nationalist armed forces, the American mission in Peking only had the status of a 'liaison office'. China felt she had been very patient over this issue, and in the talks with Vance it was unofficially reported that Deng Xiaoping·had said acerbically: 'Peking will be just as beautiful without an American ambassador.' A pro-Peking Chinese newspaper in Hong Kong said it was not, after all, China that was seeking favours from the United States. By supporting the Nationalists in Taiwan, America was, in effect, demanding the right to station troops on Chinese soil and interfere in China's internal affairs. The United States had no right to regard 'a small bunch of rascals' as the government of China and provide them with military protection.

Despite these tough statements, Deng was patient over the Taiwan issue. He knew of the island province's economic success and was ready to wait until the fruit was ripe. The Nationalist leader, Chiang Kai-shek, had died two years earlier and his son and successor, Chiang Chingkuo, showed no inclination to alienate the old-guard Nationalists who were opposed to any contact with the Communists on the mainland.

On the economic front, just how unstable the personal politics of individual Chinese leaders can be was demonstrated by the publication on 1 January 1977 of an important speech of Mao's in 1956, entitled the 'Ten Major Relationships'. In this speech, Mao had taken a practical, stop-gap approach to the problems of development which was quite different from his voluntaristic theories that fuelled the Great Leap Forward two years later.

Mao's theory of development for China was defined by him in 1956 as relying on the most developed parts of the country being given the lion's share of investment, because they were the best able to absorb it efficiently. He emphasised the development of light industry and agriculture over heavy industry, contrary to other Communist countries' development programmes which usually stress the development of steel, coal, and other heavy industries, thus slowing the rise of incomes and living standards. In 1956 he had favoured the development of China's coastal areas rather than the backward inland regions of the country because these were usually the most advanced. He wanted to cut military expenditure and raise civilian incomes and proposed greater independence for local administrative bodies with less control from the Party centre in Peking. He wanted to reduce arrests and executions for political crimes and favoured giving deviants time to reconsider and recant.

Mao's theory sounds extraordinarily like what was dubbed 'revisionism' in China in the 1960s, and it has many points of resemblance with Deng Xiaoping's policies in the 1980s. But it was almost the last time Mao had given approval to policies such as these which would slow the development of the nation-wide industrial base and encourage leniency towards political foes or deviants (*Far Eastern Economic Review*, 4 February 1977).

On 19 July 1977, wall posters in Peking had announced that Deng Xiaoping had been rehabilitated in his posts of Vice-Chairman, Vice-Premier, and Chief of Staff of the PLA — a stunning comeback. Though Hua was still nominally superior to him, Deng had gained acceptance of his demand to be restored to positions at least equivalent to those he held before April 1976. The fact that Hua was Premier and Chairman meant that he had to waste more time on airport greetings, banquets, and formal talks with visiting dignitaries whereas Deng could pick and choose whom he saw. On 22 July, the report of Deng's return to power was officially endorsed.

Provincial radio stations, probably sincerely, welcomed Deng's return. Hunan said the Gang of Four had 'feverishly attacked him and fabricated accusations against him'. It noted that Deng had been 'tested in more than half a century of struggle'. Hunan said, 'This is what we want deep down in our hearts.'

On 30 June 1977, the *People's Daily* discussed the three so far unpublicised important reports which were drafted in 1975 at Deng's instruction. These were entitled an 'Outline Report on the Work of the Chinese Academy of Sciences', 'Report on the General Programme for All Work of the Party and Country', and 'Some Problems in Accelerating Industrial Development'. The Party organ also disclosed that the Gang of Four had strongly resisted the approval of these reports on the grounds that they represented an 'encirclement and annihilation campaign' aimed at themselves and they were not far wrong. The *People's Daily* now confirmed the 'correctness' of the three and said the 'Outline Report' had been drafted in accordance with instructions given by Mao in 1974 which pre-empted leftist interference with it and the other two reports. The *Far Eastern Economic Review* of 5 August 1977 gave a review of the 'Outline Report', encapsulating Deng's thinking on the Mao cult:

'If people take a simple and violent attitude and adopt the same methods of work as the Gang of Four, or indulge in verbiage, or randomly and one-sidedly interpret Chairman Mao's revolutionary line on science and technology, they will surely cause ideological confusion and losses in work, or even seriously weaken and eliminate scientific and technological work, to the neglect of the needs of proletarian politics, the needs of socialist construction and the needs of the people.'

The report had said the precious time of scientists and technicians had been wasted by sending them down to the countryside to labour alongside the peasants, and that the people who opposed their reinstatement were 'no better than a person who occupies the privy but cannot move his bowels'. It also defended the hiving off of special scientific institutes where specialists could have peace and quiet, free of political interruptions, in order to work on such modern innovations as atomic energy and semiconductors. The *People's Daily* made no reference to the fact that less than a year previously it had said: 'The criticism of the three anti-Party and anti-Marxist poisonous weeds concocted on instructions from Deng Xiaoping is an important measure to further deepen the struggle to criticise Deng Xiaoping and repulse the right-deviationist wind of reversing verdicts.'

Deng was quoted as having told a Central Committee meeting in July or August: 'My health is all right, all working parts are in order, and I don't foresee any breakdowns in the near future.' He recalled that he had supported Mao since the 1930s and had 55 years of service to the Party to his credit. Mao, Deng reportedly said, had 'seventy per cent achievements, thirty per cent shortcomings'.

Deng's emphasis on the importance of education was asserted in a speech he made in August 1977, very shortly after his rehabilitation, but not published until 1983. He dealt especially with the effect of Mao's policy regarding education, in the deferential style which was at that time still current, being less than a year after the Chairman's death. Deng said:

'I myself believe that during most of the time prior to the

Cultural Revolution, Mao Zedong's series of directives concerning scientific research work and cultural educational work did, in their basic spirit, encourage, promote and speed the vast majority of our intellectuals as good and as serving socialism or wanting to serve socialism. After 1967, he did rather go to extremes in some of the things he said, but during the early 1960s he was still supporting the draft [report] entitled "Fourteen Opinions Concerning the Present Work of Natural Science Research Bodies", drawn up in June 1961 by the National Science and Technology Committee and the leading Party group in the Chinese Academy of Sciences, and approved for trial implementation in July of the same year by the Central Committee.'

This draft evidently stressed the importance of the work of scientists and technicians, and criticised the tendency to look down on intellectuals as being inferior to workers. Deng considered that among teachers, the work done by a primary school teacher was just as important as that of a university lecturer. Mao himself evaluated people's special talents, Deng pointed out. 'When he was evaluating me, he said: "Talented men are hard to come by." In all honesty this appraisal is too high, but this phrase does illustrate that talent is important — and that Mao Zedong respected talent.'

Deng went on to relate how the Gang of Four, in fact Mao himself, called intellectuals 'the stinking old ninth'. This referred to the 1950s list of eight types of undesirable elements: 'landlords, rich people, reactionaries, evil people, rightists, traitors, spies and those taking the capitalist road.' But even Mao, Deng pointed out, had said that 'the old ninth can't be let go', that is, the intelligentsia shall not be alienated completely. On education, Deng had said in 1975:

'Since the Cultural Revolution, the schools have lost their grip on cultural education, emphasising labour and practice,

155

disregarding the study of basic theories that the students do not know well enough, so that we are facing a situation in which there will be no successors in science and technology. . . . Since the Cultural Revolution, because the teachers do not dare to educate the students, and the schools have no fixed rules . . . even the examinations and promotion from one class to another, reward or punishment of students and attendance are non-existent, and the students are sunk in anarchy. If this goes on it may create a serious social problem, and what people will socialist China rely on to become successors?'

In 1975, referring to science and technology, he had said: 'Superficial emphasis on Marxism cannot be a substitute for science.' He proposed that on the science and technology front, the dictatorship of the proletariat should not be applied. Scientists and technologists should be 'led by enthusiastic specialists and generalists'.

'If there are to be successors, the central factors are the educational departments or what value does a university have? Whom is it rearing? If the Iron and Steel Institute is at the level of a technical middle-school what point is there in university education? The National Defence Technology Commission must organise the Technology University well. Get some upper middle-school graduates who are good at mathematics, physics and chemistry, without discriminating against the children of cadres.'

In late 1977, with new authority to act on his beliefs, Deng pushed ahead with his plans to restore the Chinese educational system, especially the universities, which had been virtually destroyed during the Cultural Revolution. 'The quality of teaching has declined drastically,' the *People's Daily* commented, blaming the Gang of Four especially for having wrecked tertiary education. There was also to be a special programme to provide university education for promising young people who had missed out because they were Red Guards during the four-year closure of the universities and therefore over-age for application under the old rules. Deng's new rules meant that they could apply up to the age of 25. Many, however, had had their minds dulled by the senseless violence of the Cultural Revolution or back-breaking labour among the peasants and were no longer fit for hard study.

So gratified was Deng by the results of the December 1978 Third Plenary Session of the Eleventh Central Committee, at which he pushed through his reform programme, that he listed it as the third major turning point in the modern history of the Communist Party. In an obviously sanctioned article in the *People's Daily* on 24 October 1983, a Party theorist said the other two landmarks were the Organisation's rise in the Agrarian Revolutionary War in the mid-1920s, and success in the anti-Japanese war from 1937 to 1945. Deng's supporters claim that the decisions of the Third Plenary Session were totally in line with Maoist principles, and assert that it decisively stopped the use of the slogan 'take class struggle as the key link'. Since this was one of Mao's most important principles it is quite illogical to say that the Plenary Session followed Mao's policies. Whilst the article said it had elected additional members to the central leadership organs, it passed over the fact that several leading figures, considered to be too left, were removed as a result of it.

In Deng's view, the Third Session's achievements were not just ideological, but organisational. After a relatively good period in the early and mid-1950s, Deng has pointed out in his *Selected Works* that Party organisational work deteriorated.

'Patriarchal phenomena like letting what a single person says go at a meeting, letting an individual decide on important matters, personality cult, placing individuals above the collective, and so forth, continuously developed. . . . A good system makes it impossible for bad people to throw their weight around, and a bad system makes it impossible for good people fully to do good, and even causes them to follow the opposite direction.'

The problem of cadres and organisational line were well aired in a film made in 1986 called *The Black Cannon Incident.* In the film, a conscientious German-speaking engineer, Zhao, arouses the suspicions of old Party hacks that he is involved in some counter-revolutionary conspiracy because he sends a telegram to a friend saying, 'Black cannon missing, please return.' The post office clerk reports this to the Party and security organs and an investigation is mounted. Meanwhile Hans, a West German engineer, has arrived to supervise the installation of some new boring equipment at the plant. He asks for Zhao who previously interpreted well for him but, because of the cloud over Zhao's activities, he is instead assigned a young and inexperienced interpreter who does not know the required technical vocabulary and, as a result, gives the workers wrong instructions. Eventually, Zhao is reassigned to the job and the plant is installed. A few days after the German's departure there is a serious breakdown. Zhao discovers that this was because of faulty instructions given to the workers by the other interpreter. Meanwhile a packet arrives in the mail for Zhao, and it is confiscated on the orders of a senior, leftist cadre, a woman, who opens it to 'expose' finally Zhao's activity. It contains nothing but a round, flat, black counter, the piece called 'cannon' in Chinese chess — Zhao's missing piece. The Party woman runs around trying to find ways in which the German can be blamed for the faulty installation, but is defeated.

The beauty of this film is in the portrayal of the various characters. The head of the Party committee is ineffectual and unwilling to take responsibility. The woman is a self-confessed leftist who cannot accept the new political trends in the country. The plant manager has little say in the matter. The young interpreter is vain, lazy, and ignorant. Zhao is an honest man, perhaps too honest for his own good. A single error may cost the state millions to put right. The German engineer is frustrated beyond belief.

Anyone who has done business in China or helped install equipment there knows these characters. They are cloned all over the country in its present state of industrial disarray, in the aftermath of the Cultural Revolution. Deng is said to have cleared the film for showing to the public but it has appeared in cinemas only sporadically. It was taken off by local leaders in the provinces because of its hard-hitting satire of the Party's failings.

An interesting change in Deng's thinking concerns the question of centralisation and decentralisation. In the 1950s he had favoured centralisation and thought decentralisation a dangerous trend. But in his 1983 critique of Party organisation, he said excessive decentralisation was caused by excessive centralisation in the past, concentration of power in the hands of a few people, and the remnants of 'feudal despotism'. He also blamed the system of life tenure for cadres and the refusal of veterans to recognise they were too old to do a good job any more. He said in his *Selected Works*:

'There are too many cadres who lack technical knowledge and skills, and too few who have them. If the revolution is not undertaken and if old and sick people are allowed to stand in the way of relatively young, vigorous and capable people, then not only is there no hope for modernisation, but there is even a problem regarding the survival of the Party and the state, with the safety of the Party and state threatened.'

Although Deng has not permitted a personality cult to be built up around himself, he is not averse to letting other senior Party members publicly praise him and his policies. One of the most remarkable tributes he received was in 1983, when General Li Desheng, commander of the vital Shenyang Military

Region adjacent to the Soviet Union, published a long panegyric on Deng's newly published selected writings and their importance for post-Mao China.

Li had held his position as military chief of northeast China since late 1973, when he was moved from his post as Military District Commander for the southeastern province of Anhui. His political stance had been the subject of much speculation among analysts of Chinese affairs. Reckoned a left-winger in the Cultural Revolution, he supported the Red Guards more willingly than any other provincial commander. Li's move to the northeast was seen as a balancing act in the interplay of radical and pragmatic forces in the early 1970s.

After Mao's death, Li's attitude towards Deng's deMaoisation programme was unclear but widely believed to be critical. Thus it was a major political victory for Deng to gain the explicit support of such an important military figure who, in co-operation with the Peking Military Region Commander, General Chen Xilian, would be charged with defending the capital and important industrial areas in the event of a Soviet invasion of China.

The *Selected Works* of Deng Xiaoping, Li wrote in the *People's Daily*, had been published to mark the anniversary of the Chinese Communist Party which was founded on 1 July 1921, and the recent conclusion of the Sixth National People's Congress. Li said Deng had responded to the hopes and fears of the Chinese people caused by the Cultural Revolution, by the Gang of Four, and by the 'whateverist' faction in the Politburo whom Deng had ousted at the critical Third Plenum of the Eleventh Central Committee.

In 1975, as Li put it, the state and Communist Party had been 'seriously undermined'. 'At this perilous juncture, Comrade Xiaoping [a respectful and affectionate way of referring to another person is to use only his given name] was instructed to take charge of the routine activities of the Party and state. In spite of the danger of being beaten down another time, he waged a resolute, blow-for-blow struggle against the

Gang of Four.' Deng had called for a 'burst of energy' to cope with the problems of the day.

It is interesting that Li pointed out that Deng's programme of reforms in the Party and state apparatus 'started with the army', which was an important key to political power at that time. The Chinese masses, he wrote, were sufficiently impressed by Deng's commitment to their interests that they staged the Tiananmen Square riots of 5 April 1976, the 'fruit of the seed' of Deng's efforts at reform and the leftists' opposition to them. The arrest of the Gang of Four in October 1976, just a month after Mao's death, showed Deng's strength as a Marxist, and General Li wrote, 'but our Party still faced the difficult situation of advancing in a hesitant manner'. The masses, he went on, wanted Deng to take charge of the nation's affairs. Deng had said during an inspection visit to the northeast: 'Whatever documents were read and signed by Comrade Mao Zedong, they must not be altered, and whatever was said or done by Comrade Mao may not be changed. Is this holding high the banner of Mao Zedong Thought? Certainly not. If we go on like this, we may damage Mao Zedong Thought.' The disgraced leftists' demand for total approval of everything Mao said was 'a false and mechanical way of holding high' the banner of Mao's Thought.

Following his victory over the leftist remnant at the Third Plenum of the Eleventh Central Committee in 1978, Deng became 'the chief designer and helmsman' of the Chinese ship of state. Li quoted him as saying: 'If a Party, a state or a nation proceeds in everything on the basis of books, is rigid in its way of thinking and practises blind worship, it will not be able to advance and its life will cease. Then the Party and state will perish.' In other words, Deng saw the Mao personality cult as threatening the end of socialism in China.

Deng's overall approach to the reform of government in China has been aimed at eliminating 'bureaucracy, excessive concentration of power, the patriarchal system, the life-long tenure system and various privileges among leading cadres.'

He was, General Li stated, particularly concerned about the lack of talented younger officials in positions of responsibility, and has said this could 'destroy the cause of the Four Modernisations'. The northeast commander said the key to the situation was Deng's 'correct' guidance, and his reputation, boldness, and influence. 'His role cannot be replaced,' Li wrote. He did not, however, offer any views on what will happen to China when Deng retires from the scene or dies.

It is instructive to examine how Deng evaluates his own role in the period just before Mao's death and into the early 1980s. The *People's Daily* printed a review of this period on 29 July 1973 and it is safe to assume that Deng saw the text and may have amended it in places. The Party organ said the main events in that period were the smashing of the Gang of Four in 1976 and the correction of 'leftist' errors at the Third Plenum of the Eleventh Central Committee convened in late 1978. In other words, the key episodes in a seven-year power struggle took place within a time-span of little more than two years. Logically speaking, then, this two-year period from late 1976 until late 1978 was the hinge on which the direction of the Party's policy-making was fundamentally changed. The years before and after it are viewed respectively as periods of preparation and consolidation.

In summary, the Cultural Revolution had been going on for over eight years when Deng responded to leftist challenges in 1975 by ordering detailed reports on some key areas of the country's life, especially education, science, and technology. By that time, the Chinese people, after loyally trying to implement Mao's policies, and after certain misunderstandings and changes of course, were disgruntled and disillusioned, the *People's Daily* admitted.

'After the various zigzags, when sincere hopes were made laughable by realities, when the successor stipulated in the Party statutes [Lin Biao] had blown himself up, many people were shocked and lost. People were getting very tired of the movement, and harboured indifferent and doubtful attitudes, even resistance, towards it. People demanded stability and hoped for the prosperity and flourishing of the motherland.'

The newspaper recalled that Premier Zhou Enlai, after eight years of exhausting efforts to stem the leftist tide, had fallen ill with cancer in 1974. Zhou said that the Party needed rectification in its policies, and Deng took on this task, starting with the People's Liberation Army. Mao, who was still just coherent between 1974 and 1975, gave Deng's stewardship his blessing, even though he knew that his wife hated Deng, had quarrelled with him openly at a Politburo meeting, and had tried to poison the old Chairman's mind against Premier Zhou and Deng.

To a certain extent, the two succeeded, according to this account. Mao realised that Deng was preparing to put into action events which would drastically affect his ideas as expressed in the Cultural Revolution. The Gang of Four took advantage of this to renew attacks on Deng. After the death of Zhou on 8 January 1976, the violent denunciations of Deng in the media, which had so far been disguised as literary criticism and historical debate, gave way to attacks on him in wall posters. The mass of people, however, were not enthusiastic about the campaign to criticise Deng and the 'sinister rightist wind of reversing verdicts'. This referred to the leftist institutions of the Cultural Revolution and to the rehabilitation of high cadres previously persecuted as 'revisionists'. In 1972 or 1973, Deng had promised Mao and the Central Committee that if he were allowed to return to work he would 'never reverse verdicts'. Now, the leftists could see he was going back on that promise and threatening their own positions of power.

The Tiananmen Square riots on 5 April 1976, sparked off by the removal of wreaths commemorating the late Premier Zhou, are now seen as a popular hostile reaction to the attacks on Deng, as well as a result of the people's affection for Zhou.

The Party has praised the Tiananmen Square riots as 'a great movement . . . in essence supporting the correct leadership of the Party with Comrade Deng Xiaoping as its representative.'

After the purge of the Gang of Four in October 1976, Hua Guofeng put forward the principle of 'two whatevers' and supported the continued application of Mao's favourite maxim: 'Never forget class struggle.' Hua stood in the way of the plans for the economy which Deng and Chen Yun wanted to implement, made excessively grandiose plans and claims of production increases, and allowed a personality cult to be built up around himself.

Deng's proposal of the principle of 'taking practice as the sole criterion for testing truth' was strongly resisted by other people who considered themselves loyal to Mao and his ideas. Their slogan was that the Dengists were 'cutting down the banner' of Mao Thought. But Deng defended himself by saying the leftist interpretation of Mao Thought was not an accurate one, and that only by studying Mao Thought more carefully could one see that it had been twisted and abused. He started his campaign to 'correct' the widespread distortion of Mao Thought with a speech he made to a work conference of PLA commissars on 2 June 1977, shortly after his rehabilitation from political disgrace on account of the Tiananmen Square riots.

Deng continued this ideological offensive with a speech at the crucial Third Plenary Session of the Eleventh Central Committee in December 1978, entitled 'Emancipate the mind, seek truth from facts, unite as one and look forward'. The result of Deng's efforts, the newspaper said, was 'to bring order out of chaos' and to concentrate the Party's attention on socialist modernisation. At a session of the People's Congress in 1979, Deng adopted a key slogan: 'Build socialism with Chinese characteristics.'

Chapter 11

THE REFORMER

T he Fifth National People's Congress was convened in late February 1978 and proceedings were announced on 6 March. The 80-year-old Marshal Ye Jianying was named Head of State and was replaced as Defence Minister by an old ally of Deng, Marshal Xu Xiangqian. Hua Guofeng retained his post of Premier and Deng continued to be the leading Vice-Premier and Chief of Staff of the PLA.

In March 1978, Deng addressed a national science conference to lay out his views on the work and treatment of Chinese scientists, a topic he had already addressed in his 1975 *Outline Report on the Work of the Academy of Sciences*. 'We cannot demand,' he said, 'that scientists and technicians, or at any rate the overwhelming majority of them, study a lot of political and theoretical works, participate in numerous social activities, and attend many meetings not related to their work.' This was a blow dealt at Mao's policy of ensuring that scientists were both 'red' and 'expert'. Deng essentially professed to follow this line, but whereas Mao emphasised the need for 'red' scientists, Deng preferred them to be 'expert'. Independence, Deng added, did not mean shutting China's door on the world, 'nor does self-reliance mean blind opposition to everything foreign'.

In the summer of 1978 signs of disagreement, if not conflict, appeared between Hua Guofeng and Deng. The main issue was political work in the PLA. At a conference held between May and June, the speeches made by Hua and Deng showed a difference of emphasis. Deng attacked the policy of making military decisions on the basis of political theories without sufficient reference to the actual circumstances. He pointed out that the nature of the PLA and the military climate in the 1970s were quite different from those of 20 or 30 years ago. 'The switch from an environment of protracted war to a peaceful environment makes the biggest difference to an army.' In an indication of things to come, he went on: 'Some people say they are afraid that the inclusion of Lin Biao among the targets for exposure and criticism of the Gang of Four might involve the risk of negating the Great Cultural Revolution and this might be construed as digging up one problem to the detriment of unity. That is wrong.'

Was Deng aware that seven years later he would be calling on the Party and the whole people 'to repudiate completely the Cultural Revolution'? Or did this grow out of his general development and disillusionment as a statesman and leader in the post-Mao era? Only he could say.

Hua Guofeng made a more conventionally Maoist speech, demanding 'revolutionism in command of modernisation' where the PLA was concerned. There were also differences of interpretation between the two men on the results of the 1929 Gutian Conference at the Jiangxi 'soviet' area. Deng said that in the debate at that time Mao pointedly opposed subjective guidance of work, pointing out that it would 'inevitably result either in opportunism or putschism'. Hua, who was too young to have attended the Gutian conference, said that it 'laid the foundations for our army's political work, and completely differentiated our army from all armies of the old type.'

The crotchety old Marshal Ye Jianying, who had recently left his job as Defence Minister to become Head of State, showed early signs of his dislike for the fast pace of political change instigated by Deng since his rehabilitation only a year ago. He said that Mao 'emphatically repudiated the purely military viewpoint, and criticised the mistaken idea of placing military affairs and politics in opposition to each other, or even giving military affairs a leading position over politics.' This was as close and as negative a definition as could be found for Deng's thinking on politics and the military, which was later made more specific through publication of some of his remarks on the subject.

A sign that the top army commanders were siding with Deng to oppose the growth of a personality cult around Hua Guofeng came on 24 June when the Army newspaper, *Liberation Army Daily*, printed an article on matters of political principle in which it quoted Deng as having said at a recent conference:

'Many comrades in our Party persevere in studying Marxism–Leninism–Mao Zedong Thought and adhere to the principle of integrating the universal truth of Marxism–Leninism with the practice of revolution. This is very good and we must continue to do so. There are other comrades, however, who talk about Mao Zedong Thought every day, but often forget, abandon or even oppose Chairman Mao's fundamental Marxist viewpoint and method of seeking truth from facts, proceeding from reality in doing everything, and integrating theory with practice. Furthermore, some people even maintain that whoever persists in seeking truth from facts, proceeding from reality and integrating them with practice, is guilty of a heinous crime. In essence their view is that one may only copy straight from Marx, Lenin and Chairman Mao, and should rest content with mechanical copying, transmitting and reproduction. They would insist that to do otherwise is to go against Marxism–Leninism–Mao Zedong Thought and the guidance coming from the Party Central Committee. What they raise is no minor issue. It involves the whole approach to Marxism–Leninism–Mao Zedong Thought.'

The Army newspaper commented: 'How well he said it!

And how profound was his explanation, driving home the truth!' This military eulogy was as close as Deng ever came to fostering a personality cult around himself, but in any case, within a year or two, he would be in conflict with some of the army chiefs over political matters.

The Third Plenum of December 1978 now became the central reference point for all Deng's reforming policies. It was the fulcrum, which he had sought for nearly two decades, with which he could move the Chinese nation dramatically on to a new track in its search for identity. Nearly ten years later, the Party media were still attributing all political and economic gains to the results of that Third Plenum, just as the followers of Mao Thought once attributed all theirs to the Great Leap Forward and the Cultural Revolution.

In foreign relations, Deng had engineered a major coup by settling the matter of bilateral relations with the Carter Administration in the United States. Washington agreed to downgrade its relations with Taiwan, and in return was able to send a fully-fledged ambassador to Peking. The biggest cloud on the horizon was the question of relations with Vietnam which were rapidly teetering towards war between the former 'fraternal allies'.

In late 1979 the 'Peking spring', represented in the cities by the Democracy Wall movement, began to fade. Democracy Wall in Changan Road, Peking had been the focal point for posters and newsheets vehemently condemning of political freedoms. The trend towards more public debate about political matters had served Deng's purpose by creating an atmosphere, at the Third Plenum of the previous December, in which his enemies in the Politburo could be neutralised. Deng's star was still rising. The Chinese people knew he was concerned with raising living standards which, after the years of political hell-raking, was the only thing most of them genuinely cared about. Some of the poster-writers of Democracy Wall miscalculated Deng's political temperament. His 'liberal' approach masked a desire for tight control which was made more tolerable by allowing the poster-writers to let off steam. When Democracy Wall began to seem like a permanent institution he gradually suppressed it, preparing the ground with articles in the media denouncing the Western idea of 'civil rights' as a fraud. The *People's Daily* commented on 22 March:

'We should not take the worn-out weapon of "human rights" — which has long become a window-dressing of the reactionary dictatorship of the bourgeoisie — as a remedy for the problems of a socialist country. . . . The imperialists brought the Chinese people cannons rather than flowers, death instead of "human rights". They instructed the Qing [Manchu] emperors, the northern warlords and the autocrat Chiang Kai-shek in killing the Chinese people, and sometimes even did it themselves. How can they be in a position to instruct us on "civil rights"?'

The best-publicised case of the suppression of Democracy Wall dissidents was the arrest on 29 March 1979 of Wei Jingsheng, a young electrician who had been producing an unofficial journal called *Tansuo* (*Explorations*). A week later Ren Wanding, another unofficial publisher, was also arrested. By the end of the year it was estimated that several dozen people in Peking had been arrested and jailed for putting up wall posters and conducting free contacts with foreigners, especially correspondents. Wei was later put on trial for allegedly selling military secrets to foreigners, a charge which was not substantiated in court. Indeed, Wei enjoyed no effective defence except his own statement, a lucid and courageous challenge to the forces of obscurantism which still largely control the judiciary in political trials. He was sentenced to 15 years' imprisonment.

The year 1980 was marked on 1 January with the introduction of six new legal codes. Deng believes in codified law, and the legal codes were a major goal of his tenure of office. They were drawn up under the supervision of Deng's ally and sometime rival for power, the rehabilitated leader Peng Zhen. After 1949, the Communist Party preferred to rule through secret directives and emergency regulations so there were very few codified laws. The new laws, which were only the beginnings of the process of codification, covered court procedures, rules of evidence, right of defence, arrest and detention, elections to office, environmental protection, and foreign investment.

Deng now moved to consolidate the political victory he had won at the Third Plenum of 1978. The Fifth Plenum was convened in Peking between February and March 1980, and one of its important decisions was posthumously to rehabilitate the former Head of State and Mao's most prominent enemy, Liu Shaoqi.

A ruling made at the Fifth Plenum that the 'four big freedoms', a creation of Mao's, were to be written out of the Chinese Constitution further shored up the position of the Secretary-General. The freedoms are defined as 'speaking out freely, airing views fully, holding great debates, and writing big-character posters'. These were the instruments by which Mao had overthrown Deng and so many other senior leaders between 1966 and 1967, and Deng was determined that this should never happen again.

Dismissed from the Politburo were General Wang Dongxing, whose ambition was to build a top leadership post for himself by trading on his former relations with Mao; General Chen Xilian, former commander of the Peking Military Region, who appeared to have fallen out with Deng although he had backed the arrest of the Gang of Four; Ji Dengkui, a left-leaning *apparatchik* and specialist on agriculture whom Mao favoured; and Wu De, former Mayor of Peking, whose misfortune it had been in 1977 to go on publicly criticising Deng when everyone else had the discretion to stop. Zhao Ziyang, a pragmatic and experienced administrator, was promoted to membership of the key policy-making body, the Standing Committee of the Politburo. Later he was to become Premier and still later Secretary-General of the Party. But in 1980 the latter post went to the diminutive former youth leader, Hu Yaobang.

Having put his desired successors in place, Deng began to talk more openly about his own resignation. He was 76 years old at the time, and he said he would like to resign from his official post as Vice-Premier although everybody knew he was the supreme leader. At the National People's Congress, held between August and September 1980, it was decided to remove Hua Guofeng from the Premiership to make way for Zhao. Hoping to salvage something of his meteoric career, Hua addressed the Congress on measures to liberalise the economy, reduce bureaucracy, and raise living standards. He announced that he would step down as Premier and that Deng had also decided to give up his post as First Vice-Premier which he did not need and found troublesome. Meanwhile, Hua remained Party Chairman and Deng Vice-Chairman.

On 28 September, Deng's revenge on the Gang of Four was disclosed. Jiang Qing, Yao Wenyuan, Zhang Chunqiao, and Wang Hongwen were to be tried on political charges. Six other men, mostly soldiers, were to be accused of plotting to kill Mao in 1971. The military men put on trial in 1980 were Huang Yongsheng, former chief of staff of the PLA; Wu Faxian, former commander of the Air Force; Li Zuopeng, former chief political commissar of the Navy; Qiu Huizuo, former director of the General Rear Services Department; and Jiang Tengjiao, former commander of the Air Force general headquarters. The other man was Chen Boda, Mao's private secretary and left-wing ideologue.

Zhang Chunqiao, who had previously been director of the General Political Department of the PLA, refused either to accept the arraignment or to speak during the trial. He and Jiang Qing were sentenced on 25 January 1981 to suspended death penalties, which meant that they would be given two years to show repentance and behave well in prison, otherwise at the end of that period they would be shot. They were not, in the end, executed. The other defendants all received long prison terms, but since they had been in jail for nine years since their arrest, some would be freed quite soon and lapse into obscurity.

By now the important problem of Hong Kong had begun to loom over Deng and his supporters. The recovery of British Hong Kong, Portuguese-ruled Macau, and the Nationalist island sanctuary of Taiwan were articles of faith to all veterans of the Chinese revolution who were as much concerned about China's integrity as a nation as they were about her internal social system. The 400-square-mile territory of Hong Kong on the coast of southern China had been forcibly annexed in 1840, 1860, and 1898 by Britain. The land grabs of 1842 and 1860 were endorsed by treaties with the enfeebled Qing dynasty in Peking, but the 1898 annexation was created in the form of a rent-free lease for 99 years. By the early 1980s, British, American, Chinese, and other investors in Hong Kong began to worry about their legal status when the lease expired in 1997. The Governor at the time, Sir Murray MacLehose, now Lord MacLehose, visited Peking to inquire discreetly about Deng Xiaoping's intentions for Hong Kong. After several visits by other British officials in 1983, the Chinese government agreed to let Hong Kong survive for 50 years after 1997 as a Special Administrative Region of the People's Republic of China. The Chinese government also agreed to let Hong Kong have its own internal political system, capitalist laws, Western life-style, and freedom of speech, print, and religion. Deng has since said that, if the people want it, it will continue with that status for 100 years.

Following further visits to Peking by Sir Geoffrey Howe, the British Foreign Secretary and Margaret Thatcher, the British Prime Minister, an agreement to this effect was signed in 1984. A similar agreement for tiny Portuguese-administered Macau, near Hong Kong, was concluded in 1987. Despite difficult points of both detail and principle involved in the Hong Kong agreement, the Sino-British Joint Declaration on the Question of Hong Kong as it is formally called, it was a remarkable document which showed a broad-mindedness on the part of Deng and his leadership group. This was greater than expected after the long years of dogmatism and political struggle within China.

There lay the nub of the question. The company secretaries, lawyers, and manufacturers in Hong Kong, who felt they needed a more solid base for their business than a leased territory after the lease had expired, had been instrumental in persuading the British government that there must be something in black and white. Similarly, Deng had to shield himself from the criticism of leftists, old guard revolutionaries, and high army commanders that he was not doing anything to recover the three territories.

However, it was impossible to seduce Taiwan into a new union with the mainland. Its people were so much better off economically than the mainland Chinese, and had such a mortal fear of communism, that the island could be regained only through military force. Deng was not about to sacrifice his new-won friendship with the United States by forcing it to defend Taiwan. He could not even stop the US selling military aircraft to Taipei, with whom the US still retains semi-official relations. As a face-saving measure, Marshal Ye Jianying, a prominent figure of the revolutionary old guard, offered Taiwan complete internal autonomy and even the right to keep its own armed forces if it would accept the Chinese flag and the Chinese National Anthem as the outward symbols of reunion. President Chiang Ching-kuo, Chiang Kai-shek's son, and the other Nationalist leaders spurned this offer.

Internally, Deng was intent on economic reform. What does economic reform mean in China? Deng was quoted in the *People's Daily* on 27 April 1987 as having said:

'Reform is a self-improvement of the socialist system. A revolutionary transformation has also occurred in reform to a certain degree, and in a certain scope. . . . There is no other road for China except reform. Only through reform can the development of China be achieved.'

Zhao Ziyang, a super-pragmatic administrator who was then Premier, was charged with the research on, and practical implementation of, the Chinese economic reform. According to the above source, he said:

'The purpose of various kinds of reforms which are in progress, or are to be carried out, is to overcome the defects and shortcomings in the previous system, which impede the development of the social productive forces; and to gradually form a new economic system suitable for our national conditions, and to build a socialism with Chinese characteristics. Although the reform is a revolution, it is, of course, not a complete change in our social system. We do not intend to shake or deviate from the socialist system. Reform means self-improvement and self-perfection of socialism itself.'

Even if socialism has failed to provide more than a meagre sufficiency for the Chinese people, and its bureaucratic practices have strangled the initiative and creativity of the inhabitants to an extraordinary degree, Deng and his team see socialism — as a system of government — as infinitely superior to capitalism. The Dengists see the superiority of socialism lying in the promise of a better future, where everyone will have equality of opportunity. They are, however, resolutely opposed to material egalitarianism which, they have discovered, stifles the productive forces both materially and psychologically.

Reform is designed to touch not only the economy, but also the political system and the guiding ideology. Agricultural reform, through the procedure of abolishing the people's communes in 1979, is the only reform to have worked well in

China so far. The communes had been the single most important factor in Mao's peacetime attempts to revolutionise China's agriculture, the basis of the country's economy. Following land reform and the setting up of peasant cooperatives in the early and mid-1950s, the first commune was formed 'spontaneously', it was claimed, by peasants at Qiliying, a town in Hebei province. The commune was named Sputnik in honour of the Soviet Union's first triumph in launching an earth satellite, but with the growth of the Sino–Soviet rift in the 1960s it reverted to its original name.

In their early form, the communes were turned into bases for massed labour forces involving thousands of people — the villagers — who had to labour communally under orders from the commune headquarters, broken down into 'production brigades' and, at the lowest level, 'production teams'.

Historically, China's peasants have been individualists, working the land they owned or rented from the landlords in family units. Some villages consist of clans of people all sharing the same surname. But among villages, and between the villagers and the landlords, or the villagers and the administrator-magistrates called in English 'mandarins', relations were often hostile, even murderous. The landlords charged such extortionist rents that the peasants became virtual slaves, labouring in poverty all their lives in order to pay rent, mostly in kind, to the landlord. A peasant who became well-to-do through his own hard work, or some stroke of luck, would probably buy land and become a landlord in his own right, and often be just as oppressive as the others. With land reform in the 1950s many landlords were killed or dispossessed by the embittered peasants with the active assistance and encouragement of Communist Party soldiers and cadres. In the 1950s, rural incomes grew, the peasants were able to eat more, and food supplies to the cities improved. But the communes changed all that. The peasants, Mao said, were 'like a blank piece of paper, on which one may draw the most beautiful pictures'.

This was not only an over-simplification, it was a misrepresentation. Peasants anywhere in the world are far from being 'poor and blank', as Mao put it. They have complex living and working customs; they have folkloric, musical, and dance traditions; they have special beliefs and religions; and above all they are the people who make vital decisions about what crops will be grown at what time of year, and where, and how and where they will be marketed. In countries where the peasantry have long been subjugated to bureaucratic or landlord rule, as in China, much of the peasants' initiative and decision-making have been blunted by the threat of oppressive measures if they do not grow what is required by their masters (and in socialist countries that means the state).

When oppressed and exploited, the peasants have one weapon: passivity. They work more quickly if they expect to enjoy most or all of the profits of their own labour. Without that incentive they can neglect small but important agricultural tasks which may make the difference between a good harvest and a bad one. There is sufficient emergency relief in modern China to ensure that hardly anybody will actually starve to death in a flood or other disaster and, to the peasant, starvation is the only true demon. Anything else he or she can bear with fortitude — for a while at least.

But even the peasants' patience has its limit — as Deng, the son of a landlord, knows very well. Mao, the young peasant rebelling against his father, could dream of the limitless power of the rural masses, if only they were properly organised. He found the theoretical answers in Marxist literature and his own experience. But somewhere along the way he lost touch psychologically with the peasants of modern China, and that was the downfall of his social and economic experiments.

The peasants did not take well to the new system of regimented labour, more equal incomes, and 'voluntary' labour on huge waterworks to prevent the recurrent droughts or floods. Despite early enthusiasm whipped up by the Party, the farmers passively resisted the more outrageous demands on their labour resources. Harvests declined by comparison with the mushrooming population caused by the absence of war and improving medical and social services. (Mao at that time did not believe in birth control.)

Deng had watched from 1958 to 1961 as the people's communes beggared the rural areas through mindless bureaucratic and military direction of the peasants' labour, which deprived them of the time and energy to apply their age-old wisdom to the matter of planting and harvesting crops.

The inevitable happened. Food supplies dwindled until 1961–62 and famine stalked the land. In the cities, there was a meagre diet, but in the countryside there was plain starvation. This was the turning point in Deng's old friendship with Mao: he could not sit idly by while Mao wrecked the nation's economy and reduced the people to starvation. With Liu Shaoqi, Peng Zhen, and many nameless collaborators, he produced the *Sixty Articles on the People's Communes* to address the severe damage done to agriculture.

Gradually, in the early 1960s, production recovered and the threat of mass starvation receded. The communes were institutionalised and looked as if they were there to stay. Technical inputs such as water, fertiliser, and new seed-strains helped boost their production, but the peasants' hearts were not in their work when its fruits went mostly to the community at large and they could keep only a tiny amount for private enjoyment or cash profit.

In early 1979, the Communist Party issued a new hardhitting document, based on the *Sixty Articles* published in 1962. The new *Sixty Articles* reduced the decision-making level to the village again, cutting down the dictatorial powers of the commune headquarters and the so-called production brigade.

Having realised that the communes were on their way out, the country's 750 million peasants began rushing to dismantle their village-level production teams. Consisting of several villages in a single accounting unit, the production brigades were already being broken up. It had been Mao's dream that all accounting of wages and distribution of products in the commune should be at the brigade level, which he considered more socialistic than having it done at the team level. However, most of the peasants preferred the team because they were naturally clannish and the next village was often regarded as a foreign country.

Many of the provincial and rural cadres did not fully realise that Deng was pushing for the disbanding even of the teams and a reversion to family farming once the land had been distributed equitably among the peasants. Some cadres who recognised what was happening could see the writing on the wall for their own jobs. Their accounting functions and their leadership and surveillance roles would become irrelevant, and the peasants hated them enough to curtail their food supplies. They tried to persuade the peasants to stop the drift into private farming. This argument was exemplified by a broadcast on Radio Changsha in Hunan province:

'Some comrades hold that the smaller the production team, the better. This view is wrong. The size of the production team in Hunan is in general not large. If further subdivision occurs, it will unsettle people's minds and lead to many new contradictions, and will also affect the development of production due to the scattering of manpower and production materials.'

But Deng had decided the communes must go, and go they did over the next few years. The commune headquarters were abolished and loose administrative control reverted to the pre-revolutionary *xiang*, or districts. The peasants contracted with the state purchasing units to grow so much grain for sale at a fixed price at each harvest. The surplus they could sell at market prices. The old private plots, always a political bone of contention and only a meagre supplement to a family's income, became unnecessary and all the land reverted to the families, not to be owned by them but to be used by them in perpetuity.

Deng and his supporters dealt the death-blow to Maoist ideas about the organisation of agriculture when they exhorted the peasants to 'enrich themselves' through sideline production, as well as grain, vegetable oils, and cotton. Mao would have considered this a reversion to capitalism, and in a way it was, since the peasants were running their own farms and investing in them with fertiliser and other inputs for profit. But it was a very primitive form of capitalism, since it was at first forbidden to hire labour except family members.

Deng also introduced the system of 'contracted responsibility' — which meant that each peasant family signed a contract with the local authorities, promising to produce a certain amount of the most nationally vital crops in the coming year and to sell them to the state at a predetermined price.

The most important crops are grain, cotton, and vegetable oils. With grain and oil alone people can survive, and with a modicum of cotton, they can dress against the elements. Other crops such as fruit, vegetables, and peanuts were sold at negotiated prices either to the state purchasing agencies at the village level or on the free market. This had been forbidden under Mao, although, of course, the peasants found ways around the ban on commodity trading.

Grain and cotton production quickly went into surplus when the reform was first introduced. By the mid-1980s, the peasants had become so involved in growing lucrative industrial or cash crops that they were neglecting the less profitable but vital grain fields, even turning them over to other crops. The state had to make propaganda for grain-growing and, more effectively, to raise the price for grain paid to the peasants.

China does not have the huge 'virgin lands' type of grain production that has been used with extensive mechanisation in the Soviet Union, although the Russians still need to import grain. In China, grain production still depends on the peasants' material interest in it. Now that so many of the country's water supply problems have been solved, they can almost always grow enough to keep themselves and their families alive. For the first time in the modern era, China became a net exporter of grain in the mid-1980s, and cotton production achieved the same feat.

In temperate or warm climates, cotton is the best and most common clothing material. It needs abundant sunshine and quite a lot of water. It grows best in flat landscapes, the plants often interspersed with the shoots of other crops that are grown for food. However, cotton is increasingly being replaced by artificial fibres. As well as possessing most of the attributes of cotton, artificial fibres have become cheaper than cotton in the West. For the Chinese, artificial fibre is expensive because their chemical industries have not yet achieved the economies of scale required to produce it cheaply, and petroleum, needed for its production, is in limited supply. Until the 1986 breakthrough in cotton production, artificial fibres were bought by the Chinese because no ration coupons were required for them even if the rationed cotton was much cheaper.

The abolition of the communes solved most of China's food and clothing problems in a way which showed how natural self-interest, generating hard work and commercial initiative, has no substitute when it comes to raising people's living standards. That is the meaning of 'reform' in Chinese agriculture. There are two other important reforms still to be carried out: in industry, and in the politics and government of the country.

Deng is not really expert on matters of industry. He joined the Chinese revolution in the rural areas, and he busied himself, after the Communist victory, with problems of man-management, ideology, politics, and agriculture more than with industry. He did work in French factories in his youth and had learned about the problems of industrial economies, especially those of a backward country like China. China had no modern industry until the second half of the nineteenth century. Her handicrafts were famous throughout the world, and she had made extraordinary scientific advances in navigation, weaving, metalwork, building, and other essential arts of civilisation. However, she had never discovered the trick by which knowledge and skill could be multiplied in their value through the organisation of large amounts of human labour — the industrial revolution. Her ships could sail only as far as East Africa, for they did not have lateen (triangular) sails, and had difficulty in beating to windward. The European ships had lateen sails which enabled the Europeans to discover America and to cross the Pacific from there to Asia.

Chinese engineers and farmers knew something about the principles of hydraulic power, but in most arable parts of China the main hydraulic problem was lifting water to the level of the cropfields, not using it to drive machinery. Most of the lifting was done by human beings, either with shoulder-pole buckets or on treadmills. The harnessing of steam power was unknown and electricity was introduced by the Europeans and the Americans. Gears were known and used to some extent (one of them enabling a 2,100-year-old horse-drawn war chariot to keep an arm pointed always southwards, whichever way it turned, on reasonably level ground). They had the magnetic compass, but did not know the world was an oblate spheroid spinning round and round in space, rotating around the sun.

The Chinese invented paper and gunpowder. The paper they put to excellent use with printing which they also invented. They were the most civilised nation in the world while Europe was in the Dark Ages. The gunpowder they used more for its sound and fury than for accurate marksmanship and, until the Europeans showed them how, they did not rifle the barrels of their guns.

To a degree, to learn from the Europeans was a logical and wise move on the part of the idealistic young Chinese who undertook the long voyage to Europe. But foreign aid and copied foreign methods are not the whole solution for China in her desperate bid to modernise and bring herself into the 21st century. Beyond a certain point, she has to do it herself. In this she is hampered by her ageing leaders' life-long faith in Marxism–Leninism and the 'Thought of Chairman Mao', none of which can tell them how to run a steel mill or an automobile assembly line. Deng's argument on this is as follows:

'After the founding of the People's Republic [in 1949], if we had embarked on the capitalist road rather than the socialist road, it would have been impossible to end the chaos in China and to overcome the situation of inflation, the extremely unstable commodity prices, and poverty and backwardness. . . . We should stick to the socialist orientation in the reform. This is a very important problem. We are now carrying out the modernisations of industry, agriculture, national defence and science and technology. However, the adjective "socialist" should be prefixed to these four modernisations. We call them the "socialist four modernisations". Now, the policy of enlivening the domestic economy and opening up the outside world is being implemented under the prerequisites of upholding the socialist principle.'

The *People's Daily*, quoting this remark, said: 'We should soberly realise the importance of his view.' However, in this passage Deng does not explain why, in completely changed economic circumstances, China must adhere to socialism. He merely asserts it dogmatically, for if he did not, his political rivals could discredit him.

Reform in the management of Chinese industry is essential if the country is to make economic progress more quickly. In the 1950s, China inherited the heavily bureaucratic Soviet model of economic planning and industrial management and, despite the disruptions caused by the Cultural Revolution, more or less adhered to it. State Council ministries lay down the nature and amount of goods to be produced, arrange for the supply of materials, labour, and plant, and take most of the profits, if there are any, when the products are sold. In some industries this practice has been abandoned in favour of the enterprise's retention of the profits of its production, and sales and payment of tax to the state at a predetermined level. The surplus left over after payment of tax is either ploughed back into the development of the enterprise or used to improve the living conditions of workers and management personnel.

Deng is in favour of the latter system, but because of the inherited bureaucratic tradition that stifles individual initiative and new ideas and bogs the whole operation down in unnecessary paperwork and meetings it has not proved easy to implement. There has been some progress in making enterprises more independent, and more able to control and plan their own production. Material incentives for the workers are now ubiquitous. During Mao's declining years he forbade incentives and they were given only covertly. The workers have grown accustomed to their bonuses which can be as high as 50 per cent of normal wages, and can become unco-operative if they do not receive them. So management pays the bonuses to all workers, except a few they wish to penalise for absenteeism, carelessness, or laziness. The bonus is chiefly a negative incentive, and it is always in danger of contributing to inflation which is now an accepted feature of the Chinese economy and hits urban dwellers more than peasants. Thus, progress towards Deng's dream of modernisation in industrial reform can only be a slow business.

The thorniest problem of all is political reform which is closely bound up with matters of ideology and old rivalries or enmities among the veteran leaders. In Marxist theory, China is ruled by the 'dictatorship of the proletariat', but in the real world this is nonsense. The country is ruled by a small group of veteran revolutionaries, a large proportion of whom came from middle-class or landlord families and became soldiers in the 1920s and 1930s. They have demanded near-military discipline from their subordinates and from the mass of the people. Until the 1980s, the country did not even have a codified legal system but was ruled by decrees proclaimed at meetings of the Politburo or the inmost caucus, the Standing Committee of the Politburo. Mao ruled by *fiat*, and so does Deng. The 'proletariat' (workers) have little say in the formation or implementation of policy. This system worked, after a fashion, in times of crisis, when unity of will and action were required from the people and the leaders to set the country on its feet. But it is now anachronistic, since peaceful economic development needs more subtlety and less brute force to succeed.

The political system Deng has attempted to reform is a pyramid, administered at all levels by 'cadres' whom we would call white-collar workers. The efficiency and morality of the cadres is essential to the functioning of the system. But in recent years there have been more complaints, especially from Deng himself, to the effect that too many cadres are corrupt, inefficient, ignorant, and oppressive. Many of them have lost their youthful idealism and just want to make a decent living and bring up their families, something it is very difficult to do without peculating some extra living expenses from the public purse. Yet it is extremely difficult to get rid of a cadre once he or she has taken root in a bureaucratic position. Since the Cultural Revolution, there has grown up a revulsion for persecuting people because of their real or suspected political deviance. This is called 'beating people with big sticks' and under Deng it is officially forbidden, though of course it continues. Usually it is the intellectuals and teachers who 'get stick' from generalist political cadres or security functionaries. A favourite way to keep the intellectuals in their place is to 'stick hats on them' — which refers to the Red Guard practice of putting tall, conical, white paper hats on officials and intellectuals when they were being harassed and denounced. Nowadays, 'sticking hats on people' means accusing them of harbouring wrong and dangerous political views — and the definition of 'right' and 'wrong' in Chinese politics remains volatile and elusive. It used to be safe to be known as a 'leftist' though not an 'extreme leftist' and, if someone wanted to bring down an enemy in his office, he could accuse him of being an 'unreconstructed rightist'. Political mud sticks when it is thrown in China. A vague or garbled old story about a person is enough to give him or her a 'queue', or pigtail, which could forever afterwards be meta- phorically 'seized'. Deng himself once said, 'I have as many pigtails as a Uygur girl.' (Uygurs come from Chinese Central Asia, where women still favour braids.)

From this imperfect and unfair system of social control, Deng has sought to create an orderly and democratic society ruled in the interests of the people. He knows that one way to hear the people's complaints and suggestions is through the election of deputies to political bodies. The chief of these is the National People's Congress (NPC), with its steering body, the Chinese People's Political Consultative Conference. Pre- viously the NPC was dismissed as a rubber stamp, but in the last few years some students of Chinese affairs have been drawn to the opinion that the NPC is slowly building up a real power- base of its own. Some observers thought Peng Zhen was trying to bring this about to challenge Deng as effective head of the Party, but Peng, at the age of 86, retired from active politics in 1988.

To set up democratic institutions in a country which has never known them, or known them only in a corrupt and ineffectual form under the Nationalists, is no small order. The Chinese leaders profess to believe in 'elections with consulta- tion' as the basic democratic road. This means that, in their elections to the NPC, the local congresses have usually only one candidate who is chosen by the Communist Party. It has become fashionable of late to put up two candidates, both of whom are chosen by the Party. This means that they will never seriously challenge the authority or policies of the Party except in small, tokenish ways. It is unthinkable that a candidate at a Chinese election should campaign at all, much less on a platform that defies Party policy or suggests kicking the Party out of power. He would not only lose his candidacy, but would also go to jail. As for elections to the Party itself, these are treated as internal Party affairs into which no-one else is entitled to enquire. The task of elected members of the national and local congresses is to act as conveyors of Party policy to the people or as a buffer zone which can respond to complaints from the public without having to involve the Party straight away. But in practice it is the Party which still rules at all levels and, whereas Deng has called for less Party interference in small, day-to-day, or routine matters, he is a man of the Party and has no intention of abolishing it. Zhao Ziyang is, in 1988, Secretary- General of the Communist Party but still under Deng's protective wing.

However, the Party has serious internal problems that are mainly related to generation gaps. Most of the veterans of the Long March are dead and, by the end of the century, their political influence will be minimal. The next generation of military people who joined the Party in the 1940s have been largely passed over for top political jobs as they, too, are becoming old. Behind them are the idealistic technocrats of the 1950s who were, to a large extent, trained by the Russians, victimised in the Cultural Revolution, but still believe, more or less, in Soviet-style planning and social institutions. This generation has a chance of real power in the early years of the 21st century. However, the Soviet economy, through its own planning system, is in deep trouble, so the Russian-trained Chinese officials may want to make modifications to what Deng calls 'socialism with Chinese characteristics'. A large number of illiterate peasants were also recruited into the Party during the land reform, the co-operative movement, and the period of the people's communes. Few of these people will gain high rank in the Party, but they will be useful stiffeners at the village level when policy changes are required by the leadership or when it seeks to defend its policies against attack from political rivals at the top. At present, the peasants are doing relatively well economically and will probably continue to defend Deng's reforms against the sniping of some leftist rural cadres.

The biggest danger for China's future is represented by the frustrated Red Guard generation. These are people who were between 16 and 22 years of age in the first part of the Cultural Revolution and are the people who denounced Deng and broke his son's back. The Red Guard recruitment into the Party lasted for about the ten-year period of the Cultural Revolution. By the early 1980s, it is estimated that the Party ranks contain some 16 million former left-wing activists out of a total membership of 41 million. They are moving up the ranks of the Party and government, and may be the rulers of China in the second and third decades of the 21st century. Deng has openly recognised this problem, originally with the intention of expelling former leftist agitators from the Party, or at least blocking their promotion.

This, it seems, he has been unable to do. Only a few hundred thousand leftists have been expelled from the Party and the logic of nature will bring the others on up the ladder. These are people most unsuited to the rational government of a huge, backward country like China. They missed most, or all, of their secondary and tertiary education, so they tend to be uneducated and suspicious of scholarship. They envy the generation after them which has been able to attend functioning universities and obtain degrees. They have spent long periods in the rural villages or in wild frontier areas, in conditions of the greatest discomfort. They were despised by the peasants and worked their fingers to the bone just to feed themselves.

With the return of Deng in 1977, a fresh look has been taken at these young people and their plight. Some had married and settled down in the rural areas, often quite near their home towns. But the majority desperately wanted to go back to the big cities where there were very few jobs for them. Unlike the Soviet Union, which has a chronic labour shortage, China has a huge labour surplus disguised by the fact that nearly 80 per cent of the population still live in the rural areas. In the cities there is about 5 per cent unemployment and workers tend to transfer their jobs to their children when they retire. Deng and his advisers created a youth employment scheme in the late 1970s when they permitted jobless young-sters to set up small business enterprises such as shops, carpentry work-shops, and transport firms. This helped to ease the situation for a few years, but the young people earned so little that they gradually found more permanent employ-ment. The 'high school graduate businesses', as they were called, shrank in numbers and ceased to be a matter of great interest to the government.

Deng's most substantial statement on the question of reform was made at the 1985 Extraordinary Conference of the Party held in Peking to discuss the forthcoming Seventh Five Year Plan for economic development. Emphasising his fa-vourite concept of 'socialism with Chinese characteristics', Deng used this conference to turn his thinking on reform into an integrated social philosophy which was less abstruse than Mao's philosophy and less difficult for the average person to understand. It has several fundamental lines of thought which are mostly related to the pragmatically conceived reality of the present day, and its soundness will determine the country's future as either a great power or merely a big, underdevel-oped country of the Third World.

The only unpragmatic element of Deng's thinking has been his continued insistence on the absolute necessity of socialism. This ignores the fact that the greatest success stories in the development of East Asian countries in the period since World War II are Japan, South Korea, Taiwan, Hong Kong, and Singapore, all of which absolutely reject socialism.

Deng said that the reform, which started in the countryside in 1978, had shown good results within three years despite heavy criticism of it from the 'Old Guard'. Reform was next focused on the cities with their multifarious industries and service trades. The principle underlying the urban reform was a combination of the predominance of the socialist public sector, state-planned attention to 'common prosperity', utilisation of foreign investment funds, and the promotion of a degree of free enterprise. This has required new and specific rules and regulations which are still being drafted and re-drafted as they are tested in practice.

The success of the reform depends on the success of the five-year plans, especially the current Seventh Plan. It has set a growth rate of 7 per cent annually for industry and agriculture. Deng explained:

> 'That growth rate may not be considered low. If the growth rate were too high, that would create many problems that would have a negative effect on the reform and on social conduct. It is better to be prudent. We must control the scale of investment in fixed assets and seek economic and social returns.'

How remote this was from the heady days of the Great Leap Forward, when China swore to catch up with the industrialised countries in a short time, and Mao 'declared war on nature' in order to make the country self-sufficient. Deng estimated that China would 'approach the level of the advanced countries' by the middle of the 21st century, and 'at that time the strength of China and its world role will be quite different'.

Turning from economics to culture and ideology, Deng said, 'We must admit that the results of our work are not very satisfactory.' He added that the main key to developing the country's civilisation was 'improvement in general Party conduct'. The Party is regarded, in any Communist country, as the leading social element, or as the Chinese sometimes put it, 'the ox's nose'. If Party members do not set a good example of honesty, thrift, discipline, and unity, there is no hope that the rest of the country will practise such virtues. However, the old methods of correcting moral, cultural, and ideological errors are not, Deng said, to be used again. There are to be no more scurrilous attacks or secret denunciations of individual members or groups, no more mass criticism, and no more violent political campaigns aimed at the overthrow of one's rivals. The Party must develop what it has never yet had — a smooth and orderly succession with the timely resignation of veterans and the training of younger and more vigorous successors.

Deng's labour policy has been firmly based on the Marxist definition of socialism which is 'distribution according to work'. In a speech to the political research workers of the State Council reported in the Peking *Workers' Daily* on 2 July 1983, he conceded that political attitude was also important in assessing a worker, but added: 'It must be clearly stated that a good political attitude must be manifested chiefly in the fact that they should work well and make more and better contributions to socialism.' The Maoist idea was that if a worker's political attitude were correct, he or she would naturally work well. Deng explained:

'We are carrying out a low-wage policy. This is a policy which we are implementing for a considerable period of time. At present the wage ceiling of a grade-eight worker [the highest of grades] is a little more than 100 *yuan* [about US$50 per month at 1988 prices]. With the development of production, wages will be raised step by step in the future . . . the wages of primary school teachers are too low. . . . A special wage scale should be set up for every trade and profession. . . . Those who pass an examination should have their wages upgraded and skip a grade on the wage scale.'

The Dengist leadership has reinstituted the system of

bonus payments for workers that existed before the Cultural Revolution but had been outlawed under Mao. Special payments are also to be made to inventors and innovators, and writers are to have their fees increased.

On 18 December 1985, at a meeting organised by *Time* magazine, Deng told a group of American businessmen that 'a fundamental contradiction does not exist between social-ism and a market economy.' It was a major exposition of his economic thinking. He went on:

'The question is what methods should be used in order to develop the social productive forces more effectively. We have always engaged in planned economy in the past, but practice over the years has proven that, in a sense, engaging exclusively in planned economy will hinder the develop-ment of the productive forces. By integrating the planned economy with a market economy, we shall be in a better position to liberate the productive forces and to speed up economic development. . . .

As you know, for a long time following the founding of the PRC, the average [annual] income of the peasants was just 60 *yuan* — a level below the poverty line — it really means they did not have enough to eat and to wear. The reforms have, in effect, aroused the enthusiasm of the peasants and emancipated the productive forces. If you want to bring the initiative of the peasants into play, you should give them decision-making power. That is why we put an end to the system of communes, and have intro-duced the responsibility system, advocated scientific man-agement and developed a diversified economy. The region where reforms were started had results in one or two years' time at the most, and the living standard there doubled, and in some regions was raised many times higher.

At present people abroad are closely watching whether or not there are different views among us regarding the reforms. Differing views do exist. However, compared with

191

seven years ago when the reforms in the countryside were just started, the differing views are on a much smaller scale. At that time, at least one-third of the regions of China lagged behind in starting reforms or were not enthusiastic about the reform. All along we have had to wait. Some regions waited one or two years before they started to catch up with the reforms. Those which managed began to have results in one or two years' time.'

'Democracy', in socialist countries, means something quite different to what it means in capitalist countries, and in the phrase 'democratic centralism' the emphasis is on the 'centralism'. This means the central Party authorities insist on the implementation of all their decrees and policy decisions all over the country.

In March 1987, the *People's Daily* urged its readers to study an unpublished speech of Deng's given 25 years ago at a meeting referred to as the 'conference of 7,000' — a conference of some 7,000 leading figures in the Party and society. The reason for republication of this speech, hitherto unknown in the rest of the world, was to help people to understand the situation stirred up by the student demonstrations of the preceding December. Deng said then:

'The problem is that some Party organisations and Party-member cadres have failed to observe strictly the requirements laid down in the Party statutes and the guidelines that Comrade Deng Xiaoping put forth in his speech. . . . Some of them are in a state of disunity and are showing poor efficiency and slackness, with their responsible persons all going their own way and the system of collective leadership failing to work. . . . How well the system of collective leadership works depends on the mutual supervision between members of a leading body and the head of a leading body in particular plays a decisive role.'

The Party organ also quoted Deng as saying:

'Our Party is unified, united and powerful. Without democracy, there will be no centralism and unification; without centralism and unification, the Party will have no fighting power. Our Party must remain centralised and unified for ever. Such a Party is truly powerful. However, only on the basis of democracy and fully developing socialism is it possible to build such a unified, disciplined and powerful body.'

Deng could not have foreseen, when he made that speech, that within four years the Party would be tearing itself apart in its greatest-ever schism. This act of near-suicide continues to be reflected to some extent in the rivalries and power-plays of the leaders today. The use of the term 'democratic' is also misleading. From Deng's speech it was clear that what he considered important was full consultation *within* the Party which nowadays makes up about 4 per cent of the population of China. His references to consultation of people *outside* were perfunctory to say the least. Indeed, it is only in the past few years that even a pretence of 'democracy' has been nurtured in China. In fact, where only one candidate was standing for office all the fraudulence of totalitarian countries' 'elections' was being tediously rehearsed again. If there is more than one candidate standing, most people are afraid to vote even though there is a 'secret' polling booth. They are afraid to voice opposition because it would be taken to mean that they were spoiling their ballot papers or that they were sending them in blank because they did not like either of the candidates.

Several times Deng has repeated his position that the reforms begun in 1978 will continue unchecked. In September 1985, he told Austria's visiting President Rudolf Kirchschlager that if the reforms were correct there would be no need to change them, but if they were incorrect they would be scrapped. The reforms had popular support, and the Party ranks were being filled with younger cadres while the older ones were retiring in a more timely manner. But he conceded, 'A few old cadres will remain in their posts. I myself will still hold office for a while.'

One of the most besetting problems of the economic reforms in China has been the growth of 'economic crime' such as graft, corruption, embezzlement, black marketeering, and smuggling. Like Gorbachev in the Soviet Union, Deng believes it is best to discuss these problems openly and not sweep them under the rug. This means that, to a certain extent, things are being disclosed now which were kept secret in the past. Like other socialist countries, there is no doubt that there has been a general easing of social discipline in China which, since the death of Mao, is seeing the spontaneous growth of a business class that often breaks state laws and regulations in the interests of trading and profits. The return of Hong Kong to China in 1997 will further test this. Citing Deng, Henan's provincial radio station said in 1986:

'Facts have proved that in a unit of enterprise which attaches importance to the work of cracking down on economic crimes and grasps it well, reform will be smooth and economic results high; otherwise, violations of law and unlawful practices will run wild, operation and management will be chaotic, and reform and production cannot be carried out well. Therefore, we must not set cracking down on economic crimes against enlivening the economy. We must not do one thing and disregard the other.'

Deng's own recipes for curing economic crime have been better education, police and customs work, and steady economic growth.

With the regrowth of his political power, Deng took it upon himself to restore the good name of Liu Shaoqi. Liu's works were republished in China, and a string of press articles emphasised his important role in the revolution. The Peking *Guangming Daily* wrote in December 1983: 'Comrade Liu Shaoqi devoted great efforts to finding a suitable path for China's socialist construction. As he pointed out: "We must learn to walk with our own feet and adopt methods suitable for China's specific circumstances in our construction."' This was also a tenet firmly adhered to by Deng. Liu was quoted as having said: 'The socialist economy is characterised by planning. It is a planned economy. However, planning can only cover a number of fields. There are tens of thousands of variations in socio-economic life. If we only emphasise planning, to the neglect of flexibility and diversity, the economy will become over-simplified and rigid.' Again, this is an example of thinking which is typical of Deng.

Deng Xiaoping's target for the Chinese economy, modest though it is in real terms, is highly ambitious in absolute terms. He wants China to quadruple her total output between the mid-1980s and the year 2000. While talking to foreign visitors in 1984, he said:

'This quadrupling we speak of can be attained. In the past we dared not say this: we only said that it could possibly be attained, but would require very great effort. In the past four years, the main production targets of the Sixth Five Year Plan have been fulfilled in three years, and the plan for this year will be over-fulfilled. In the past we said that if the average growth in the first ten years could reach 6.5 per cent, and reach 7.2 per cent over the 20 years [1980–2000], the task of quadrupling could be accomplished. It seems that the momentum in the first ten years may exceed 7.2 per cent, because in the past three years it was almost eight per cent.

Quadrupling is very significant. It means that by the end of the century annual output value of the national economy will reach 10,000 billion dollars (US). By then, we will be in the front rank of the world in total economic output value, but not in average per capita. Reflected in the people's daily life, this 10,000 billion will mean what we call a comfortably well-off level. Reflected in national strength, it will mean that we shall be a relatively strong country. . . . By that time, China's international impact will also be much different from now, and our national strength will be truly powerful.'

The Western reader will see nothing very grand in China's ambition to produce a national average per capita income of something less than US$800 by the year 2000, allowing for population growth. With the slashing of the armed forces and military production in the 1980s, China is clearly aiming at more high-technology national defences; her own technology, however, is still relatively backward and her ability to purchase large quantities of advanced arms from abroad is strictly limited by her cash reserves. It is possible to make a case that the China of the 1950s and 1960s, with her huge military manpower resources and her hostile attitude towards most of the outside world, was a greater force in the international arena than she is now or will be for many decades to come. In August 1984, *Observation Post* published some of Deng's remarks on the reform:

'The Third Plenary Session of the Eleventh Central Committee has placed heavy tasks on those who are young and strong. Now important matters are attended to by Hu Yaobang and Zhao Ziyang. Those who are a little advanced in years are placed in an unconventional position. We are now working on the third echelon. We are selecting some people under sixty and more people in their forties. Young people lack experience, but after working for two or three years they will have experience and prove themselves equal to their work. This arrangement of personnel will ensure the continuity of our policies. We will soon hold a Party Representative Conference, at which the central issue of selecting young people for the CPC Central Committee, the Political Bureau and the Secretariat will be discussed. Of course, the conference will decide on the Seventh Five Year Plan. Our opening-up policy will not change. If there is a change, it will be a change for the better. We have been opening up wider and wider to the world over the past few years. The Four Modernisations will come to nowhere without the opening-up policy. Therefore, apart from adhering to the opening-up policy, we will also ensure the continuity of other policies by strengthening the personnel system. We will form the fourth and fifth echelons. . . . There will be no readjustment for China's opening-up policy. Opening up to the world is a new thing. Since we want to open up to the world, we should understand the positive results the policy will bring to us. That is, it will promote the productive forces. In addition, we should also be fully aware of the negative effects it will cause. So, it is necessary to sum up experience in each stage of reform. Apart from opening up to the world, we should also carry out economic structural reform in an overall way. This involves more problems than opening up to the world. Price system reform, wage system reform, and management system reform are new things. Opening up to the world and economic structural reform are also new things, in which risks, obstacles, and mistakes are inevitable. So, we are required to sum up experience in a timely manner and to correct mistakes as soon as they are found. . . . China will continue to pursue the established principles. Some foreign newspapers said that China's opening up to the world and its structural reform are unalterable. This is correct. It has been five years since structural reform started in the countryside. This reform is a success. The rural economy has increased by nine per cent. This is marvellous in the rural areas. Urban economic reform has been under way for over half a year. It involves wider and more complicated fields, and problems have arisen. For example, money has been excessively issued and income from foreign exchange has been reduced. But on the whole, the trend is good. Better than expected.'

In all Communist movements, the trade unions have been theoretically regarded as the expression of the aspirations of the working class but, in practice, they have merely been instruments of Party policy. The Chinese leadership and media have paid little attention in recent years to questions of labour and trade unions, by comparison with the minute attention they have accorded to agriculture, the political line in art and literature, the misdeeds of the erstwhile leftists, and the relationship between Deng Xiaoping's political thinking and Mao's thought.

Chapter 12

THE STATESMAN

Deng is not just an internal politician, but an international statesman of note. Chinese foreign policy between 1972 and 1973 was dominated by Zhou Enlai's strongly anti-Soviet stance. He blamed Soviet premier Alexey Kosygin for having gone back on his promise to remove Soviet troops from the river frontiers of Manchuria in order to prevent recurrences of the armed flare-ups which had almost led to war in Northeast Asia in 1969.

While referring to the United States and the Soviet Union, the 'two superpowers', as the main factors that would lead to global war, Zhou sided with the Americans, saying that the Soviet Union was the more dangerous superpower. Later Deng was to correct this imbalance. Zhou was particularly disturbed by the 1973 coup in Afghanistan, as he saw the Russians ousting American influence from Asia and strategically encircling China.

Zhou's anti-Sovietism brought him into a conflict of views with other world statesmen who were pinning their hopes on the process of *détente* and arms control. One of these was the late French president, Georges Pompidou, who visited China in September 1973. The *People's Daily* on 4 October gave a warning that the Soviet Union was contemplating an invasion of Xinjiang (Chinese Turkestan). The Xinhua News Agency said a Soviet proposal for a 10 per cent cut in arms spending by the nuclear powers to aid underdeveloped countries was 'cheap propaganda' and accused Moscow of falsifying its defence expenditure figures. Canada's premier, Pierre Trudeau, like Pompidou, found himself at variance with Zhou's extreme anti-Soviet stance. Undeterred, Xinhua accused the Soviet Union of 'nakedly pursuing big power politics' at the expense of the Arab nations.

At the Tenth Party Congress in August 1973, Zhou accused the late Lin Biao of having plotted with the Soviet Union, and he said elsewhere in his speech, 'US–China relations have improved somewhat.' Washington's military aid to Taiwan continued to be the main bone of contention between China and the US.

Deng Xiaoping had increasingly taken charge of China's global relations in 1974, as Premier Zhou Enlai succumbed to cancer. In domestic affairs, however, he and Zhou were being sniped at more and more by left-leaning members of the Politburo grouped around Mao's wife, Jiang Qing. At the year's end, Zhou, perhaps in consultation with the still unrehabilitated Deng, had switched around most of the eleven regional military commanders, with the aim of breaking up cliques and provincial alliances which could threaten the stability of the Communist Party and government. The leftists, for their own reasons, attempted to disrupt formal education again, but with less effect than in 1966. Their attacks were also levelled at imports of foreign technology and 'decadent' foreign culture. The people's mood turned irritable and somewhat anxious, as they sensed the possibility of a fresh round of the Cultural Revolution.

China's anti-Soviet stance remained firm, and she made numerous verbal attacks on her big neighbour's policy of global expansion, while the new relationship with the United States was on the whole fostered, since that country was considered the lesser threat. It was reported by Xinhua on 8 January 1974 that China also condemned the Russians for their mistreatment and incarceration of political dissidents.

This attitude seemed somewhat inappropriate for a totalitarian country.

In mid-January Deng had received a big promotion. He was restored informally to the Politburo which put him in a position to deal more strongly with the increasingly weird and wonderful antics of the leftists. Beethoven was denounced in the leftist-inspired press as a 'bourgeois', while Shakespeare's *The Tempest* was attacked as 'propagating the capitalist theory of human nature'.

Meanwhile, a measure of order was being restored in the educational system at Deng's instigation, with Peking University graduating its first classes for eight years. Leftist influences, however, remained strong. The May 4th Central Arts Academy issued a statement claiming that performance of Western music was a means of 'reversing the verdicts of the Great Cultural Revolution'. This was aimed at Deng who had allegedly disclaimed any such intention in his pre-rehabilitation letter to the Central Committee. The *People's Daily* denounced 'class enemies' for 'maliciously attacking revolutionary dramas, rejecting the Great Proletarian Cultural Revolution and the revolution in literature and art, and babbling that our productions are few, the quality is not high, and so forth.' Again, Deng was an obvious 'culprit' in the attack, though Zhou Enlai had also been critical of Jiang Qing's 'revolutionary' stage works.

Even Mao, it seemed, had been tiring of the internal bickering, and said later that he had not lived together with Jiang Qing for several years. Wall posters went up in some places quoting him as saying: 'The Cultural Revolution has been going on for eight years now. It is time to settle down. The entire Party and army should unite.' But China was incapable of ridding itself of political factionalism, however much time and money it wasted.

The campaign to denigrate the late Marshal Lin Biao was blended with the anti-Confucius campaign, thus enabling the leftists to deny any intention of attacking Zhou Enlai or Deng.

It became more and more absurd, however, as obscure classical Chinese slogans were loudly chanted by workers and peasants who had not the faintest idea what they meant.

The leftists also mounted attacks on the system of bonuses in Chinese industry, which were considered 'revisionist' or 'capitalist'. This was also an attack on Deng who, after his final rehabilitation in 1977, made bonuses a nation-wide policy for paying the workers and giving them more incentives to do their jobs well. But in 1974 bonuses were still highly controversial.

In the provinces there were reports of demonstrations and strikes, as well as wall-poster attacks on local dignitaries and office-bearers. In Peking, a whole street was given over to posters which were mostly obscure or concerned with parochial issues. The posters also spoke of trouble in the provinces, especially in Liaoning, where the military region commander, General Li Desheng, was accused of being a 'sworn follower' of Lin Biao. However, the attacks on him soon simmered down and he remained at his post until his semi-retirement in 1983 which was accompanied by an admiring tribute he made to Deng Xiaoping.

The high point of Deng's rehabilitation was reached when he was chosen to go to New York in the summer of 1974 to attend the United Nations' General Assembly. He took with him the new theory of world affairs that was more than likely thought up by Mao with some input from Premier Zhou. Previously, the Chinese had seen the world in which they aspired to a leading role in rivalry with the Soviet Union as divided into the two superpowers and their respective supporters and allies, neutral nations, and the Third World. Now, as Deng explained it to the General Assembly, the official view was changed. There were now considered to be two superpowers, a 'Second World', and a Third World. The Second World was seen as the developed capitalist nations, such as Western Europe, Canada, Australia, and Japan. Their friendship was sought by China, because they could help her modernise her economy and were a factor for peace. But their complacency in the face of Soviet expansionism was criticised by the Chinese who, at the same time, were urging the Third World countries to raise their national incomes by forming producer cartels for primary commodities.

Later in 1974 Deng was explicit about the Soviet threat: 'The US is not so dangerous as the USSR up to a certain stage,' he told a visitor. 'The reason is that the US is at present devoting its power to the point of maintaining its own rights and interests at various places in the world, and is standing on the defensive. The USSR is standing on the offensive.' It is not known whether Deng himself accepted this new view of the world, even though he read it out at the UN. It was the first time he had been abroad since his last trip to the Soviet Union in 1974.

In the mid-1970s, Deng and other Chinese leaders were forced to face the fact that they could not have their cake and eat it. They might differ with the US over Taiwan (that was a long-term problem which would be solved in its own good time), but with neighbours closer to hand there was a paradox in China's policy. The Chinese wanted to have close and friendly relations with the nations of Southeast Asia. This could hardly be reconciled with their support for Communists and revolutionaries inside those countries, especially Malaysia, where the leftist insurgents were encouraged by a radio station in southwest China. The Indonesians had not forgotten China's role in the attempted pro-Communist coup in 1965, and Singapore's leader, Lee Kwan Yu, was well-known for his anti-Communist views. Thailand also had a leftist insurgency, though the monarchy seemed fairly stable, even with the recurrent military *coups d'état*. The Philippines had the Muslim Moro insurgency in the south, and the Chinese were acutely embarrassed when one of their agents was caught raising funds for them on the eve of a visit to Peking by Mrs Imelda Marcos. The Thais and Malays were the first to open diplomatic relations with Peking, despite their objections to

Chinese support for revolutions in their countries. Deng and other leaders, when challenged about this, would say that ideas knew no frontiers, that verbal support was not the same thing as military supplies, and that China sent no arms to Southeast Asian countries. The Indonesians have not risked another close relationship with the Chinese and diplomatic relations have remained closed. Peking's real anxiety was that, if its encouragement of rebels in Southeast Asian countries was discontinued, the Soviet Union might step in to fill the breach.

In late 1978, Deng visited Thailand, Malaysia, and Singapore. With their chronic fear of communism and subversion, these countries needed some reassurance about Peking's policies towards the Southeast Asian countries. His most successful visit was to Thailand, where he was greeted in a relaxed manner reflecting the government's good relations with its prosperous Chinese minority and the relative stability of the monarchy. Deng attended a 90-minute Buddhist ceremony for the symbolic entry of the Crown Prince into monkhood.

At the same time, Deng Xiaoping was apparently taking a pessimistic attitude towards the future of the West. He told a visiting West German youth group that war in Europe was inevitable, and could only be postponed temporarily. He was quoted as saying in *The Times* on 2 May 1974 that disarmament talks could not avert war, for both the superpowers regarded control of Europe as the key to world domination. The threat to China from the more than a million Soviet soldiers stationed on her borders was less immediate than the threat to Europe, against which the Russians had organised three times as many forces.

Deng's anxieties about the situation in Europe were brought up again when Archbishop Makarios of Cyprus visited Peking in May 1974. Deng said then that the Russians' claim to be a Mediterranean country was 'preposterous'. He was quoted in *The Times* on 20 May 1974, accusing the Soviet Union of sending ships there regularly 'to make a show of force'.

Edward Heath, leader of the Conservative opposition in the British Parliament, visited China a few days later and was warmly greeted by the Chinese leaders, especially Deng Xiaoping. Mao Zedong also received Heath, to emphasise China's high regard for the man who took Britain into Europe and expelled 105 Soviet spies from London at one go in 1971. In his banquet speech, which was reported in *The Times* on 26 May 1974, Deng again returned to his European theme. He said the Soviet Union was 'making a feint in the East' by reinforcing its border with China 'while planning an attack in the West'. Similar themes dominated the two men's private talks.

Zhou Enlai, by then very ill, made the effort to meet Heath at the official guesthouse. As a reminder that all was not well beneath the seemingly smooth surface of China's political life, a senior military officer in the southwestern city of Kunming was attacked in wall posters which were put up outside a theatre where Heath watched a song-and-dance performance on a provincial tour. A month later in Nanchang, capital of Jiangxi province, rival political factions brawled with sticks, stones, and iron bars, as was disclosed by a fresh rash of wall posters in Peking. Posters also attacked the municipal Party committee, without mentioning the mayor, Wu De, by name. From Henan province it was reported that the authorities had banned mass 'struggle movements' such as had characterised the Cultural Revolution. The situation was highly confused.

Meanwhile, the Politburo faction supporting Deng Xiaoping received a filip in October 1974 when Xiao Hua, former chief political commissar of the PLA, was rehabilitated. In 1967, the Red Guards had denounced him for 'counter-revolutionary double dealing' — one of their favourite meaningless phrases.

In talks with West German parliamentarians visiting Peking, Deng returned to his theme of the inevitability of war in

Europe, but said the Third World countries could survive if they pooled their commodity exports or agreed on fixed prices, as OPEC had done. Deng added that China had several times feared she would be attacked by the Soviet Union, but he believed this threat was just to distract attention from Europe, Russia's main target. Denmark's Prime Minister, Poul Hartling, was flown to a secret destination to meet Mao, who in the official photograph of their meeting appeared visibly senile. Hartling also found Mao in favour of stronger defence efforts by the West Europeans.

It seems likely, in view of subsequent developments in Deng's global strategic thinking, that his tough line over the Soviet Union and Europe was intended to please the old Chairman, and had not been thought up by Deng at all. In fact, Deng told other foreign visitors in October that the number of Soviet troops on the Chinese border were 'not even enough to defend themselves'.

In November 1974, US Secretary of State, Henry Kissinger visited Peking, following talks he and President Ford had held in Vladivostok, the Soviet Union's main naval base in the Far East. Some analysts believed the Chinese would see this as undiplomatic, although clearly the leaders would benefit from a briefing on some of the things the Russians had to say to Kissinger and Ford. Deng needled Kissinger by asking how much his voluminous position papers weighed, and added that China did not have such things — 'only guns and millet'. Kissinger quipped, 'we outnumber you', referring to the size of the American diplomatic team. Deng replied, 'You cannot outnumber us — we are 800 million!'

The late Qiao Guanhua, who had recently been appointed Foreign Minister, jokingly referred to Kissinger's attempt to speak a few words of Chinese at the previous evening's banquet. Qiao, who had a pre-war doctorate in philosophy from the University of Tübingen, said, 'Mr Secretary, when next you try to speak a foreign language, use German. I will understand you better!' Sources in Kissinger's party disclosed to correspondents that the Chinese had told the Americans that their perception of the Soviet threat was naïve. On a visit to the east China beauty spot of Suzhou, he was taken to a formal Chinese landscaped site whose name can be translated roughly as 'the garden of the foolish politician'. Kissinger and Deng, it seems, had developed a healthy dislike for each other.

In mid-January 1979, the deeper shadow of future Chinese frictions with North Vietnam fell over the two countries' previously described 'close as lips and teeth' relationship. In November 1975, China took a more assertive stance towards her claims to the archipelagos of the South China Sea. Some of them were as far as 1,000 miles away and were claimed by other countries, essentially North and South Vietnam, Taiwan, Malaysia, and the Philippines. The most serious dispute was over the Paracel (Xisha) Islands which China had already garrisoned in 1974. An official statement put out in Peking said that the more than 200 islands of the South China Sea were 'our sacred territory, and we have a responsibility to defend them and build them up.' Most of the islands are uninhabited, but some have military garrisons maintained there by rival claimants. Ludicrously enough, in 1974, Jiang Qing tried to take personal credit for driving the South Vietnamese navy away from the Paracels in 1974. The Chinese Navy was rewarded shortly afterwards when its officers were again permitted to wear white and the ratings were issued sailor suits instead of the lumpy green army uniforms they had worn since the Cultural Revolution. Chinese naval vessels clashed with South Vietnamese warships once again at the beginning of 1979 near the Paracels in the South China Sea and the Chinese took a number of Vietnamese prisoners. North and South Vietnam also claimed the Paracels, as well as the more southerly Spratlys to which China laid claim. There would be plenty more causes of conflict with Vietnam in the succeeding years, and Deng's hatred of the stubborn, militaristic regime in Hanoi was to lead to tragic blood-letting in those years.

Deng's view of the inevitability of global war, which he voiced strongly in the 1970s, underwent significant change in the 1980s. In February 1985, he was officially quoted as saying:

'There has now been some change in our view of the danger of war. We feel that the factors inhibiting the outbreak of world war are on the increase. War is still a possibility, and it is essential to remain vigilant, but the factors for averting the outbreak of war are on the increase.'

In 1979, China's foreign policy, as moulded by Deng and his supporters, became firmer in outline than ever before. Vietnam, whose quarrel with China over the expulsion of ethnic Chinese was at its height, invaded Cambodia and seized the capital Phnom Penh. China responded to this by invading Vietnam in a 16-day 'punitive' war, with casualties numbering some 25,000 men on both sides.

Deng was caught by the Cambodia situation. It would cost him prestige and respect in the eyes of the world if he gave open support to the brutal Pol Pot regime that had massacred hundreds of thousands of its own people. The previous November, while visiting Thailand, Deng had succeeded in condemning the Vietnamese interference in Cambodia without actually naming any of the top 'freedom fighters'. Khieu Samphan, the other top leader of the Cambodian revolution, was still welcome in Peking, however, as was Prince Norodom Sihanouk, the deposed Cambodian monarch. Laos was also under Vietnamese and therefore Soviet influence, but Deng did not have to take the blame for the poor Chinese relations with the Indochinese countries which originated in the period between 1967 and 1973 when he was exiled in the countryside.

Meanwhile, Deng was working hard to improve relations with the United States. Dr Henry Kissinger had again visited Peking in 1975 and Deng had accepted an invitation from

President Carter to visit America. Deng had also publicly invited US Senator, Barry Goldwater to come to Peking and 'get to know' about China. Goldwater was one of the strongest supporters of Taiwan. The Chinese government was initiating a 'smile campaign' aimed at Taiwan. It consisted of low-level friendly gestures, such as harmless TV shots of the 'beautiful island' of Formosa, as the Portuguese had christened it in the sixteenth century. It was officially said that China could let Taiwan keep its social system if it would only enter into another political union with the People's Republic. Three years later this offer was made official.

In 1979, Deng stated that it was Peking's policy to reunify Taiwan with the mainland by peaceful means. He would not entirely rule out the use of force on the grounds that to do so would 'reduce the prospects for Taiwan entering into serious negotiations'. Taiwan, however, continued to spurn all offers of links or contacts with the mainland.

In late January 1979, Deng went to Washington and somewhat embarrassed his American hosts by talking about the aggressive nature of the Soviet Union at a time when President Jimmy Carter was putting the emphasis on defence in US–Soviet relations. Stephen Barber reported in the *Far Eastern Economic Review* on 8 February 1979 that Deng had referred to the Soviet Union as a 'hotbed of war', and said the US was in a posture of 'strategic retreat'. He also said: 'We are in favour of *détente* — a genuine *détente* which truly reduces the danger of war and safeguards the security of all nations, not a false *détente* used by some countries as a cover to carry on war or to commit aggression and expansion.' He also repeated his familiar theme that Europe was the target most at risk from the Soviets.

In terms of his image in the West, Deng's US visit was a huge success despite disagreements over Taiwan and *détente*. The master-stroke was his donning of a ten-gallon hat in front of photographers at a rodeo in Houston, Texas, which, as one reporter put it, 'made him look like an over-ripe mushroom'. Deng made no secret of his belief that the SALT II treaty then under negotiation would be futile. He even offered Chinese support for American military measures to check Soviet potential aggression.

Anti-Vietnamese propaganda had become increasingly menacing in the Chinese media. In February, shortly after Deng's return to Peking, six divisions of the PLA supported by tanks and artillery struck across different points on the Vietnamese border. Overcast weather made close ground support by Chinese-built MIGs difficult. The fighting was fierce, and the Vietnamese fell back on Lang Son, about 80 miles northeast of Hanoi. China justified the invasion as a 'self-defensive lesson' for the Vietnamese. At one stage four provincial capitals in Vietnam were occupied by Chinese soldiers. The Foreign Ministry told resident diplomats in Peking that the invasion was of 'a limited nature', and that Chinese troops would be withdrawn 'after Vietnam has been taught a lesson'. On 27 February, Deng told American correspondents in Peking that China could not tolerate 'Vietnam's swashbuckling in Laos and Cambodia and even on the Chinese border', and said the attack had shown that 'the myth of the invincibility of Vietnam is no longer reliable'.

Deng said that he thought the Soviets 'will not take too much action, but if they should really come, there's nothing we can do about it, but we are prepared against that.' This was the height of Deng's anti-Soviet hawkishness in the post-Mao period. According to *Observation Post* magazine, an influential journal published fortnightly in Beijing, Deng told West Germany's Chancellor Kohl in October 1984:

'We believe that China is a force for peace, and this is a very important point. We often say, and our international friends say, that China hopes least for war, because it is too poor and it can only develop itself in an environment of peace. In order to gain that, it is essential to cooperate with all forces for peace in the world. We hold that Europe is precisely a force for peace [though previously Deng had called it the most likely theatre of war]. This hope is based on the fact that Europe wants peace, that we have always hoped for a united, combined and powerful Europe. The strength of Europe is a factor for peace, a factor inhibiting war. Similarly we believe that the development and strengthening of China are also factors for peace and inhibiting war.'

All in all, Deng has proved a highly able statesman, pragmatic and flexible in dealing with other world leaders without showing exaggerated respect for anyone. He has a keen sense of humour and an excellent grasp of world affairs and China's role in them. Because he travelled widely in his youth, the outside world is a living entity to him and not just an aspect of internal Chinese politics.

Chapter 13

THE COMMANDER-IN-CHIEF

T o understand Deng's role in the military today it is necessary to be reminded of where he had come from, and how from the 1950s onwards he responded to Mao's dictates and the role of the People's Liberation Army. Central to Deng Xiaoping's thinking as statesman and politician is his view of the PLA, the roughly three million-strong armed forces which include the air force, navy, frontier guards, and all the military forces of the People's Republic. Deng's military career was brilliant, especially in the 1940s, and there can be little about commanding men in action that he does not know. At the same time, his position as a top political commissar serving with the one-eyed General Liu Bocheng gave him a certain detachment from purely military matters, and he is no respecter of military fetishes.

In 1952, when he was recalled to Peking from Chengdu, Deng's role as a soldier was terminated for a time. He spent the 1950s and most of the 1960s working in civilian administration. Unlike Mao, when no longer actively serving, he did not aspire to be a leading light of the PLA. Under Mao he saw the armed forces transformed from a fighting force into a semi-imaginary host of haloed crusaders whom the Chairman used to increase his own glory and stature. Part of this enforced worship of the PLA was a product of its original role as a guerrilla force. It had to rely on the local peasants to keep it supplied with food, to provide intelligence on enemy movements, and to perform logistical support. As a result, it developed a cult of 'serving the people': if the peasants helped the PLA, the PLA would get rid of their landlords and the heavy tax burden. True, the landlords might return and take their revenge when the PLA moved on, but the general trend was towards freedom from crippling debt and forced labour for the peasants.

It was no easy task to make the army popular. Chinese peasants and intellectuals alike shared a millennia-old hatred of soldiers, their cruelties and exactions. The Nationalists' armies and local bandits had reinforced this feeling. Mao laid down a whole set of rules for his troops — for example, they should replace the doors of peasants' huts removed to sleep on and pay for what they took. These were sound policies for a revolutionary army, and Deng doubtless endorsed them thoroughly. Unity with the peasants was the road to victory. Most of the PLA rank and file were illiterate peasants. From 1949 onward the PLA occupied the cities, where the residents looked down on and mistrusted them as country bumpkins. In the absence of a proper police force, law and order were enforced by soldiers, many of whom spoke incomprehensible dialects. But Mao would not let go of his control of the moral strength of the PLA. In the 1960s, cults were instituted, emphasising self-sacrifice and adaptability. A cult developed around a young man called Lei Feng who was killed in a peacetime accident, and whose diary was found to contain exemplary notes on obeying Mao and serving the people.

The PLA exercised nation-wide control of the population through its political commissars who could be more powerful than the local Party Secretary in times of trouble. The PLA grew much of its own food and manufactured much of its own equipment, and even officers' wives had to labour in work-shops. Training and technology were backward, however, and Mao relied on the strength of will of the common soldier to prevail in battles.

Deng had a shrewder view of the situation than this. He knew all about the problems and discipline of the rank-and-file. He knew soldiers were not saints, and he knew they could often be very stupid, egotistical, self-glorifying, and hidebound by worn-out traditions. In the 1960s and early 1970s, the PLA was so protected by Mao and had so many of its top commanders in the political leadership that even Deng could not do much to criticise or reform it, especially as he no longer had a military rank.

In any case, the army was the only force that could quell the Red Guards between 1967 and 1968. Even though the Defence Minister, war hero Marshal Lin Biao, was posthumously denounced for attempting to murder Mao in a *coup d'état* in 1971, the PLA still functioned as a tool of Mao, although naturally some senior commanders were purged following investigation of their roles.

Between 1980 and 1981, five top commanders were tried and sentenced to long gaol terms for their part in the Lin Biao affair, and this served to link them with the Gang of Four, tried at the same time. The PLA was morally on the defensive. On the other hand, Deng owed some high commanders a debt for having backed the purge of the Gang in 1976 and a year later supporting his own rehabilitation.

Caught between old loyalties and the need for reform and modernisation of the PLA, Deng chose the latter, thereby offending some of his erstwhile allies. These included General Xu Shiyou, who gave him protection in Canton between 1976 and 1977; General Wei Guoqing, who had pushed for his rehabilitation; General Chen Xilian, the Peking Military Region Commander, who must have agreed to the arrest of the Gang of Four; General Wang Dongxing, the commander of the special 8431 guards unit which was Mao's personal bodyguard; and Marshal Ye Jianying, the ageing veteran who thought Deng was going too far in his political reforms and who reputedly used to thwack the Politburo table with his walking-stick. Characteristically, once embarked on a course

215

of reform, Deng did not let himself be swayed by these personal debts. From 1975 onwards he talked and wrote about the need for modernisation and reform of the PLA.

Deng's active military career had extended over some 22 years and he was known to be a formidable soldier, decisive, methodical, practical, and far-sighted. As Liu Bocheng's health worsened, he began to assume direct command and made some of his closest friendships and comradely relationships while he was a political commissar. However, in the 1950s, his direct concern with military affairs had receded as he took on more and more responsibility as Secretary-General of the Communist Party. During the seven years of political exile that followed his fall from power in 1967, he had much to reflect on regarding his past career and the lessons he had learnt from it. He had seen how old and trusted comrades Peng Dehuai and Luo Ruiqing could be pulled down by Mao. We do not know to what extent he was informed of the alleged Lin Biao plot to assassinate Mao in 1971, or of the assumption of nation-wide military control through the appointment of officers to the revolutionary committees which rule every school, factory, and province of China, or the gradual removal of military control from these bodies as Zhou Enlai and his supporters gained the upper hand in the early 1970s.

Deng had been rehabilitated for barely two years when he began to criticise the PLA in 1975, which at that time still bore the shining image of victor in the revolutionary war. In March 1980, Deng pursued his campaign against inefficiency in the armed forces with a speech to an enlarged session of the Military Affairs Commission. He announced his theme of 'cutting the fat' and demobilising and retiring officers who were too old to be effective. In the past there had been no system of automatic retirement and pension in the PLA, and senior commanders retained their positions, if only nominally, into their seventies and even their eighties.

According to Deng, the PLA was over-staffed, by which he meant there were too many officers relative to the number of common soldiers. Costs were too high, affecting the modernisation programme for the whole country. New equipment could not be purchased in sufficient quantities and too many aged officers were still in charge at all levels. He told his audience of army officers and commissars:

'I am afraid that most of the people here, if not all, will find it difficult to carry on their work after five years. You will all be over seventy five – eight years from now. . . . If there were a war, would you be able to stay awake three days and nights at a stretch?. . . It is necessary to lift the lids in the current streamlining, including the lids on regiments, battalions and companies, to create conditions for the promotion of newly emerging forces.'

Senior officers going into retirement need not feel useless, Deng emphasised. The army would build houses for them and they would be recommended for various types of civilian jobs. For instance, they could take part in legal, political, and administrative work, drawing on their experience while in the service. They could become schoolteachers and a few might lecture at universities. Managerial skills could evolve from their knowledge of command systems. Apart from the question of retirement, such important organs as the General Political Department, the General Staff, and the General Logistics Department were over-staffed and training in the PLA was outmoded, according to Deng.

'It should not rest always at the level of firing practice, bayonet fighting and throwing hand grenades. How to deal with tanks, airplanes and so on — every fighter should know about such things. In addition, municipal authorities must stop drafting young delinquents into the PLA [as a form of discipline or punishment].'

An important aspect of the demobilisation programme was

to find jobs for the roughly one million men who were being returned to civilian life. This was particularly important for demobilised officers because, for the most part, they did not want to go and work in the rural areas. They had skills and experience which made them suitable for industrial work, and they knew a lot about rules, regulations, and discipline, but now they would have to be retrained.

After the key policy-making military organ, the Military Affairs Commission, met in 1984 with Deng presiding, a plan for reorganisation of the PLA was drawn up, creating civilian job assignments for military officers. A national work conference on retraining was held. He later told the *Observation Post* magazine in an interview: 'In an effort to realise the four modernisations, we should train and bring up, through various channels, a contingent of cadres who are better educated and have both professional knowledge and managerial skills. . . .' The journal said: 'As far back as 1979 Comrade Deng Xiaoping pointed out that it is necessary to run training classes for a large number of cadres [officers] who leave the army in civilian posts, so that they can learn various branches of knowledge, such as industry, finance and trade, politics and law, culture and education.' Deng also gave specific instructions on the period, method and organisation of the forms of training.

In November 1984, Deng gave his views on the PLA's role in civilian construction and production. Deng has insisted that the PLA contribute to the fruits of the civilian economy. There is nothing fundamentally new in this. Mao had ordered the army to help the peasants at busy periods of the crop-year and to undertake key construction projects. But Deng has gone further by turning a large part of the PLA's industrial concerns over from manufacturing arms and equipment to providing more consumer goods for the civilian population. He explained his policy at a meeting of the Military Affairs Commission in November 1984:

'The armed forces are related to national construction in various fields. They should consider how to support and to participate actively in national construction. All of them, whether the Air Force, the Navy or the Commission for Science, Technology and Industry for National Defence, should consider the question of releasing their forces to support the development of the national economy. For example, the Air Force can set aside some airfields to help the state develop civil aviation, by turning them into joint military-civilian airfields or civilian ones. The ports of the Navy can also be used jointly by army and civilians, or transformed into civilian ports in order to increase their capacity. With its good equipment and strong technical force, the National Defence Ministry should make full use of this force in overall national construction, and energetically develop civilian production.'

Deng also discussed the question of training: 'This is a question of taking the overall situation into consideration. If the armed forces succeed in doing a really good job in training people, it will be easy for army cadres and soldiers to be transferred to civilian work or reimbursed.' Demobilised soldiers, Deng said, were particularly useful as pig-breeders and drivers.

In July 1983, Deng laid down his basic policies for the armed forces at a meeting of the Military Affairs Commission. He stressed the need to combat economic crimes such as black-market dealings in the PLA. Officers often have access to scarce or restricted goods, and many of them had 'gone into business' in their own right, sometimes involving their family members in shady deals with army property and resources. In pursuing organisational reform, Deng said, the army 'is a little bit behind' other state organs. He proposed greater simplification of the command structure.

'The present system of leadership and institutional system

of the army are not so good, and very elaborate. There are a military commission, a standing committee, office meetings, and on top of that, several general departments. . . . When fighting battles in the past, there were just a few people responsible for leading a field army, an army corps, an army or a division. In some divisions, the division commander also served concurrently as the political commissar, and the division was quite well run with the help of a handful of deputy commissars. . . . It was most convenient! Now we have a big group of people.'

Deng also demanded a reduction in the average age of serving military men with faster promotion for the bright ones.

'Among all present [at the MAC meeting], is there anyone under the age of 60? If this problem is put off for a year [in age], the debt we owe in age will be greater. If we put it off for five years, what is to be done? Making the cadres younger in average age should be regarded as a key objective of system reform. . . . A large number of Red Army men, myself included, are sitting at the top. It will not do if this question is not solved.'

He called on the 'dukes and princes' (old commanders) to prepare a list of names of younger officers for promotion. In 1986, Deng instituted a new form of organisation of the PLA: the group army. The PLA's basic fighting units had hitherto been the infantry, with only relatively small special corps of armour, engineers, artillery, missiles, and naval and air forces. The old Field Army structure had become obsolete. Deng's recently created personal organ, *Observation Post,* commented:

'Group armies are the combat units which organise and coordinate the troops fighting in a certain direction or region. . . . This has combined various types of originally independent troops into a comprehensive combat unit. After being combined into a combat unit, these troops can carry out military training together, promote understanding among one another, strengthen their concept of unity, and raise their standard of combined operations through training in peacetime. In wartime, these troops can simplify coordination methods and reduce command levels through their coordinated relations.'

The magazine, which is frequently used to float Deng's more advanced ideas, noted that group armies first appeared in Europe in the nineteeth century, and during World War I they were the basic combat troops. In World War II, different kinds of troops were merged into group armies and have operated on that basis ever since. Modern tactical missiles, armed helicopters, and other types of new weaponry have been added, overall manning strengths have been reduced, while mobility and firepower have been greatly strengthened. The new PLA would have group armies consisting of infantry, motorised divisions, tanks, artillery, anti-chemical corps, anti-aircraft units, engineers, signallers, logistics units, and helicopter forces.

Against whom will all this hardware and manpower be used in the event of war? The only serious military threat to China in the foreseeable future is the Soviet Union, with its one million men, missiles, armour, and aircraft on China's northern and northwestern borders. Since the armed border clashes in 1969, resulting in hostility and bitterness, the tension between the Soviet Union and China has been gradually wound down. The Russians have actually talked of making minor concessions on the river frontiers and China has shown willingness to restore, if not Party-to-Party relations, more extensive state-to-state contacts with the Russians.

Nonetheless, the Russians do perceive a long-term threat in China's continuing population growth compared with their own falling birth rates in the urban areas. This is compensated by the huge numbers of children born to the Soviet Union's Asiatic peoples in Central Asia. The Soviet agricultural performance is stagnant and inadequate. From a geopolitical point of view, there are factors in the future which might make the Soviet Union anxious to seek a new, dominant relationship with China, even if at present all appears to be going well, though slowly, towards the restoration of their former friendly relationship.

On a wider scale, China represents an obstruction on Russia's road to her goal of domination of the Western Pacific through her fleets based at Vladivostok and Cam Ranh Bay in Vietnam. Deng has shown himself only too aware of this drive towards domination and has been strongly opposed to the Soviet support for Vietnam in its occupation of Cambodia, as well as the Soviet intervention in Afghanistan, which threatened the stability of China's old friend, Pakistan.

The idea of a war with the United States has receded into improbability since, after two decades of bitter hostility, Zhou Enlai and later Deng cultivated the Americans as friends and suppliers of advanced technology and education for China's brightest young people. However, the US is still committed to the defence of Taiwan against any military threat from China and, with the problem of Hong Kong and Macau basically solved, it is not ruled out that some future Chinese leadership may attempt by force of arms to increase its prestige by restoring effective mainland sovereignty over Taiwan, something it has been unable to do by political means. Such an armed clash in the Taiwan Strait could set Sino–American relations back by decades; fortunately, Deng's leadership group evidently understands this and is exercising patience over the Taiwan issue.

China must still be on its guard against border clashes with Vietnam which have burdened her with hundreds of thousands of ethnic Chinese refugees. Vietnam is vociferous in its condemnation of Chinese foreign policy. The Vietnamese army, though smaller than China's, has infinitely more battle experience, as well as equipment supplied by the Soviet Union that is in some ways superior to that of the PLA.

Deng does not show the same degree of personal bitterness towards India as the late Zhou Enlai did concerning the quarter-century-old dispute about the Himalayan frontiers between the two Asian giants. But neither is he in a hurry to make concessions to the Indians. The difficulties of the terrain and logistical support suggest that any future fighting that may take place on the Sino–Indian border will be restricted in scale.

Meanwhile, China has become a large exporter of inexpensive, easy-to-operate arms which its military factories churn out in excess of its own needs. These include small arms, anti-tank weapons, and mortars. Chinese weapons can be found in most parts of the Third World, often on opposing sides. The Chinese deny any political inconsistency in this, saying that once a weapon is sold it may turn up anywhere. Nonetheless, this is in contradiction of its previous policy of selling arms or supplying them only to Third World countries engaged in anti-colonial or 'anti-imperialist' struggles. Persistent reports of Chinese collaboration with Israel to improve its weapons design and materials are fiercely denied for the sake of its image in the Arab world.

Chapter 14

THE THOUGHTS OF DENG

T o what extent is Deng a Marxist? How does he see the future of China? How have his ideas been modified by experience? His thoughts on education and economic development are telling.

Deng is all too aware of the tremendous damage done to the Chinese educational system by the Cultural Revolution. In the late 1960s the system was shaken to its foundations, and is still backward, conservative, and lacking in proper buildings and teaching materials. In an article published in May 1977, just as he was again being rehabilitated, Deng pointed out that the United States had 2.1 million scientists and technicians, the Soviet Union had 900,000, whilst China had only 200,000, including the old, infirm, and weak, not many of whom can actually be employed. He also called for an improvement in the living conditions of intellectuals and scientists. 'At present, some of these people have old folk and children in their homes, and their monthly pay is only a few dozen *yuan*. They have to spend a lot of time doing daily chores and cannot find a quiet place for reading in the evenings. What is the good of that?' Deng also criticised people who looked down on intellectuals and scientists, saying the latter were also workers. 'There are many workers whose work consists of standing and pressing buttons for several hours; this is tense mental labour, and is also arduous physical labour.' In March 1983, Deng elaborated his ideas about education:

'Recently, I made a tour from Jiangsu to Zhejiang and then
returned to Shanghai. Throughout the journey, I found an
excellent situation: the people were full of joy; many new
houses had been built; the markets had a sufficient supply
of goods; and the cadres were full of confidence. This shows
that the Four Modernisations are full of promise. In order
to realise the target of quadrupling the output value by the
end of this century, all provinces and municipalities should
have concrete plans and should have a pretty clear idea of
their situations. We should help various provinces and municipalities solve their respective prominent problems and
help them create conditions for fulfilling their plans.

At present, Jiangsu's industrial and agricultural output
value has topped 73 billion *yuan*, showing a per capita
figure of 1,200 *yuan*. This is nearly double the 1976 figure.
I asked the comrades in Jiangsu how they achieved this
result. They said that there were mainly two points. First,
they relied on Shanghai's technological resources. Jiangsu
has hired many retired workers from Shanghai. These old
workers are capable, and they do not demand high pay. As
long as the authorities assign housing to them, they will be
glad to work and will be able to play a great role in
production. Now the technological conditions in many
Jiangsu enterprises and cities are not less sophisticated
than those in Shanghai. For many years, the comrades in
Jiangsu have highly valued knowledge and the role of the
intellectuals, and they have properly given play to the
intellectuals. Second, they have paid attention to the
undertakings owned and run by collectives and to the
development of small and medium-sized enterprises.

Comrade Zhao Ziyang has proposed the establishment
of some [domestic] economic cooperation zones, and
everybody is glad to hear that. This is the right way. In my
view, we should not just set up two economic cooperation

zones in Shanghai and Shanxi, and should not just rest at the stage of conducting pilot projects. If we only conduct pilot projects in the handling of concrete matters, we will fail to settle quite a few issues in a number of years, and we will advance too slowly. During the liberation war, Comrade Mao Zedong proposed that the Second and Third Field Armies take joint action. He said that with two field armies joining hands in action, their strength would increase many times rather than just double. This is also true of economic cooperation. However, many problems in people's minds have yet to be solved with regard to economic cooperation, and it is now time to get things started.

The development of intellectual resources is an important matter. This should include training of workers. More attention should be paid to this matter. More institutions of higher education should be developed. If the number or size of these institutions cannot be doubled in the near future, it should at least be increased by fifty per cent. At present we have the ability to do so. There are not too many difficulties in doubling the number of students enrolled by key universities and colleges. There is no lack of teaching staff. The main difficulty is the shortage of living quarters for the students. So we should allocate some money to build more schoolhouses and student dormitories. I think that we have money for doing this. We can make a calculation to see how much money this will take.

Our present problem is that we have too few intellectuals; in addition, young and middle-aged intellectuals in some places find it hard to display their abilities and talents. We must be determined to implement the policies towards the intellectuals and improve their living conditions.'

Literature and art are also extremely vexed questions in modern China. Traditionally the preserve of scholars and administrators, they have been used in the twentieth century to propagate or oppose revolution and other political movements. Writers and artists have been so frequently persecuted for political reasons over the past three decades that most of them are timid, imitative, and lack self-confidence and creative freedom. Despite Deng's rehabilitation of old writers who were disgraced or exiled to the countryside in the 1950s, the present state of literature and the arts in China is dismal indeed.

Deng has not made many pronouncements on literary and artistic questions. Like the Soviet Union's former dictator Khrushchev, he recognises that the arts can be a morale-booster, that they stimulate independence of mind and creativity, raise the country's prestige internationally, and generally brighten people's lives. Like Khrushchev, he has had the experience that a small let-up in strict Party control of the arts can encourage artists and writers to expose unpleasant social truths. When the inevitable clamp-down comes again, the opinion of the outside world is one of disappointment, and the censorship of the Soviets and the Chinese is regarded as ludicrously oppressive. In 1987 the dilemma was exemplified, in a small way, by a controversy that arose over Chinese women body-builders wearing bikinis. The old Party hacks said bikinis were not allowed in China, and the body-builders said: 'If we don't wear bikinis, the judges won't be able to judge our torsos!'

Deng, considered by some to be relatively liberal in matters of art and culture, has been rather inconsistent over the problem, presumably because he has never really decided in his own mind how to solve it. He has rejected the leftists' argument that more cultural freedom breeds, or brings in from abroad, decadent influences which are harmful to Chinese people, especially the youth. He has argued that good police work and education can protect the morals of the Chinese people from insidious, supposedly vicious, influences such as pornographic videos, while 'healthy' foreign performers and writers may still be admitted to the country. That at least is an advance on the position of Mao and his widow, Jiang Qing, who thought that foreign influences were irretrievably harmful for the masses, although Jiang Qing relished them in private.

It is not just foreign arts and books that bother the leadership. There is the ever-present problem of Chinese intellectuals wanting to resume and contribute to the study of classical and modern Chinese literature. Anyone who studies Chinese culture can easily see what unscholarly nonsense the pro-Party 'scholars' of the past thirty years have made of their literary history and can understand the inapplicability of Marxist teachings to a country of China's size, traditions, and culture. That is a matter which bothers the Party: it fears the intellectuals may pick on its numerous errors from past history. It is impatient with academic pedantry and wants a single, agreed interpretation of history in a Marxist mould, albeit 'with Chinese characteristics'. As the 1980s progressed, the critique of Marxism continued and widened until it was little more than a meaningless slogan.

Between 1978 and 1979, Deng experimented with freer public expression when he allowed the so-called 'Democracy Wall' in Peking to be plastered with essays by would-be intellectuals and political polemicists. This helped to fuel a new phase of modern Chinese writing, particularly by younger authors, the so-called 'literature of the wounded'. It sought to reveal the terrible sufferings imposed on individuals, and on the nation as a whole, during the Cultural Revolution. The army chiefs in particular objected to this, since they regarded it as an attack on Mao, their hallowed leader. The contents of bookstores in the late 1980s are infinitely more interesting than they were under Mao. Even though Chinese writing shows only a limited degree of cultural freedom, people now at least have access to the works of some famous Chinese and foreign authors which were nearly all banned by Mao.

In the summer of 1983, the Central Committee issued a circular setting out guidelines for the study of Deng's views which were published in his *Selected Works* in 1984. The circular first laid down that all Deng's thinking on this subject was conditioned by adherence to the 'four basic principles' defined by Deng in March 1979: socialism, the people's democractic dictatorship, leadership of the Party, and Marxism–Leninism–Mao Zedong Thought. Art and literature, according to Deng, should 'serve the people and socialism', which could mean almost anything, but Deng says observance of the 'four principles' is essential to the 'four modernisations'. So his fundamental view of the arts, as was Mao's, is utilitarian, rather than devoted to class struggle.

In the West, people interested in art and literature regard them on the whole as serving no purpose other than to give pleasure and enlightenment. To view art and literature as serving the purpose of economic modernisation would be considered by most educated people to be philistinism. Deng balances his utilitarianism by calling on Chinese writers and artists to 'emancipate their minds', one of those nice-sounding, liberal ideas which, since the 1950s, has tripped up so many cultural figures in China and led to the destruction of their careers and the wasting of their talents. The Hundred Flowers campaign of the mid-1950s is an outstanding example.

In capitalist society, Deng has said, there is 'the tendency to bourgeois liberalisation and the completely commercialised tendency of putting money first in everything', while no attention is paid to the social effects of 'bad' literature and art. In China, Deng says, 'the arts serve the needs of the people in their spiritual life, for fostering new socialists, and for heightening the ideological, cultural and moral levels of society', a sentiment with which some people in the West would concur even if it does not appeal to aesthetes.

Deng concedes that in literary and artistic circles there are 'impurities of ideology, style and organisation, of bourgeois liberalisation, of extreme individualism, of the scramble for fame and wealth, of anarchism, of paying no attention to professional ethics, personalities, the national image, economic and cultural crimes, and so on.' He also opposes mass movements and political campaigns aimed at involving the populace in criticism of works of literature or art considered by the Party to show bad political errors. It is the tactics of opposing 'bad' works that he dislikes, not the need to oppose them. In practice, severe censorship is still in effect in China and by no means all the censors are as relatively broad-minded as Deng makes himself out to be.

The Peking *Guangming Daily*, which is designed to appeal to intellectuals — *Guangming* meaning enlightenment — has published an analysis of Deng's views on literature and the arts. It considers the danger of 'ossification' as the antithesis of liberalisation. The concepts of political left and right are inevitably involved in criticism. In speeches made in 1981 and 1984, Deng has said that left and right 'erroneous' tendencies must be equally criticised. This is disingenuous. Anyone who has observed Chinese literature and art since the death of Mao can see that it contains more liberal and rightist trends than it did before, and that Deng has been more censorious of the left than of the right. Sometimes he has had to sacrifice an author's career in the interests of harmony with other senior power-holders, especially the army chiefs who are more authoritarian than he is in these matters. Deng has, on the other hand, been able to work towards the principle that intellectuals and artists should not be victimised if their products are disapproved of by the authorities. It is enough to criticise them and remove the offending work. It is then up to the writers to show that they have taken the criticism to heart; otherwise their promotion on the academic or artistic ladder may be hampered.

In 1956, Mao used a particular phrase to express the need for variety and free play in artistic and literary work: 'Let a hundred flowers bloom and a thousand schools of thought contend.' A year later, in 1957, he went back on this policy, astonished at the chorus of intellectual opinion which put in doubt many hallowed tenets of the Party. The worst offenders among the writers were judged 'rightists'. Some well-known literary figures were imprisoned or exiled to remote parts of the country. The majority drew the obvious conclusions and fell silent.

In the mid-1970s, the Hundred Flowers slogan was revived to mask the extreme anti-liberal policies of the Gang of Four. Chinese intellectuals again came under pressure to conform 100 per cent, with the result that they were again intimidated. The Hundred Flowers was a policy both insincere and dangerous to those who took it literally. Party policy over such became known alternately as *shou* (tightening up) and *fang* (loosening up). Between 1978 and 1979, the Democracy Wall chapter, which resulted in a sizeable number of arrests, was a third experience of false permissiveness. In late 1986, there was a repetition of this with the student demonstrations in Peking and other university cities.

Deng is quoted as having said that art and literature should not be asked to 'be subordinate to *ad hoc*, concrete and immediate political tasks'. He has also said that literature and artwork should aim to effect social change gradually and subtly. Further, 'we should not continue the call for art and literature to be subordinate to politics, because this call can very easily become the theoretical basis for wilful intervention in them.' On the other hand, in Deng's view, 'all progressive and revolutionary artists have to consider the social effects of their work, and they have to consider the interests of the people, the state, and the Party.' Deng further clarified his thinking on literature and art in a speech, published in July 1983, to a congress of people active in these fields. His central theme was that 'The people need art, but art needs the people more.'

He explained:

'It is our hope that more and more comrades among literary and art workers will become real engineers who can rebuild the human soul. In order to educate the people, they should first be educated. In order to provide the people with mental food, they themselves must first absorb nourishment. Then who will educate literary and art workers? The Marxist answer can only be: the people. . . . However, in the recent period, a small number of literary and art workers have deviated from the needs of the people and the needs of the socialist cause. In their eyes, 'everything is for the purpose of making money', so they regard their works and performances as merely a means of seeking personal fame and gain, have carried out their artistic work in a slipshod manner, and have even offered the masses shoddy works of a vulgar style.'

Deng writes in his *Selected Works*:

'Workers in literature and art who are responsible to the people should unfailingly and consistently face the people, keep improving, refrain from producing in a rough and slipshod way, seriously assess the social effects of their productions and strive hard to provide the people with the best spiritual food.'

However, Deng is not in favour of fierce, ideological attacks on writers who are deemed to have strayed from the right path: 'Methods of criticism should be tasteful,' he writes. 'The criticism should be appropriate in extent; do not mount an encirclement attack or organize a campaign.'

This is very different from the views of Mao, who started the Cultural Revolution with virulent attacks on prominent writers of the 1960s, and who subjected nearly all well-known authors of the post-revolutionary period to public humiliation, exile, or imprisonment, banning their works or causing psychological pressure to the point where they committed suicide. One of the most pathetic sights of the post-Mao period was to see distinguished novelists like Ba Jin and Ding Ling emerging from their long spells in the wilderness still proclaiming their faith in socialism and youth. One could sense that they were doing this in order to cling to their newly-recovered self-esteem and to avoid, at all cost, a repetition of their previous suffering.

What is Deng Xiaoping's ideology today? Does he really have an ideology other than some Marxist prejudices and a dislike of most aspects of Maoism? In the ideological sphere, is he merely a debunker or is he really an original thinker? Anyone acquainted with senior cadres in China is aware of their desperate desire to steer a middle course and never again be hoisted with the petard of Maoism or other extremist philosophies. Under Deng, they have considerable freedom to say what they think, if it is founded on common sense and realism, but many will not even do that for fear of falling victim to some future leftist convulsion. Deng has taken it upon himself to persuade all generations of Chinese people, and foreigners too, that no such convulsion will take place, although, at his age, it is hard to see that he can stand surety for what may happen in the 21st century.

The most solid, if not stodgy, Chinese journal of ideology is the now-defunct fortnightly, *Hong Qi* (*Red Flag*), whose task used to be to give a mental system to, and clarify points on, the policies of the current leaders. In the mid-1970s, it managed to retain just a little independence from the leftists around Mao who consequently set up their own political journal, *Xuexi yu Pipan* (*Study and Criticism*) in Shanghai. One analyst of Chinese affairs, himself a Chinese, succeeded in following the course of the left–right struggle simply by counting the number of recurring leftist slogans in *Red Flag* and comparing them with the number of these clichés in *Study and Criticism*. Some aspects of 'China-watching' are amazingly simple. By the late 1970s, *Red Flag* was being written and edited by Dengists or by theoreticians who saw there was no future in opposing Deng and continuing to over-glorify Mao and his achievements. Its central task was to convince politically-minded people that Deng's policies were not a contradiction of Mao's, but actually a logical continuation of them.

The theorists in Peking seem to feel it is important to show that there is continuity between the policies of Mao and Deng, otherwise the whole nation would lose face for having gone along with Maoism for a quarter of a century, only to watch Deng throw it out of the window when he won supreme power. These questions of face, both personal and national, are still taken extremely seriously in China. It should be noted that Chinese officials reject the use of both the terms 'Maoism' and 'Dengism'.

In July 1983, *Red Flag* made a stab at justifying Dengism as merely a new form of Maoism by taking as its text Deng's maxim that 'seeking truth from facts, proceeding from the actual conditions to everything, combining theory with practice, and persisting in the principle that practice is the criterion for truth, such is the ideological line of our Party.' The journal said Mao was not only the author of the phrase 'seek truth from facts', but had also said, during the 1943 'rectification' campaign at Yan'an, 'discover the truth through practice, and again through practice verify the truth. . . . Practice, knowledge, more practice and more knowledge — this form repeats itself in endless cycles, and with each cycle the content of practice and knowledge rises to a higher level.' Mao had also said: 'We should proceed from the actual conditions inside and outside the country, the province, county or district, and derive our guide to action from them.' *Red Flag* commented: 'Comrade Deng Xiaoping's concept of seeking truth from facts as part of the content of the ideological line has included in it rich experiences and lessons, and there is no mistaking that it is aimed at the actual conditions.' What one almost senses as the anti-ideological ideology of Deng is rationalised in the *Red Flag* article:

'If theory is not combined with practice, and if theory is not regarded as the guide of action but as dogma to be applied indiscriminately regardless of the time, the place and the conditions, there will be no proceeding from the actual condition and no seeking truth from facts to speak of . . . this fine tradition of combining theory with practice was gravely damaged during the Cultural Revolution.'

In September 1985, Deng was quoted, in an optimistic mood, as telling the visiting Austrian president, Rudolf Kirschschlager:

'There are two main factors deciding whether our policy can be carried on: first, the correctness of the policy. If the policy is correct, nobody can change it: otherwise, it is not necessary to keep it. Our practice in the past seven years has proved that the current policy is in keeping with the interests of the state and the people. As all the people have trust in this policy, no one can change it. Second, since the very beginning when we drew up the policy, we have taken organisational measures and introduced the program of making the ranks of cadres younger in average age to guarantee its continuity. We laid down this guideline and started establishing a second echelon a few years ago. Now we are building up our third echelon, equipped with professional knowledge and full of energy. Young cadres are most aware of the advantages of the current policy. . . .'

One of the campaigns launched with Deng's approval was the 'spiritual civilisation movement' which reached its height in 1985. This aimed to eliminate anti-social habits, such as public spitting, and to make people more serious and responsible in their behaviour. Deng said of the campaign: 'If we do not strengthen our building of spiritual civilisation, our building of material civilisation will be disrupted and suffer from setbacks.' From a political viewpoint, the aims of this campaign were ambiguous. It was welcomed by leaders and cadres with leftist leanings because, in view of the continued problems of low living standards, it was one more way to keep the general public under control and stop them from becoming openly disgruntled or rebellious. It was also a device with which the rightists and centrists, headed by Deng, could draw the fire of the opposition and give the latter a chance to busy themselves relatively harmlessly. This is typical of Deng's pre-emptive tactics in political struggle.

Alongside the moves to promote 'spiritual civilisation', however, Deng has insisted on continuing the policy of opening China to the outside world — which the leftists and Old Guard have proclaimed to be the reason for the growth, or persistence, of anti-social behaviour. A high-level commentator wrote in the *Observation Post* on 11 November 1985:

'In history, China has pursued opening-up policies as well as closed-door policies. It can be said that China has a profound knowledge of their advantages and disadvantages. . . . One of the problems that warrants our attention is that in society the blind worship of foreign things has become an epidemic. In the eyes of those who blindly worship foreign things, smoking imported cigarettes means an enhanced social status. Riding in an imported automobile gives one a sense of pride, and riding in a China-made automobile gives the impression of "low socio-economic status". By refusing to remove the labels on their imported sunglasses, these people have become spiritual slaves. . . . It is a good thing to acknowledge inferiority on seeing that the things produced by others are better than ours. However, an even more important thing is that we should modestly learn from others and strive to do better. This broadmindedness is characteristic of the Chinese nation.'

Unfortunately for China, her people have not proved as capable of absorbing foreign ideas and techniques as have other countries, particularly the Japanese. The most plausible explanation for this is that traditional Japanese society was feudal, with the retainer owing absolute allegiance to his lord, which was easily translated into company loyalty in industry. The Japanese have been skilled imitators for a very long time. They have copied half their civilisation and their script from China and Korea. When it came to 'spiritual civilisation', the Japanese imposed draconian punishments for anti-social behaviour. The ruling class had absolute freedom to dispose of their retainers as they wished and, at one stage, one could be beheaded for spitting in the street. The Chinese, by contrast, were more touchy and mutinous towards their land-lords, neighbours, and rulers, insisting on total propriety and filial respect for the elders at home, while paying little attention to hygiene and the environment affecting people outside the extended family.

Unlike some of his peers, Deng never studied in Japan and, until the 1980s, had never visited Japan. His personal experience of the Japanese is of their sadism, aggressiveness, and violence during their occupation of China from 1937 until 1945. Deng has never been slow to reproach the Japanese for short memories or bad faith when, in recent years, the two countries have quarrelled. He does not regard them as an economic model for China to follow, preferring instead to give measured praise to the economic success of South Korea, Hong Kong, and even Taiwan.

China is a nation nowadays obsessed with self-reproach for its inability to keep up with the modern developed countries, especially Japan. Her leaders, however, continue to refuse to face facts in assessing her backwardness. An official commentary on Deng's 1985 speech on the reforms said:

'In the history of world cultural development, the Chinese nation has made glorious contributions. It suffered from setbacks and became backward in many fields only during a relatively recent period. However, the Chinese people have written a glorious chapter of Chinese history in the past century. The founding of the People's Republic of China brought to an end the history of China as a feudal, semi-colonial country. As a result, China has been standing in the forefront of Asian, African and Latin American national liberation movements. Our achievements in socialist construction have drawn attention from all over the world. Since the Third Plenary Session of the Eleventh Central Committee, we have been carrying out reforms. Our economy has been steadily developing. Our country has become increasingly prosperous, and our national prestige has been on the rise.'

The token reference to Asian, African, and Latin American countries and their revolutionary movements is a little surprising. China, in the interests of good-neighbourly relations with other Asian countries — for instance Thailand, Malaysia, and the Philippines — has almost ceased direct aid to their leftist insurgent movements. They may permit some of their home-made arms to reach selected groups of dissidents in modest quantities, but what they really want is to see the Southeast Asian countries strengthen themselves internally and resist Soviet infiltration. In Latin America, many of the insurgent movements look to Cuba for help. China is on very bad terms with Cuba because of the latter's adherence to the Soviet Union's global policies and the help it gives to Moscow in setting up pro-Soviet regimes in Angola and Mozambique, African countries previously ruled by Portugal.

Apart from building a railway to help ship out the copper of land-locked Zambia through the ports of Tanzania, China has almost lost interest in sub-Saharan Africa to whose newly independent countries she used to give modest amounts of technical aid. Unfortunately, copper is now like a drug on the market, and both those countries are close to bankruptcy. Until 1971, Taiwan held China's place on the Security Council of the United Nations so China only courted African support in the 1950s and 1960s to gain votes for her own admission to the United Nations. To talk about China as a champion of Third World countries, especially since she is selling shore-to-ship missiles to the theocratic regime in Iran against the interests of the socialist-inclined Third World country Iraq, is nowadays grotesque.

Deng and his supporters, indeed the whole Chinese Communist Party, have a real problem with their public attitude towards the late Mao Zedong. In the present political atmosphere one cannot praise him highly without danger of being regarded as a 'leftist', and in the 1980s that is almost as undesirable an appellation as 'rightist' was in the 1950s. The present leaders cannot denigrate him totally, however much they feared him or loathed his policies in the past. The Chinese, like most citizens of totalitarian states, have perforce adopted a form of doublethink with which they can almost believe the things they have been taught to say, but make unexpressed mental reservations about them for the preservation of their own individual identity. The Chinese have been turned by their history, as numerous travellers down the ages have noted, into past-masters of the art of political dissimulation. The people prefer to leave politics to the higher-ups, and one of the most horrifying things about the Cultural Revolution was that its leaders insisted on recruiting almost everybody for activism in the leftist course. Nobody was allowed to be 'neutral'.

This account of Deng's life so far has shown the metamorphosis in his political beliefs since the early 1930s, when he became one of Mao's close associates. This he remained until three decades later when he had to help sort out the mess left by the Great Leap Forward and the formation of the people's communes. Together with Peng Zhen and Liu Shaoqi he worked out the modified regulations for the communes, called the *Sixty Articles*. The *Sixty Articles* deeply offended Mao, who asked 'What Emperor has written this?' when he read them. When Deng had the communes disbanded completely from 1979 onwards, he did it without vituperation or apologia. The obvious reason for this was that Deng had supported Mao strongly when the communes were instituted, and loyalty to

Mao while he was alive was more important than any decision *per se*.

However, it was not just Deng's 'face' that needed protection: the 'face' of the entire Chinese nation needed restoring. In China, more easily than in any other country, the people can preserve an unspoken understanding that something has to be put up with, or some foreigner has to be lied to, because the leaders have made it a question of national security and, most important, national pride to show a united front and conceal problems and failures. After Mao's death, a foreigner who commented to individual cadres that they had told lies during Mao's lifetime would be met with the bland response: 'Of course you understand I was not free to speak my mind then.' Nowadays it is legitimate, indeed obligatory, to talk about the 'decade of chaos', the Cultural Revolution led by Mao. Participants and victims are considered to have been in the same fog of political confusion, and the most active perpetrators of left-wing violence and injustice have now been killed, gaoled, or expelled from positions of influence. It was only for a brief period in the late 1970s that the leadership smiled on the publication of works of literature that realistically exposed the horrors of the Cultural Revolution. Army chiefs protested at too much debunking of Mao, since their own public image and morale were supposed to be intimately bound up with his favour and patronage.

The chosen approach has been to weigh Mao in the scales of history, to recognise his achievements as a revolutionary, but to criticise severely his later political activity, especially in the last decade of his life. 'In our appraisal of Comrade Mao Zedong,' Deng has said, 'we should regard his contributions as primary and his mistakes as secondary. This is in accordance with the facts, and it cannot be doubted or denied.'

As Deng states in his *Selected Works*, 'the appraisal of Comrade Mao Zedong and the exposition of Mao Zedong Thought relate not only to Comrade Mao personally, but also to the entire history of our Party and country.' Further on, Deng gives a warning: 'To exaggerate, under the sway of emotion, Comrade Mao's mistakes, can only mar the image of our Party and country, impair the prestige of the Party and the socialist system, and undermine the unity of the Party, the Army and our people of all nationalities.'

There lies the crux of the matter. Something similar happened in the Soviet Union in 1956, when some of Stalin's misdeeds were exposed by Khrushchev and later smoothed over partly to prevent embarrassing questions on how involved the post-Stalin leaders themselves had been. Once the new wave of Russian intellectual self-expression had trickled into the sands of conformity, authors were persecuted for continuing to write about the effects of Stalin's rule. Deng dealt with the problem of responsibility of leaders in power who could have moderated the dictator's acts. 'When we talk about mistakes, we should not speak only of Chairman Mao. For many other leading comrades in the Central Committee made mistakes too,' he writes. Deng had good scapegoats to blame for oppressive acts committed in Mao's name.

'Because Lin Biao and the Gang of Four distorted, cut up and falsified Mao Zedong Thought under the pretext of "holding it aloft", the Party's guiding ideology was for a time confused, and the reputation of Mao Zedong Thought was disastrously ruined. After the smashing of the Gang of Four, Comrade Hua Guofeng, who was in charge of the work of the Central Committee at that time, proposed and insisted on the "two whatevers".

When our Party [in 1978] repudiated the "two whatevers" in depth, and corrected the "leftist" errors of Comrade Mao in his later years, some comrades confused Comrade Mao's errors in his later years with what had been distorted, and counterfeited by Lin Biao and the Gang of Four, and jumbled them up with Mao Zedong Thought. They doubted the scientific value of Mao Zedong Thought and negated its guiding role.'

Deng, on the other hand, had 'stood high and seen far' during this period and had upheld the truly valuable things in Mao Thought. This evaluation was published in a Peking monthly, which added that Deng 'in many of his speeches and writings has repeatedly stressed the tremendous guiding significance of Mao Zedong Thought to the Chinese revolution and [economic] construction'. Mao's contribution to the revolution and the defeat of the Nationalists is beyond challenge. But his policies, not just from 1966 but from 1957 onwards, showed the mania and even paranoia that has overcome many dictators in their later years.

In December 1978, the apologia was made to sound hollow when the Dengists' alleged devotion to Mao Thought was held up as an important result of the crucial Third Plenum of the Eleventh Central Committee. It was at that Plenum that Deng secured the demotion from the Politburo of several leaders considered most committed to Mao and his thought. The results of the Plenum, an official philosophical journal said, had 'brought order out of chaos' in the Party's guiding ideology.

EPILOGUE

I n the 1980s, Deng enjoyed the fruits of his campaign to eliminate leftism from economic planning in China. He operated mainly through general instructions and left the detailed implementation to Premier, subsequently Party Secretary, Zhao Ziyang.

Initially there was marked success in agriculture following Deng's abolition of the people's communes in 1979. The peasants reacted well to their new freedoms, with a surge in production, especially of what was previously considered 'sideline' products. In the late 1980s, however, the planners ran into trouble again with rice supplies, as the peasants forced up the price and city-dwellers had to be paid food subsidies.

In industry, even with the help of the Special Economic Zones in which foreign investment was encouraged, the projected reforms were slow in getting off the ground. The reasons were not hard to find: obstructive, bureaucratic cadres who were afraid for their jobs and authority if they permitted reconstruction of Chinese industrial management. In addition, the workers became apathetic since their increased wages seemed inevitably to be eaten up by the rising prices of food and consumer goods. The educational system continued to suffer from the demoralisation of the Cultural Revolution and the low salaries paid to academics. Deng, however, remained quite optimistic, continued to receive foreign visitors, and clearly maintained a very strong grasp of national affairs despite his chief concern, the Military Affairs Committee.

The Twelfth Congress of the Communist Party was held in September 1982. At that Congress several veteran leaders were dropped, perhaps because they opposed Deng's new programme of reform of the People's Liberation Army. In 1984, a programme of rectification of sub-standard cadres began. It was intended to continue for three years. It turned out to be an ongoing campaign, however, with no particular end in sight as high and middle-level cadres continued to engage in corruption and graft and underhand commercial dealings, as well as failing to implement the reform programme. In 1985, Deng denounced the Cultural Revolution as an entirely negative phenomenon with no good points whatsoever. But, as though to impress on the public that anti-social behaviour was a serious crime, a nation-wide programme of judicial executions was stepped up to the point where an estimated 10,000 criminals were shot over a one-year period.

In late 1987, a National People's Congress was held at which a start was made on Deng's planned political reform, aimed at making the Chinese government more open and democratic. Although an unprecedented number of criticisms were raised at the Congress, it was still a long way from what anyone in the West would call 'democracy'.

The Thirteenth Congress of the Communist Party, in early 1988, was used by Deng to effect a genuine clearance of over-age leaders. President Li Xiannian was replaced as President by Yang Shangkun; Peng Zhen retired from his NPC post; and numerous others admitted the limitations of their age and either took sinecure appointments or retired altogether. Deng, nothing abashed by the fact that he was himself 84 years old, continued to exercise decisive power over national affairs through his domination of Party Secretary-General Zhao Ziyang and the newly-appointed Premier Li Peng.

Despite the obstacles ahead, Deng can look back with

satisfaction at the initiation of most of his schemes for the reform of Chinese politics and the economy. He has sacrificed the mass regimentation favoured by Mao for a more persuasive approach to the general public, and it has partly worked. Socially, however, the consequences have been much as the 'Old Guard', especially the aged economic planner Chen Yun, forecast they would be. Youth unemployment and moral decadence have become serious problems. Imported Western fashions in clothes and hairstyles have become the watermark of 'modernity', especially in the big cities like Shanghai. Illegal currency dealings, 'discomania', and other phenomena are evident in the urban areas. Even pornographic video-tapes from Hong Kong are penetrating the Chinese market.

Deng evidently does not see any reason why, if they did their job properly, these manifestations should not be controlled by the police and other authorities. He is not prepared to view them as a natural consequence of a more open society.

Deng had a problem in deciding who would succeed him politically. The Long March veterans, as well as being lukewarm about Deng's reform programme, were getting too old and ridden with prejudices and rivalries. He chose instead Zhao Ziyang, a tough, no-nonsense administrator who had suffered in the Cultural Revolution and who had strong views on the need for reform. He liked wearing Western business suits and playing golf.

Having made Zhao Prime Minister, Deng watched over him throughout the 1980s, lending strength and prestige to his image until, in 1987, he promoted him to the position of Secretary-General of the Party. Deng had by then resigned all his official positions, including chairmanship of the powerful Military Affairs Committee which he relinquished and gave to Zhao. The smooth transition and transfer of power was re-markably effective. The dull, bureaucratic, but necessary qualities which Zhao lacked were supplied by the dour Li Peng, a Soviet-trained administrator who was said to have been sponsored from youth by the late Premier Zhou Enlai. Some observers forecast an eventual power struggle between these two men.

Mao Zedong did amazing things for China. He pulled it together as a nation when it seemed ready to fall apart. He imparted the idea of constant progress. But over a period of time he failed to involve the masses in sacrifices necessary for his programme.

Deng has built on Mao's successes and corrected the wrong direction which he took. In the process, many people think he has set China on the road to abandoning Marxist ideas in favour of modern systems of management and industrial efficiency. In history he may well go down as a greater man than Mao, even without the latter's semi-religious cult and use of mass hysteria as a political weapon. As a revolutionary, he may lack Mao's extraordinarily charismatic effect, but over the long term will probably be seen to have built more than he destroyed, whereas it can be argued that Mao destroyed more than he built. Mao was the demolition expert, but Deng is the architect.

BIBLIOGRAPHY

Bartke, Wolfgang and Peter Schier, *China's New Party Leadership* (London: Macmillan, 1985).

Bonavia, David, *The Chinese — A Portrait* (Harmondsworth: Penguin, 1980).

Bonavia, David, *Verdict in Peking* (New York: Putnam's, and London: Hutchinson, 1984).

Chang, Kuo-t'ao, *The Rise of the Chinese Communist Party* (2 volumes) (Wichita: University of Kansas Press, 1971).

Ch'en, Jerome, *Mao and the Chinese Revolution* (Oxford: Oxford University Press, 1965).

Ch'en, Jerome, 'Reflections on the Long March', *China Quarterly*, No. 111, September 1987.

Ch'en, Jerome, 'Resolutions of the Tsunyi Conference', *China Quarterly*, No. 40, October–December 1969.

Ch'en, Jerome, 'The Zunyi Conference as One Step in Mao's Rise to Power — A Survey of Historical Studies of the Chinese Communist Party', *China Quarterly*, No. 106, June 1986.

China Directory Radiopress, Tokyo, 1979–1987.

Chung, Hua Lee, *Deng Xiaoping: The Marxist Road to the Forbidden City* (Princeton: Kingston Press, 1985).

Deng Xiaoping Xuanji (*Selected Works of Deng Xiaoping*) (Hong Kong: Sanlian Shudian, 1984).

Fairbank, John K., Edwin O. Reischauer, and Albert M. Craig, *East Asia: The Modern Transformation* (Boston: Houghton Mifflin Co., 1965).

Fang Percy Jucheng and Lucy Guinong J. Fang, *Zhou Enlai — A Profile* (Beijing: Foreign Languages Press, 1986).

Fuzhi Shimo, Sima Changfeng, *Deng Xiaoping* (Hong Kong: Bowen Book Co., 1980).

Han, Shanbi, *Deng Xiaoping Zhuan* (Hong Kong: East West and Culture Publishing Co., 1985).

Hook, Brian (ed.), *The Cambridge Encyclopaedia of China* (Cambridge: Cambridge University Press, 1982).

Hsu, Immanuel C.Y., *The Rise of Modern China* (Hong Kong: Hong Kong University Press, 1983).

Kaplan, Fredric M. and Julian M. Sobin, *Encyclopaedia of China Today* (New York: Eurasia Press, 1980).

Klein, Donald W. and Anne B. Clark, *Biographical Dictionary of Modern Communism 1921–1965* (Cambridge: Harvard University Press, 1971).

Lary, Diana, *Region and Nation — The Kwangsi Clique in Chinese Politics 1925–1937* (Cambridge: Cambridge University Press, 1974).

MacFarquhar, Roderick, *The Origins of the Cultural Revolution* (Oxford: Oxford University Press, 1983).

Mackerras, Colin, *Modern China — A Chronology from 1942 to the Present* (London: Thames & Hudson, 1982).

Rice, Edgar E., *Mao's Way* (Berkeley: University of California Press, 1972).

Salisbury, Harrison E., *The Long March — The Untold Story* (New York: Harper & Row, 1985).

Snow, Edgar, *Red Star over China* (revised edition) (London: Victor Gollancz, 1968).

Trivier, Leon, *La Chine de Deng Xiaoping* (Paris: 1979).

250

Wang, Jian, *Hua Guofeng yu Deng Xiaoping* (Hong Kong: Ming Pao Publishing Co., undated).

Whitson, William W., with Che-Hsia Huang, *The Chinese High Command — A History of Communistic Military Politics — 1927–71* (New York: Praeger, 1973).

Who's Who in Communist China (2 volumes) (Hong Kong: Union Research Institute, 1970).

Who's Who in the PRC (Harveder Press Ltd, 1981).

Wu, Yuan-li (ed.), *China, A Handbook* (Newton Abbot, David and Charles, 1973).

Yang Guozhi, Chen Feiqin and Wan Wei (eds.), *Liu — Deng Zhen Zhanli* (Yunnan: Yunnan People's Publishing House, 1984).

Zagoria, Donald S., *The Sino-Soviet Conflict* (Princeton: Princeton University Press, 1962).

Zhou, Xun, *Deng Xiaoping* (in Chinese) (Hong Kong: Wide Angle Publishing House, 1983).

GLOSSARY

A
Anhui (province) 安徽省

B
Ba Jin 巴金
Bai Chongxi 白崇禧
baigan 白干儿（白酒）
Baise (Guangxi province) 百色
Baotou (Inner Mongolia) 包頭
Bo Gu (alias Qin Bangxian) 博古（秦邦憲）

C
Cai Chang 蔡暢
Cai Hesen 蔡和森
Changsha (Hunan province) 長沙市
Changzhi (Shangdang) (Shanxi province) 長治（上黨）
Chen Xilian 陳錫聯
Chen Boda 陳伯達
Chen Duxiu 陳獨秀
Chen Geng 陳賡
Chen Shaoyu (alias Wang Ming) 陳紹禹（王明）
Chen Yi 陳毅
Chen Yun 陳雲
Chengdu (Sichuan province) 成都市
Chi Guang (Red Light Magazine) 《赤光》
Chiang Ching-kuo (Jiang Jingguo) 蔣經國

Chiang Kai-shek (Jiang Jieshi)　蔣介石
Chongqing (Chungking)　重慶
Ci Xi (Empress)　慈禧

D
Dabie Mountains　大別山
Dajun (Grand Army)　（劉鄧）大軍
Deng Fa　鄧發
Deng Gen　鄧墾
Deng Guozhong　鄧國忠
Deng Pufang　鄧樸方
Deng Shuping　鄧蜀平
Deng Wenming　鄧文明
Deng Xianlie　鄧先烈
Deng Xiaoping　鄧小平
Deng Xixian　鄧希賢
Ding Ling　丁玲
Dong Biwu　董必武
Donggu (Jiangxi province)　東固
Donglan (Guangxi province)　東蘭
Douzheng (struggle)　鬥爭
Du Yuming　杜聿明

F
Feng Qing (affair)　"風慶輪"事件
Feng Yuxiang　馮玉祥
Fujian (province)　福建省
Fuzhou (Fujian province)　福州市

G
Gansu (province)　甘肅省
Gao Gang　高崗
Gelao Hui　哥老會
Guangan County (Sichuan province)　廣安縣
Guangchang (Jiangxi province)　廣昌
Guangdong (province)　廣東省
Guangming Daily　《光明日報》
Guangxi (Zhuang Autonomous Region)　廣西壯族自治區

Guangzhou (Guangdong province) 廣州市
Guiyang (Guizhou province) 貴陽市
Guizhou (province) 貴州省
Guo Moruo 郭沫若
Guomindang 國民黨
Gutian (Fujian province) 古田

H
Hainan (province) 海南省
Hangzhou 杭州市
He Kequan 何克全（凱豐）
He Long 賀龍
Hechi (Guangxi province) 河池
Henan (province) 河南省
Hongze Lake (Jiangsu province) 洪澤湖
Hu Qili 胡啟立
Hu Yaobang 胡耀邦
Hua Guofeng 華國鋒
Huai-Hai Campaign 淮海戰役
Huai River 淮河
Huang Fan Qu (area flooded by Yellow River) 黃泛區
Huang Shuai 黃帥
Huang Wei 黃維
Huang Yanpei 黃炎培
Huang Yongsheng 黃永勝
Hunan (province) 湖南省

J
Ji Dengkui 紀登奎
Jiang Qing 江青
Jiang Tengjiao 江騰蛟
Jinggangshan (Jiangxi province) 井崗山
Jin-Ji-Yu-Lu Jun 晉冀豫魯軍
Jinzhang 緊張

K
Kaifeng (Henan province) 開封市
Kang Sheng 康生

L

Lanzhou (Gansu province) 蘭州市

Laoye hilltop (Shanxi province) 老爺頂

Lechang River (Guangdong province) 樂昌河

Lei Feng 雷鋒

Li Da 李達

Li Dazhao 李大釗

Li De (alias Otto Braun) 李德

Li Desheng 李德生

Li Fuchun 李富春

Li Jingquan 李井泉

Li Lisan 李立三

Li Mingrui 李明瑞

Li Peng 李鵬

Li Shizeng (see Li Yuying) 李石曾

Li Su 李蘇

Li Xiannian 李先念

Li Yuying (also called Li Shizeng) 李煜瀛

Li Zhuoran 李卓然

Li Zongren 李宗仁

Li Zuopeng 李作鵬

Liaoning (province) 遼寧省

Lin Biao 林彪

Liu Bocheng 劉伯承

Liu Lantao 劉瀾濤

Liu Shaoqi 劉少奇

Liuzhou (Guangxi province) 柳州

Longchuan (uprising) 龍川

Lowu (Guangdong province) 羅湖

Lu Dingyi 陸定一

Luo Fu (alias Zhang Wentian) 洛甫（張聞天）

Luo Mai (also called Li Weihan) 羅邁（李維漢）

Luo Ming 羅明

Luo Ruiqing 羅瑞卿

M

Mao Anying 毛岸英

Mao Zedong 毛澤東

Mao Zetan　毛澤覃
Mo Wenhua　莫文驊
Mopan Hilltop (Shanxi province)　磨盤頂

N
Nanjing　南京市
Nanning　南寧市
Nie Rongzhen　聶榮臻
Nie Yuanzi　聶元梓

P
Paracel (Xisha) Islands　帕拉塞爾（西沙）羣島
Peng Dehuai　彭德懷
Peng Zhen　彭眞
Pengdian (Henan province)　彭店
Pingma (Guangxi province) (see Tiandong)　平馬（田東）

Q
Qian Long (Emperor)　乾隆
Qian Ying　錢瑛
Qiao Guanhua　喬冠華
Qiliying (Hebei province)　七里營
Qin Bangxian (alias Bo Gu)　秦邦憲（博古）
Qin Jiwei　秦基偉
Qin Shi Huang Di　秦始皇帝
Qing Dynasty　清代
Qing Ming (festival)　清明
Qinghua Daxue　清華大學
Qiu Huizuo　邱會作
Qu Qubai　瞿秋白

R
Rao Shushi　饒漱石
Ren Wanding　任畹町
Ru River　汝河
Ruijin (Jiangxi province)　瑞金

S
San Guo Zhi Yan Yi (Romance of the Three Kingdoms)　三國志演義
Sha River　沙河

Shaanxi (province) 陝西省
Shandong (province) 山東省
Shangdang (Shanxi) (see Changzhi) 上黨（長治）
Shanghai 上海
Shanxi (province) 山西省
Shenyang (Mukden) (Liaoning province) 瀋陽市
Si Qing (Four Clean-ups Campaign) 四清運動
Sichuan (province) 四川省
Song Jiang 宋江
Song Renqiong 宋任窮
Su Yu 粟裕
Sun Chuan-fang 孫傳芳
Sun Yat-sen 孫逸仙
Sun Yefang 孫冶方

T
Taihang Mountains (Shanxi–Hebei border) 太行山
Tan Zhenlin 譚震林
Tansuo (Explorations)《探索》
Tao Zhu 陶鑄
Tiandong (Pingma — Guangxi province) 田東（平馬）

W
Wang Dongxing 汪東興
Wang Hairong 王海容
Wang Hongwen 王洪文
Wang Jiaxiang 王稼祥
Wang Ming (alias Chen Shaoyu) 王明（陳紹禹）
Wei Baqun 韋拔羣
Wei Guoqing 韋國清
Wei Jingsheng 魏京生
Wu De 吳德
Wu Faxian 吳法憲
Wu Peifu 吳佩孚
Wu Xiuqian 伍修權
Wuchang (Hubei province) 武昌
Wuhan (Hubei province) 武漢市
Wuyuan 婺源

X
Xi Zhongxun 習仲勳

Xia Bogen 夏伯根
Xi'an (Shaanxi province) 西安市
Xiang 鄉
Xiang River 湘江
Xiang Ying 項英
Xiang Zhongfa 向忠發
Xiao Hua 蕭華
Xiao Jin Zhuang (Hebei province) 小靳莊
Xie Jinbi 謝金碧
Xiexing (Guangan county, Sichuan province) 協興鄉
Xikang 西康
Xin County 新縣
Xinhai Revolution 辛亥革命
Xining (Qinghai province) 西寧市
Xinjiang (autonomous region) 新疆維吾爾自治區
Xisha Islands (Paracels) 西沙羣島
Xixian 息縣
Xu Shiyou 許世友
Xu Xiangqian 徐向前
Xuexi Yu Pipan (Study and Criticism) 《學習與批判》
Xuzhou (Jiangsu province) 徐州市

Y
Yan Xishan 閻錫山
Yanan 延安
Yang Chengwu 楊成武
Yang Kaihui 楊開慧
Yang Shangkun 楊尚昆
Yang Yong 楊勇
Yangmingbao (Shanxi province) 陽明堡
Yao Wenyuan 姚文元
Ye Jianying 葉劍英
Yinchuan (Ningxia province) 銀川市
Yongxing (Jiangxi province) 永興
Youjiang (Right River) 右江
Yu Qiuli 余秋里
Yu Zuoyu 俞作豫
Yuan Renyuan 袁任遠
Yunnan (province) 雲南省

Z
Zhang Chunqiao　張春橋
Zhang Guotao　張國燾
Zhang Qianyuan　張茜元
Zhang Wentian (alias Luo Fu)　張聞天（洛甫）
Zhang Yunyi　張雲逸
Zhang Zuolin　張作霖
Zhao Ziyang　趙紫陽
Zhejiang (province)　浙江省
Zhengzhou (Henan province)　鄭州市
Zhou Enlai　周恩來
Zhou Rongxin　周榮鑫
Zhu De　朱德
Zhuang (minority)　壯族
Zhuo Lin　卓琳
Zunyi (Guizhou province)　遵義
Zuojiang (Left River)　左江

INDEX

Bai Zhongxi   21, 57
Barefoot doctors   139
Beijing Review   112
Black Cannon Incident (film)   158–59
Bo Gu   22, 23, 24, 25, 28, 29, 30, 31, 32
Dong Biwu   63, 110
Braun, Otto (alias Li De)   28, 29, 30–31

Cai Hesen   20
Chen Boda   121, 122, 123, 171
Chen Duxiu   11, 14
Chen Xilian   160, 170, 215
Chen Yi   9, 53, 54, 57, 58, 110
Chen Yun   28, 63, 67, 164, 247
Chiang Ching-kuo   136, 151, 173
Chiang Kai-shek   11, 14, 15, 23, 27, 37, 42, 43, 44 46, 47, 56, 58, 136 (death)
Chinese Communist Party   10, 15–16, 19, 27, 53, 73, 74, 75, 84, 90, 102, 111, 131, 146, 177
Comintern   11, 28
Criticise Lin Biao & Confucius Campaign   201–02
Cultural Revolution   113–27, 129, 201, 233 (see also Mao Zedong, Deng Xiaoping and Liu Shaoqi)

Democracy Wall   168–69, 229, 232
Deng Fa   28
Deng Gen   2, 70
Deng Guozhong   49
Deng Pufang   126
Deng Shuping   2–3, 68, 69, 70

Deng Xiaoping
    agriculture 87–88, 95, 97–98, 174–75, 178–80, 191–92, 245
    Anti-Rightist Campaign 79
    appointments 60, 62, 63, 64, 65, 67, 135, 138
    arts and culture 189–90, 201, 227–34
    Baise uprising 16–18
    birth 1
    brothers, see Deng Gen and Deng Shuping
    cadres 90, 103–04, 158, 184, 236
    Chi Guang (Red Light) 9
    children 14, 120 (see also Deng Pufang)
    CCP member 14
    CCP Secretary General 65
    crime 194, 246
    Cultural Revolution 117, 118, 119–27, 166, 246
    Dabie Mountains 40–41, 43, 46, 52
    democracy 92–94, 104–05, 192, 193, 229–34, 246
    economy 96, 102, 107, 142, 150, 173–74, 189, 191–92, 194, 195–96, 197, 202
    education 154, 155–56, 226–27
    father 1–2, 5
    Feng Yuxiang and (see Feng Yuxiang)
    foreign policy 137, 168, 199, 202, 203, 204–11, 209–10 (in America) 239–40
    France 7–10
    Gang of Four 132, 136, 138, 139, 140, 153, 163, 166, 171
    Gao-Rao purge 68
    Guangdong campaign 21
    Guangxi 15—19, 22–24
    Guangzhou 146–47
    Huai-Hai Campaign 47, 53, 54, 55
    Hundred Flowers Campaign 231–32
    ideology 103, 156–57, 174, 189–90, 234–37
    industry 98–99, 102, 150, 180–83, 245
    intellectuals 90, 91, 155, 230–31
    Jiang Qing 132–33, 134, 139, 145, 163
    Jiangxi 22, 23, 166
    labour 190–91
    legal codes 169–70
    Li Dazhao and 13
    Liu Bocheng and 40, 42, 44, 45, 46, 47, 52, 53, 54, 60, 62, 63, 201, 215
    Longchuan uprising 17
    Luo Ming line 25, 26, 29, 83

mass movements 106–07
Mao and 22, 23, 26, 76, 77, 79, 80, 83, 86, 131, 139, 140, 143, 153, 154,
   163, 177, 240–43
Mao's brother 25
Mao Zedong Thought 74, 101, 153, 161, 164, 198, 230, 242, 243
modernisation 92, 161–62, 164, 197, 226, 238
mother 2
   step-mother, Xia Bogen 69, 126
Moscow 12, 75, 109
names 1, 2
Party policy 89, 91, 92, 149, 157, 159, 185–86, 187, 246
Party relations 77, 78, 79, 81, 193
People's Communes 95, 96–97, 175, 177–78, 180, 240, 245
PLA 89, 163, 166, 167, 168, 213–23, 246
political reform 183–86, 192, 193
science and technology 154, 155, 156, 165
Selected Works 157, 159, 160, 229, 233, 241
sister 69
political disgrace 23, 24, 25–26, 77, 78, 126, 136, 137, 138, 139, 140,
   142, 144
Rectification Campaign 84–87, 88, 235
Red Army 20–21, 24, 34–35
Red Star 22, 26, 33
rehabilitation 29, 130, 131, 134, 144, 145, 146, 152, 153
Shanghai 14, 17
Shanxi 34, 36, 48, 49
Sino-Soviet 83, 109, 110–12, 203, 204, 209
sister, see Deng Xianlie
study and criticism 234
Tan Zhenlin and 25–26
wives 14, 126
Wuhan 14
Xian 12–13
Yan'an 39
youth 9, 100, 187–88
Zhou Enlai and 14, 131
Zunyi Conference 29, 30, 33–34
Deng Xianlie 2

Far Eastern Economic Review 119, 152, 153, 209
Feng Qing Affair 133
Feng Yuxiang 12–14

foreign policy 137, 151, 199, 202–11 (see also Deng Xiaoping, Sino-Soviet, US-China)
Four big freedoms 170
Four Clean-ups movement 114–16
France 5, 10 (see also Deng Xiaoping and Zhou Enlai)

Gang of Four 79, 116–17, 131, 143, 146, 153, 155, 171, 215, 242
Gao Gang 66, 67, 68
Gao-Rao purge 66–68
Guangming Daily 130, 142, 195, 231
Guo Moruo 63
Guomindang 3 (see also Nationalists)
Great Leap Forward 92, 96, 99, 107

He Kequan 28
He Long 34, 62
Hong Kong 172–73, 188, 194
Hong Qi (Red Flag) 234, 255
Hu Qili 9, 148
Hu Yaobang 99, 147, 151, 171
Hua Guofeng 130, 135, 138, 140, 142, 144, 146, 147, 148, 149, 152–53, 164, 165, 166, 171, 242
Huai-Hai Campaign, see Deng Xiaoping
Huang Yanpei 63
Huang Yongsheng 171

Ji Dengkui 130, 170
Jiang Qing 79, 129, 130, 132-33, 134, 138, 139, 142, 143, 144, 145, 163, 171, 200, 201, 207, 229 (see also Deng Xiaoping and Gang of Four)
Jiang Tengjiao 171
Jinggangshan 18

Kang Sheng 109, 120
Khrushchev Nikita 66, 75, 82, 228, 242
Kissinger Henry 137, 206–07, 208

Lei Feng 214
Li Da 56
Li Desheng 159–60, 161, 162, 202
Li Fuchun 9, 25, 28
Le Heying 8, 9
Li Jingquan 64, 65, 115
Li Lisan 19, 20, 24, 35

Li Mingrui   15, 16
Li Peng   246, 247
Li Shizeng, see Li Youyong
Li Xiannian   246
Li Youyong (or Li Shizeng)   5, 6, 8
Li Zhuoran   28
Li Zongren   14, 58
Li Zuopeng   171
Liberation Army Daily   167
Lin Biao   18, 28, 34, 53, 59, 67, 114, 127, 129, 162, 166, 201, 215
Liu Bocheng   28, 34, 35, 36, 40, 43, 44, 45, 46, 47, 48, 49, 53, 54, 55, 57, 60,
     62, 63, 147, 213, 216 (see also Deng Xiaoping)
Liu Lantao   65
Liu Shaoqi   8, 28, 66, 68, 79, 80, 99, 103, 108, 110, 136, 177,
     194–95, 240
   Cultural Revolution,   114, 118, 119–25
   death   130
   dismissal from Party   121
   posthumous rehabilitation   170
Long March   27–28, 41, 62
Luo Fu (alias Zhang Wentian)   23, 28, 29
Lu Dingyi   26
Luo Ming   24–26, 29
Luo Ruiqing   120, 216

Macau   172
Mao Zedong   23, 32, 56, 57, 68, 131, 136, 142, 152, 154, 205, 206, 231, 233
   brothers   25
   conflict with Party   19–20
   death   143
   Deng and   22, 23, 76, 77, 79, 80, 83, 86, 131, 134, 139, 140, 143, 144,
        163, 177, 235, 204–43
   Cultural Revolution   113–14, 118, 124
   early life   17–18
   Luochuan Meeting   35–36
   peasants   175, 176
   PLA   213, 214, 215, 216
   son   64
   Soviet Union   82, 83, 110,
   wife 64 (see also Jiang Qing)
   Zunyi Conference   28, 29, 30, 31
Mao Zedong Thought   74, 75, 117, 131, 149, 161, 164, 167, 198, 242, 243
May Fourth Movement   4–5

Mo Wenhua 21

Nationalists 10, 11, 13, 14, 27, 29, 32, 43, 45, 54, 56, 67, 58, 151, 173
Nei Rongzhen 9, 28, 59, 147
Nixon, Richard 138, 139

Observation Post 196, 210, 218, 220, 237
Open-door policy 197, 237
Peking University 116, 118, 121, 123, 126, 137
Peng Dehuai 19, 28, 36, 58, 60, 67, 216
Peng Zhen 67, 68, 99, 109, 118, 119, 170, 171, 185, 240, 246
People's Daily 102, 139, 140, 150, 153, 154, 156, 157, 160, 162, 169, 173, 182, 192, 201
PLA 89, 114, 121, 135, 138, 213–23, 246 (see also Mao Zedong and Deng Xiaoping)

Qiao Guanhua 206
Qin Jiwei 59, 147
Qinghua University 91, 116, 123
Qiu Huizuo 171
Qu Qubai 20, 26

Rao Shushi 66, 67, 68
Red Army 17, 20, 23, 27, 29, 30, 32, 34, 58 (see also Deng Xiaoping)
Red Flag 102 (replaces *Red Star*), 121, 150
Red Guards 80, 113, 119, 121, 123, 187, 215
Ren Wanding 169

Salisbury, Harrison 27, 28
Sino-Soviet relations 66, 82–84, 109–12, 137, 199–200, 203, 209, 221–22 (see also Deng Xiaoping and Mao Zedong)
Solinger, Dorothy 62
Song Renqiong 56, 65
Su Yu 57, 58
Sun Chuanfang 11
Sun Yat-sen 1

Taiwan 74, 151, 168, 173, 188, 200, 209, 222
Tan Zhenlin 25–26, 53, 57, 58, 65
Tang Wensheng (Nancy) 132
Tangshan earthquake 143
Tao Zhu 119, 123
The Times 142, 145, 204, 205

Tiananmen Square   118, 138, 140–42, 163, 164
Twenty-eight Bolsheviks   22, 24, 109

US-China relations   83, 137, 138, 139, 151, 168, 173, 199, 200, 208–10, 222
    (see also Kissinger, Henry and Nixon, Richard)

Vietnam   168, 207, 210, 222

Wang Dongxing   150, 170, 215
Wang Hairong   130, 132
Wang Hongwen   131, 132, 133, 143, 171 (see also Gang of Four)
Wang Jiaxiang   28
Wang Ming   22
Wei Guoqing   54, 215
Wei Jingsheng   169
Worker's Daily   117, 190
Wu De   148, 170, 205
Wu Faxian   171
Wu Xiuqian   29

Xiang Zhongfa   20, 22
Xiao Hua   205
Xiao Jin Zhuang   139
Xinhai Revolution   4
Xu Shiyou   144, 147, 215
Xu Xiangqian   147, 165

Yan Xishan   39, 48, 49
Yang Chengwu   120
Yang Shangkun   28, 65, 109, 246
Yang Yong   148
Yao Wenyuan   129, 130, 132, 133, 135, 139, 141, 143, 171 (see also Gang
    of Four)
Ye Jianying   146, 147, 165, 166, 173, 215
Yu Qiuli   148

Zhang Chunqiao   129, 130, 131, 132, 133, 135, 138, 143, 171 (see also Gang
    of Four)
Zhang Guotao   20, 28, 32, 36
Zhang Wentian (alias Luo Fu)   29 (see also Luo Fu)
Zhang Yunyi   15–16, 19, 20
Zhang Zuolin   13
Zhao Ziyang   170–71, 174, 186, 226, 245, 246, 247

Zhou Enlai   20, 23, 28, 36, 39, 58, 83, 92, 110, 132, 140–41, 143, 163, 199, 201
    Cultural Revolution 114, 121, 127
    death 138
    Deng and   14, 131, 135
    France 8, 9
Zunyi   28, 31, 32
Zhou Rongxin   137
Zhu De   18, 19, 23, 28, 35, 36, 58, 75, 110, 143 (death)
Zunyi Conference   26, 28–37